The Metropolitan Museum of Art Symposia

Afghanistan

Forging Civilizations along the Silk Road

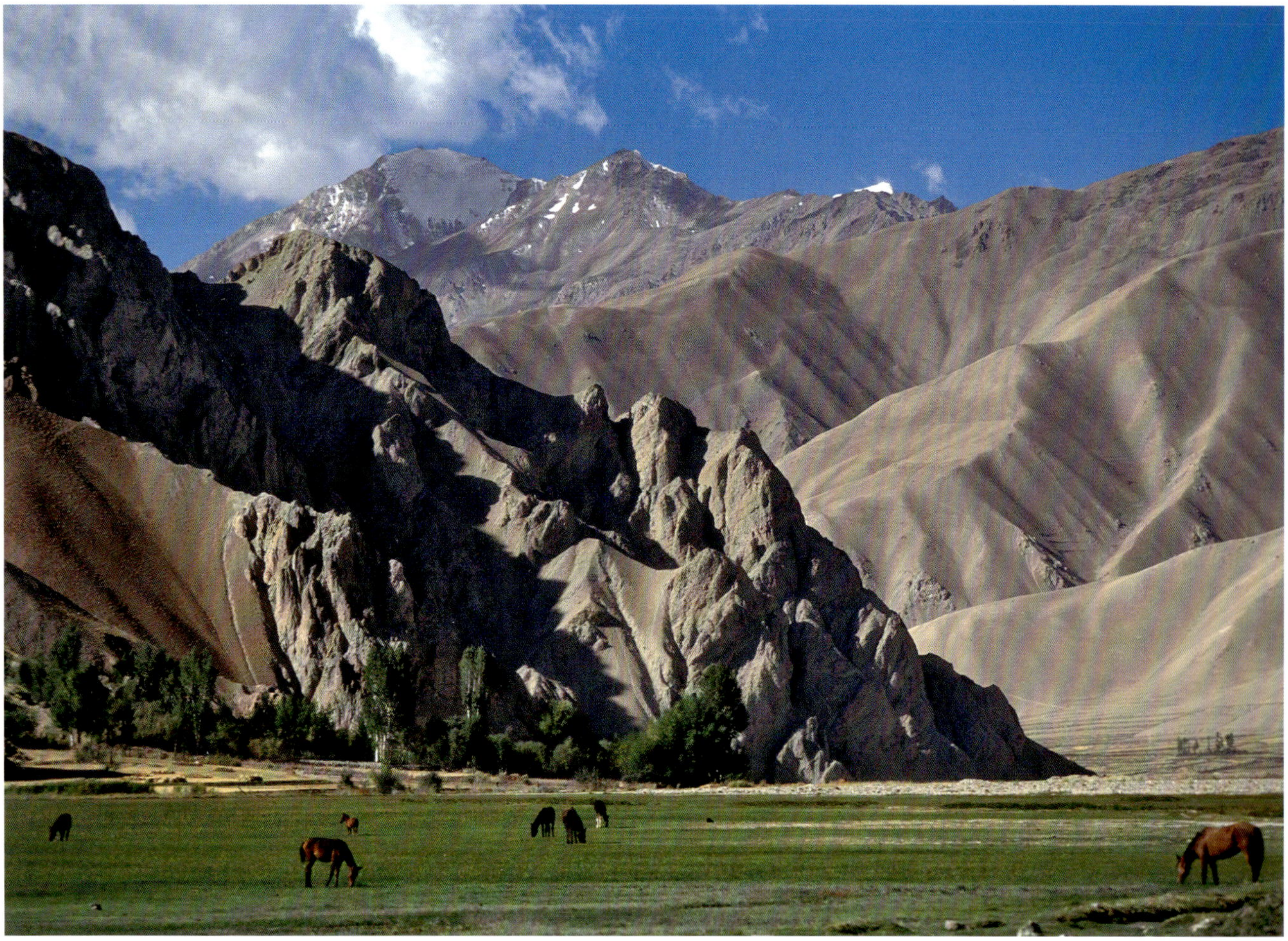

The Metropolitan Museum of Art Symposia

Afghanistan

Forging Civilizations along the Silk Road

Edited by
Joan Aruz
and
Elisabetta Valtz Fino

THE METROPOLITAN MUSEUM OF ART, NEW YORK
DISTRIBUTED BY YALE UNIVERSITY PRESS, NEW HAVEN AND LONDON

Most of the essays published in this volume were presented at the symposium "Afghanistan: Hidden Treasures from the National Museum, Kabul," held at The Metropolitan Museum of Art, New York, on September 10, 2009. John Boardman's essay was part of the Charles K. Wilkinson lectures held on September 9, 2009. Omara Khan Massoudi's essay is based on a lecture that took place at a meeting of the Friends of Inanna on June 17, 2009.

The symposium was made possible by The Hagop Kevorkian Fund and the Friends of Inanna.

Published by The Metropolitan Museum of Art, New York
Mark Polizzotti, Publisher and Editor in Chief
Gwen Roginsky, Associate Publisher and General Manager of Publications
Peter Antony, Chief Production Manager
Michael Sittenfeld, Managing Editor
Robert Weisberg, Assistant Managing Editor

Edited by Elizabeth Powers
Production by Douglas Malicki

Printed on 130 gsm Lumi-Silk Matte Artpaper
Design implemented by Douglas Malicki and Steve Chanin based on a format established by Tsang Seymour Design Inc.
Typeset in Bembo Std and Lotus Linotype
Separations by Professional Graphics, Inc., Rockford, Illinois
Printed and bound by Oceanic Graphic Printing, China

Maps (pp. vi–vii and p. 17) by Anandaroop Roy
Chronology (pp. 28–29) by Steve Chanin

Jacket illustrations (front): Clasp showing Dionysius and Ariadne on a lion-griffin (detail). Tillya Tepe, Tomb VI, second quarter of the 1st century A.D. Gold, turquoise, 6.5 x 7 cm. National Museum of Afghanistan, Kabul (04.40.53); (back): Bracket in the shape of a lion-griffin. Begram, Room 13, 1st century A.D. Ivory, H. 30 cm. National Museum of Afghanistan, Kabul (04.1.116)

Frontispiece: Horses graze in green fields at the foot of northern Afghanistan's rugged Pamir Mountains. Photographer: Michael Yamashita

First printing, 2012

The Metropolitan Museum of Art
1000 Fifth Avenue
New York, New York 10028
metmuseum.org

Distributed by
Yale University Press, New Haven and London
yalebooks.com/art
yalebooks.co.uk

Cataloging-in-Publication Data is available from the Library of Congress.

ISBN 978-1-58839-452-1 (pbk: The Metropolitan Museum of Art)
ISBN 978-0-300-17954-5 (pbk: Yale University Press)

Contents

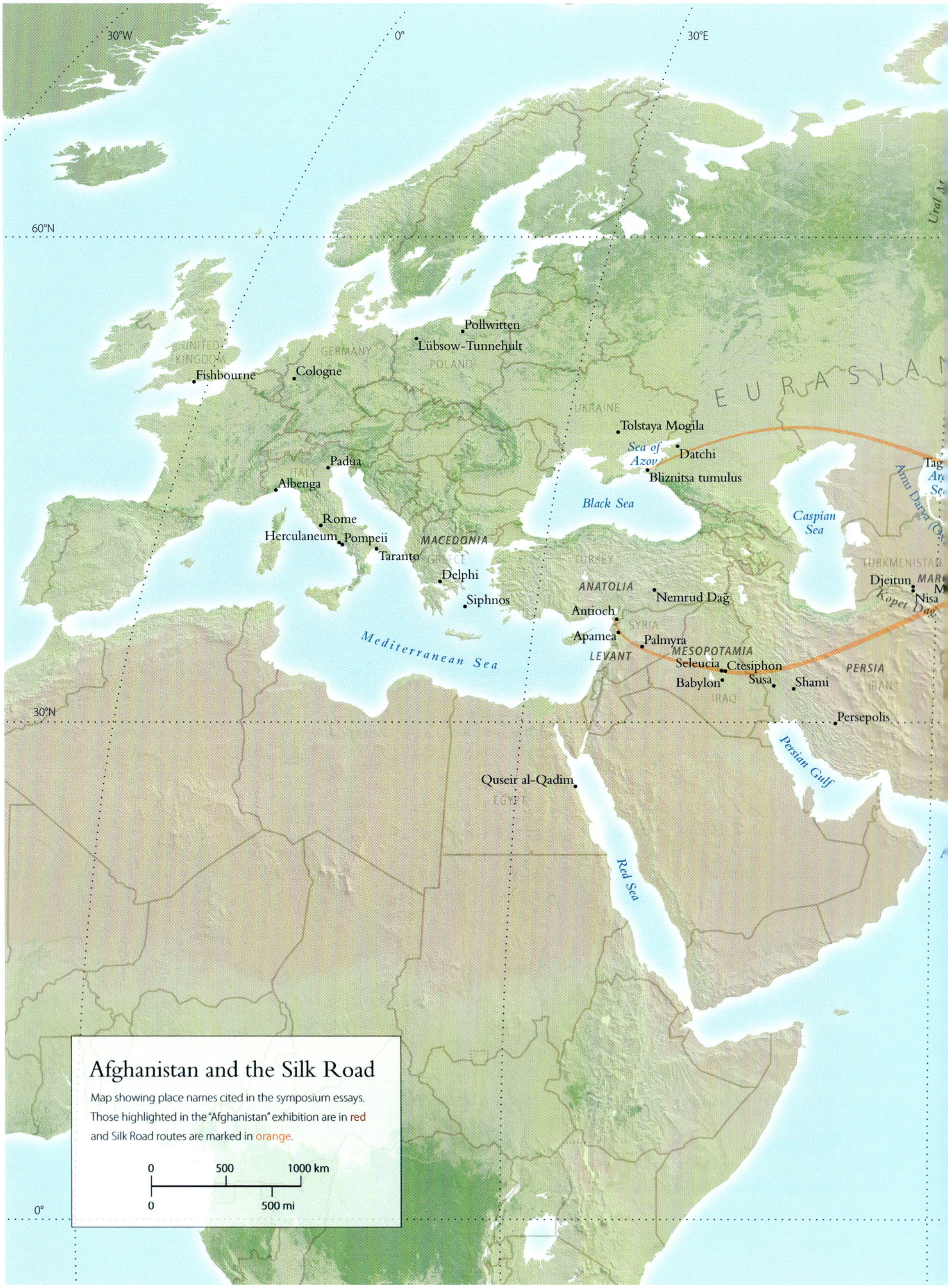

Afghanistan and the Silk Road

Map showing place names cited in the symposium essays. Those highlighted in the "Afghanistan" exhibition are in red and Silk Road routes are marked in orange.

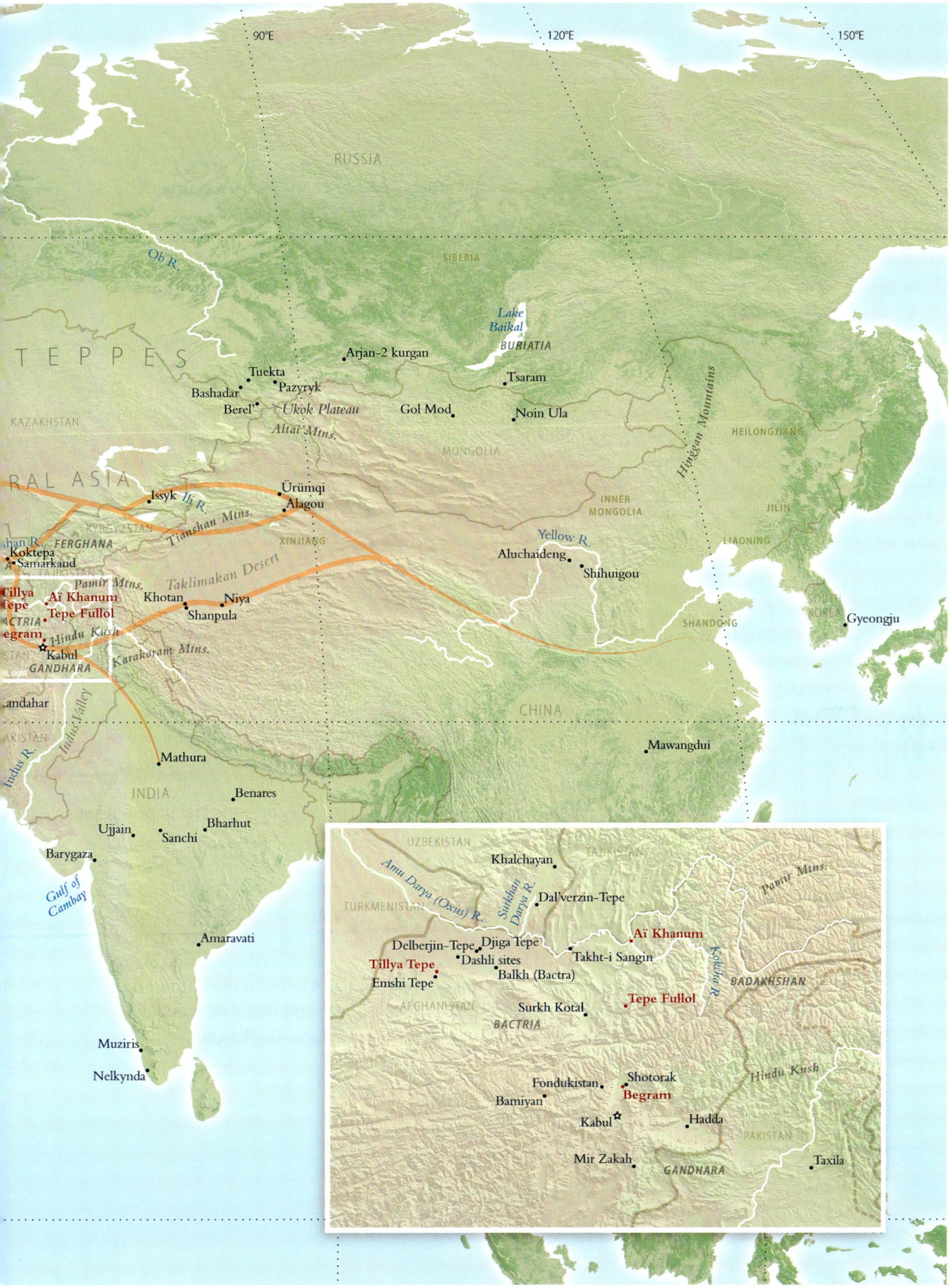
90°E
120°E
150°E
RUSSIA
Ob R.
SIBERIA
Lake Baikal
BURIATIA
Arjan-2 kurgan
Tuekta
Bashadar
Pazyryk
Berel'
Ukok Plateau
Altai Mtns.
Tsaram
Gol Mod
Noin Ula
KAZAKHSTAN
MONGOLIA
Hinggan Mountains
HEILONGJIANG
Issyk
Ili R.
Ürümqi
Alagou
INNER MONGOLIA
JILIN
KYRGYZSTAN
Tianshan Mtns.
XINJIANG
FERGHANA
LIAONING
Yellow R.
Koktepa
Samarkand
Aluchaideng
Shihuigou
Taklimakan Desert
Pamir Mtns.
Aï Khanum
Khotan
Niya
Shanpula
Tepe Fullol
SOUTH KOREA
Gyeongju
SHANDONG
Hindu Kush
Kabul
Karakoram Mtns.
GANDHARA
CHINA
Indus Valley
Indus R.
Mathura
Mawangdui
INDIA
Benares
Bharhut
Ujjain
Sanchi
Barygaza
Gulf of Cambay
Amaravati
Muziris
Nelkynda
UZBEKISTAN
TAJIKISTAN
Khalchayan
Amu Darya (Oxus) R.
Surkhan Darya R.
Dal'verzin-Tepe
Pamir Mtns.
TURKMENISTAN
Aï Khanum
Delberjin-Tepe
Djiga Tepe
Dashli sites
Takht-i Sangin
Kokcha R.
Tillya Tepe
Emshi Tepe
Balkh (Bactra)
BADAKHSHAN
AFGHANISTAN
Surkh Kotal
Tepe Fullol
BACTRIA
Fondukistan
Shotorak
Hindu Kush
Begram
Bamiyan
Kabul
Hadda
PAKISTAN
Mir Zakah
GANDHARA
Taxila

Acknowledgements

We would first like to thank Thomas P. Campbell, director of The Metropolitan Museum of Art, for his commitment to fostering the appreciation of the magnificent cultural heritage of Afghanistan through the symposium and lectures that accompanied the landmark exhibition "Afghanistan: Hidden Treasures from the National Museum, Kabul"—which was on display at the Metropolitan Museum in 2008 and 2009. The symposium was funded by the Hagop Kevorkian Fund and the Friends of Inanna, the support group of the Department of Ancient Near Eastern Art. We are very pleased that, with these papers, we are able to make another contribution to the Museum's symposium series, six years after the publication of *The Golden Deer of Eurasia*. We would like to thank Mark Polizzotti, Gwen Roginsky, Peter Antony, Michael Sittenfeld, and Robert Weisberg of the Editorial Department for their assistance in bringing this volume to completion. Elizabeth Powers devoted much time and energy as copy editor, and Doug Malicki, assisted by Steve Chanin, deserves special thanks for his attention to complex issues relating to images and layout. Anandaroop Roy created a new map to cover the vast distances discussed in the book.

In the Department of Ancient Near Eastern Art, we would like to thank many members of the staff. Yelena Rakic, with the help of Virginia Verardi, was instrumental in ensuring the accuracy of the map designations. Virginia also did a superb job in creating a chronology chart that reflects the breadth of this volume, in collaboration with the editors and Denise Leidy, and we thank Henri-Paul Francfort for his suggestions. She began with a preliminary draft prepared by Friedhelm Pedde, who also worked on the captions and bibliography. Sarah Graff produced the final version of the bibliography and also took on the time-consuming task of tracking and securing permissions for images, seeking the advice of Jane Tai in the process. Elizabeth Ann Knott provided essential proofreading assistance, and Susanna Lee coordinated the distribution of the many versions of the manuscripts.

We would like to express special thanks to the National Museum of Afghanistan, and to the photographer Thierry Ollivier for generously sharing many of the beautiful photographs that enhance this publication. Finally, we would like to voice our appreciation of Fred Hiebert, who played an invaluable role as curator of the Afghanistan exhibition in the United States and who facilitated contacts with our Afghan colleagues.

Joan Aruz and Elisabetta Valtz Fino

The Metropolitan Museum of Art Symposia

Afghanistan

Forging Civilizations along the Silk Road

Joan Aruz

Introduction

This volume of symposium papers—stimulated by the extraordinary exhibition "Afghanistan: Hidden Treasures from the National Museum, Kabul"—is more than a scholarly treatise on aspects of the history and culture of this land. It also serves as a tribute, not only to a nation seared by war and destruction for centuries, but also to a land of heroes. One who honored us by his presence and lecture to celebrate the opening of the exhibition at the Metropolitan Museum in 2009 is Omara Khan Massoudi, Director of the National Museum in Kabul, who with select members of his staff realized the risk to the collection already in the late 1980s and made the enlightened decision to hide these precious objects in a secure bank vault. They maintained a code of silence for about twenty years in the face of hostile warlords and the Taliban, who threatened their lives. The Afghanistan exhibition and the scholarship it has inspired demonstrate to the world the power of the belief emblazoned across the museum's façade: "A nation stays alive when its culture stays alive."

The hidden treasures were for years referred to as the "lost" treasures, until 2003. It was then thought safe enough to reveal to the world that—despite the destruction that reached its climax with the obliteration of the Bamiyan Buddhas and the smashing of thousands of sculptures in the museum—a large part of the cultural heritage of Afghanistan had been saved. In his introductory essay, Dr. Massoudi recounts the poignant story of its survival in the context of the fascinating history of the Kabul museum and of the many attempts to keep the country's precious artifacts safe during turbulent times. The museum was founded in 1924, and its collections survived a coup d'etat in 1978, Soviet invasions of 1979, and security threats that invited looting in the 1980s and early 1990s, before the unthinkable devastation that was wrought by the Taliban. The key to the future, in Dr. Massoudi's words, is international cooperation—the first steps being events such as the exhibition and symposium, which have focused positive attention on Afghanistan.

The symposium, like the exhibition, leads us through the long, rich, and diverse history of Afghanistan, with a special focus on four of the over 1,500 sites excavated—dating to a period before the rise of Buddhism and Islam in the region. Even at the outset—around 2000 B.C., during the so-called Bactrian Bronze Age—Afghanistan served as a crossroads of cultures between the great river valleys of the Indus and Mesopotamia. Its lapis lazuli deposits in the mountains of Badakhshan were highly valued in the Near East and as far away as Egypt and traded from at least the fourth millennium B.C. Fredrik Hiebert traces the development of the region and equates its cultural identity with a rich and vast exchange network, composed of elite centers and allied pastoral groups that extended across Central Asia. He stresses the importance of geography in the formation of the Oxus civilization and its routes of contact. Famous for superb metalwork, this phase of cultural development in Afghanistan was represented in the exhibition by gold bowls from Tepe Fullol with distinctive figural designs, among them the image of the Mesopotamian bearded bull (see Hiebert essay, fig. 4).

History is largely silent regarding the immediate aftermath of the Bronze Age. Symposium contributions resume after the Assyrian and Babylonian imperial ages in the Near East; the conquest of the ancient land of Bactria—bounded in the north by the Oxus River and encompassing northern and central modern Afghanistan—by Cyrus in the sixth century B.C.; and the eventual defeat of the Achaemenid Persians by Alexander the Great in 331 B.C. The remaining papers explore the effects of the conquests of Alexander and his successors, focusing attention on the arts and culture of Aï Khanum, Begram, and Tillya Tepe, as well as on one body of material omitted from the exhibition: the rich array of Bactrian coins.

The coins are the subject of the contribution by Frank Holt, who draws on a 19th-century source referring to them as "the very backbone on which the frame of Central Asian history is supported." As he demonstrates, the messages encoded in these tiny and portable disks, with their royal and divine images, inscriptions and symbols, are of profound importance. The variety of designs and impressive sizes—including the largest gold and silver coins in the ancient world—not only provide avenues for the exploration of the social significance of these objects among the elite but also afford a window into the humbler world of workers in the mints, whose technical skills and creative processes are made evident through the careful analysis of the coin corpus. Moreover, as Holt demonstrates, Bactrian coins provide critical evidence for the history of the region following the conquests of Alexander the Great and his Macedonian commanders, the *diadochoi*, who took control of Alexander's empire in the years following his death. According to Plutarch, Alexander founded over seventy cities in the midst of barbarian tribes and spread Greek institutions across Asia. Aï Khanum, a city founded around 300 B.C. during the reign of his successor, Seleucus Nicator, is situated at the foot of the Pamir Mountains facing the Eurasian steppes, at the confluence of the Oxus and Kokcha rivers. Even at a distance of around 3,000 miles from Greece and Macedonia, Hellenic culture is preserved here in an extraordinary fashion. It is manifest in the form and architectural details of the buildings that preserved the social institutions of the homeland, its sculptures, monuments, and scientific instruments, as well as texts bearing inscriptions that express Hellenic philosophical principles and preserve Greek literature. And yet, as is so dramatically pointed out in the essay by Paul Bernard, there was also an acceptance of eastern forms and ideas, which led to creative experimentation in the royal, religious, and domestic architecture of Aï Khanum, where Greek prototypes were lacking or considered inappropriate. Bernard notes that the consequences of Alexander's intrusion into Central Asia were profound, with the Greek alphabet transforming Bactrian into a written language and Greek artistic traditions stimulating a flowering in the arts of the region.

Aï Khanum survived for 150 years before nomadic horsemen moved in from the northern steppes to destroy it, dealing the city its first blow by piling their unburied dead on the stage of the Greek theater. But the nomadic presence in Afghanistan did not completely obliterate the Greek legacy, so vibrant at Aï Khanum, as is very evident from two archaeological sites that illuminate the succeeding period, from the last centuries B.C. to the first centuries A.D.: Begram and Tillya Tepe. This was an era of great empires: Romans in the west, Parthians in the Near East, and the Han dynasty in China. They were connected by the complex network of trade routes we know as the Silk Road, which carried silk and lacquer, horses and gemstones, carpets, and other exotic goods to the west and luxury wares and statuary to the east. Situated at the nexus of these routes was the Hellenistic city identified as Alexandria ad Caucasum (modern Begram), later known as Kapisa, the summer capital of the Kushan king Kanishka. In the trove of luxury goods found in two sealed rooms at the site—which Sanjyot Mehendale and others have interpreted as a merchant's collection rather than a royal treasury—were metal sculptures, ivory furniture elements, and works of cast, fused, and blown glass. Among the most spectacular Roman works were painted, relief-cut, and gilded glass vessels with figural scenes, but, as David Whitehouse points out, other works in glass are not so easy to assign to the Roman world. His valuable paper not only presents us with a catalogue of Roman examples that can be dated but also tackles the complex issue of interpreting the more ambiguous pieces in the glass corpus, which, based on their forms and chemical composition, sometimes appear to provide contradictory evidence. The meeting of east and west at Begram, as he notes, may involve yet another dimension, with the possibility of the transport of raw Roman glass to be worked in Central Asia. Trade in this raw material can be documented as far back as the Bronze Age, as witnessed by the glass ingots discovered in the Uluburun shipwreck.[1]

Turning eastward, Sanjyot Mehendale's contribution on the Begram ivories again raises the issue of the production of works outside the main artistic and cultural centers that drove trade along the Silk Road. The elaborately carved ivory panels that once adorned chairs, footstools, and other luxury furniture from Begram certainly appear, in their technique, style, and iconography, to be associated with the arts of India. Their imagery, as Mehendale points out, offers a fascinating glimpse into the female world, with women depicted in familiar Indian-looking architectural settings. Nevertheless, by attempting to distinguish inspiration from import and the possible role of itinerant craftsmen, she challenges traditional definitions of Indian art and its regional schools. Mehendale's work is based on a careful examination of the panels that comprise individual sets of furniture. While they exhibit a diversity of stylistic approaches, often interpreted as Indian regional variations, she concludes that they must have been made together in a single workshop, located most probably in the vicinity of Begram.

Further illuminating the artistry of Afghanistan at the beginning of the first millennium A.D. are the unparalleled discoveries made by Viktor Sarianidi on the Hill of Gold, or Tillya Tepe. The grave shafts discovered here on the desert plains close to Afghanistan's border with Turkmenistan may provide a historical missing link between the end of Aï Khanum—laid waste by nomads and effectively ending the political authority of the Greeks—and the establishment by nomads of the Kushan kingdom and a sedentary lifestyle. Still, the precious contents of the Tillya Tepe tombs testify to the survival of the Hellenic artistic legacy and its transformation in the context of eastern traditions. Much attention has focused on the assemblages of golden adornments that covered the bodies of the chieftain and five females buried at the site. Of primary importance is their technical analysis, as presented by Jane Hickman, who had the rare opportunity to examine them carefully during the de-installation of the exhibition in Washington D.C. Her article focuses attention on the materials used—mainly gold from Bactrian rivers and turquoise—and on those materials surprisingly not favored, in particular lapis lazuli, one of the most prized and ritually charged minerals in ancient western Asia, with its source in the nearby mountains of Badakhshan. Her examination of the details of manufacture illuminate essential issues regarding the workshop practices that led to the production of the Tillya Tepe corpus, which incorporated imported elements, re-used heirlooms, and exhibited wear patterns on many pieces.

The Tillya Tepe ornaments reveal great skill in their execution and a local style that incorporates traditions handed down by the Greeks, combined with nomadic animal-style imagery and features that may be traced to China. Three authors attempt to unravel these various elements, which ultimately may lead not only to a better understanding of long-distance interrelations of the time but also to the identification of the peoples buried at Tillya Tepe.

The relationship of ethnicity and artistic forms and styles is a major focus of the work of Henri-Paul Francfort, who brings a deep understanding of the arts of Eurasian nomads to his penetrating study of the finds in the tombs. His careful analysis of individual works and assemblages, such as those in the burial of the chieftain—whom he identifies perhaps as one of the small kings of western Bactria—highlights the creative contribution of steppe cultures to the distinctive "Scytho-Bactrian" style at Tillya Tepe. Francfort points to the surviving elements of the chieftain's high Eurasian headdress and his ceremonial weapons, embellished with distinctive "animal-style" motifs, which would have been suspended from his golden belt while on horseback. As Francfort notes, the gold-clad sheaths, along with related appliqués, were embellished with images of predators and prey in contorted and coiled postures, some with segmented body parts, revealing the integration of such artistic conventions over a long span of time into the repertoires of nomadic cultures from the Sea of Azov to China. This view is reinforced by his analysis of the extraordinary rendering of the ancient Near Eastern composition of the Master of Animals on a pair of pendants in a local style, expressing the interaction of ancient traditions over the vast expanse of Asia. The pendants are also the subject of a fascinating discussion by Sir John Boardman, who recognizes the figure as a Master of Divine Horses.

The purely Greek elements in the artistic admixture at Tillya Tepe are best elicited by Boardman. He draws attention to the female in one of the graves, who is distinguished not only by her spectacular nomadic gold crown but also by the coin in her mouth, in accordance with Greek funerary customs. Her garment clasps present us with a quintessentially Bactrian image in which Dionysos and Ariadne, crowned by a winged Victory (Nike), are rendered in a local style, riding on a Near Eastern lion-griffin, while underfoot is a faun-skinned satyr holding a Greek drinking cup or *kantharos*. This image—beautifully drawn by the author—provides us with perhaps the most eloquent artistic expression of the lady's apparent connections to a distant Greek heritage as interpreted in her Central Asian world.

Both Boardman and Denise Patry Leidy also address the Chinese elements at Tillya Tepe, among them the boot buckles worn by the chieftain, executed in the distinctive "lost wax–lost textile" technique, and the imagery on his dagger and its sheath. Leidy's work on the rich tombs of the later Silla kingdoms of Korea leads her to draw further attention to the collapsible nomadic crown that distinguished the female whose burial and effects evoked Hellenic customs and artistic traditions. The tall, impressive crowns found in Silla tombs, with elements representing trees, antlers, and birds, may suggest the continuity of such nomadic traditions into the fourth to sixth centuries A.D. in eastern Asia.

Symposium contributors include primary researchers—archaeologists working in Central Asia—as well as historians, art historians, and experts in glass and jewelry technology. They have shared their own individual perspectives on the dynamics of cultural interaction and its manifestation in the arts. They have explored such issues as the impact of and response to the Hellenic presence in Bactria; relations between nomadic and sedentary populations and the infiltration of "animal styles" into the repertoires of major civilizations across Asia; contacts with Rome, Iran, China, and India; and the creation of a unique Bactrian culture, with styles of expression that reflect the variety and intensity of such interconnections. Inspired by the brilliant display of the arts of Afghanistan in the exhibition, they have come together and reinvigorated the discussion of the exceptional nature and significance of the cultural heritage of Afghanistan.

1. See Cemal Pulak in Aruz, Benzel, and Evans 2008, p. 293.

Omara Khan Massoudi

At the Crossroads of Asia: A History of the National Museum of Afghanistan

The National Museum of Afghanistan, founded in 1924, was first housed in Koti Baghcha, a royal palace in Kabul. The museum displayed art objects belonging to the royal families, including manuscripts, miniatures, and weapons, as well as archaeological objects from the excavations of the newly formed Délégation Archéologique Française en Afghanistan (DAFA). The National Museum divided the archaeological finds with DAFA through the policy of *partage*, and the best examples, which stayed in Afghanistan, were proudly displayed there. In 1931, the museum moved to a previously constructed administrative building on the outskirts of Kabul, in a neighborhood called Darulaman. By mid-century, archaeological objects from excavations represented the bulk of the museum's collections, which included more than 100,000 pre-Islamic, early Islamic, and ethnographic objects. Around 700 of the best and most iconic objects on display in the museum showcased the unique culture of ancient Afghanistan, which exhibited stylistic and intellectual influences from all over Asia but, at the same time, represented a unique melting-pot culture, one distinct from its neighbors.

Following the coup d'etat of April 27, 1978 (the Saur Revolution), these treasures—of immense world historical and cultural value—became caught up in the political turmoil affecting the country and suffered terrible damage as a result. Ironically, it was just at this moment that one of the great discoveries of Afghan archaeology was made. In the fall of 1978 Viktor Sarianidi found intact nomadic burials at Tillya Tepe in northern Afghanistan. Dating to the first century A.D., these burials were bejeweled with thousands of distinctive gold ornaments. Working through the winter of 1979, Sarianidi was only able to excavate six tombs. A seventh and possibly others had to be left, and the contents disappeared into unknown hands as the country tumbled into turmoil.

Because of the chaos following the Saur Revolution, objects from the National Museum were transferred, on April 17, 1979, to the home of Minister Sardar Mohammad Naim Khan on the western outskirts of Kabul. The works of art were removed hastily and handled without care, without regard for the scientific and technical standards that ought to have governed their packaging and transport. The transfer operation took twenty-five days, and the objects remained in storage for a year. Artifacts were piled in sitting rooms, hallways, and the basement; the library was housed in the garage; the showcases, office furniture, and storage crates were left outside in the garden, while the staff moved into the servants quarters. The objects themselves were not broken or damaged, but the glass cases and wooden and metal containers suffered badly from the effects of unsuitable storage space, rain, and snow.

Following the Soviet invasion in late December 1979, a new political order was established in Kabul. With the beginning of

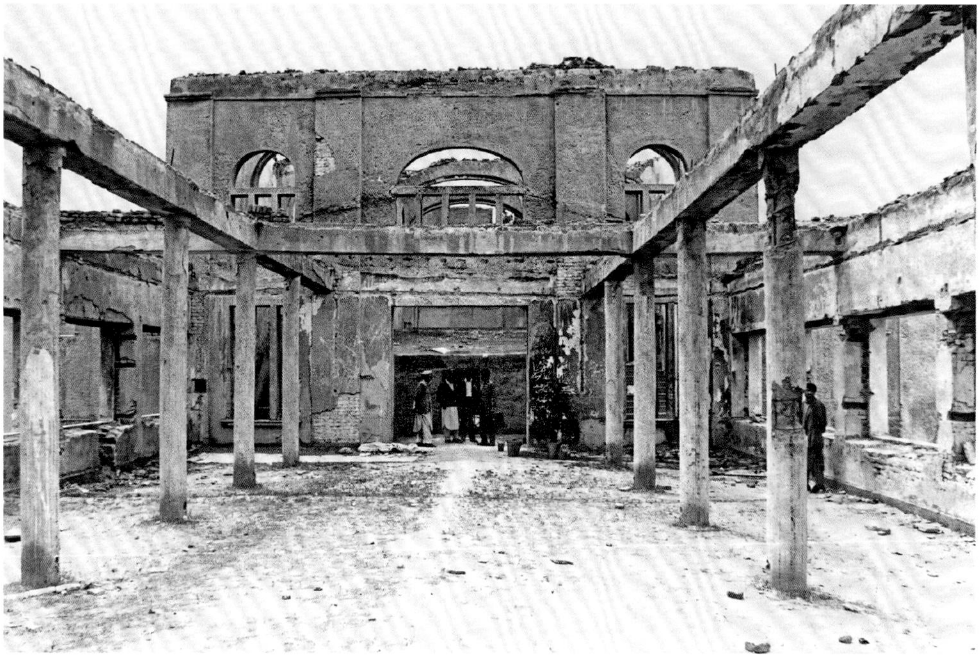

Fig. 1. National Museum, Kabul, after its destruction in 1994

the new regime, the museum was renovated and conservation undertaken for the objects. Months of effort by the conservators of the National Museum and the staff of the Archaeological Institute of Afghanistan put the collections back in order, and, in October 1980, the pieces were transferred to a restoration center near the museum in Darulaman. During these early months of the Soviet occupation, the museum was reopened, and artifacts from new excavations were installed: frescoes from the Soviet excavations at Delberjin-Tepe, objects from the French excavations at Aï Khanum, and a magnificent sculpture of the Hindu god of the sun from Khair Khana that had been found by Soviet soldiers. Some of the treasures from Tillya Tepe were briefly exhibited at the National Museum in 1980. The museum even invited the renowned excavator of the site, Viktor Sarianidi, for several months in 1982, when he meticulously documented the Bactrian gold that was later published in the sumptuous volume *The Golden Hoard of Bactria* (1985).

The situation was not the same elsewhere: the Soviet invasion also led to the destruction of the economy and of the cultural infrastructure throughout the countryside. At Hadda, eight kilometers east of Jalalabad, the superb outdoor site museum was plundered and burned in 1981, a loss that can never be made good. Like the many treasures discovered by Afghan archaeologists at Hadda, those stored at Jalalabad were likewise looted and are lost forever. Most ominous, in 1982, the venerable research compound of DAFA shut its doors after sixty years of continuous existence in Afghanistan.

Throughout the 1980s the security situation in Afghanistan continued to deteriorate. Finally in 1988, officials of the National Museum, in consultation with the Ministry of Information and Culture and the security forces, proposed that a number of works from the museum be transferred to the custodianship of Mohammad Najibullah, then president of the Republic. President Najibullah ordered the museum closed and the collections once again packed up. This was done in secret, with the best objects (those on display or with high value) placed in a bank vault and others dispersed, so that if one collection was damaged, others might escape such a fate. Selected objects from Begram, Aï Khanum, and Hadda, as well as the gold from the Bactrian hoard, were transferred to a secure vault. Finds from Fondukistan and Bamiyan and others from Hadda were taken to the Ministry of Information and Culture. Most of the objects in the storerooms remained in the now-closed museum, along with the frescoes, large pieces of sculpture, most of the vast coin collection, and the collection of Islamic pottery and metals.

The fall of the communist government in 1992 brought hope of a more peaceful future, but this was short-lived and civil war ensued. The long war years made the lives of Kabul's population hellish. Industry, all marks of civilization, state provisions, and private assets were plundered or left in ashes. Thousands of Afghan families had to leave the country.

Darulaman, on the outskirts of Kabul, became home to rival militia groups. During this time, museum staff were arrested, mistreated, and even killed for a variety of reasons. At the end of 1992, the personnel of the National Museum were placed on non-active status because of the dangers of the road accessing Darulaman. Their absence left at peril the collections still in the museum. On the evening of December 31, 1992, two major works from Shotorak, which had pride of place in the hallway of the upper floor of the National Museum, were stolen. One piece, carved in slate and dating from the second or third century A.D., depicted a Buddhist legend, the adoration of the Buddha by the three Kashyapa brothers. It was eventually bought in Peshawar, Pakistan, by a Japanese benefactor, and is intended to be returned to Afghanistan. The other was a bas-relief (depicting the *Dipankara Jataka*) dating from the same period. The government failed to respond with any action, thereby increasing the likelihood of future thefts. Only days later the windows of the main storeroom of the National Museum were broken, and many pieces were stolen.

People wondered about the fate of the museum's masterpieces, leading to a private one-day exhibition of the Bactrian gold in Kabul in 1991. This collection was again checked at the end of 1992 to nullify rumors that the Soviets had taken the gold back to Moscow.

Looting at the museum building in Darulaman began in earnest in 1993 and continued each time the militia groups in Darulaman shifted control. On March 12, 1994, the museum, which was being used as a military base and defensive position, was struck by a rocket during the fighting and burst into flames (fig. 1). Fires destroyed office records, inventories, photographs, the frescoes from Delberjin-Tepe, the Bronze Age finds from Dashli, and most of the Islamic glass and metal objects. On the evening of May 13, 1994, a BBC report declared that "Afghanistan may have buried its children, but should not be burying its culture." This message created a great stir among the national and international cultural organizations, including the United Nations, and a worldwide alarm was raised.

On November 29, 1994, the Special Representative of the Secretary-General of the United Nations, Sotirios Mousouris, arrived in Kabul and visited the leader of the militia holding this area. Mousouris asked his permission to implement a plan for restoration of the looted museum. Mr. Mousouris' visit provided an opportunity for journalists, diplomats, and members of the United Nations and the Red Cross to visit various departments of the museum. Mousouris observed that a large number of works had been stolen from the National Museum, in particular the magnificent coin collection (fig. 2). The same was true of a large portion of the floor coverings, including the superb Afghan carpets that had decorated the entrance hall and exhibition galleries. Display cases, some donated by UNESCO, had been damaged by fire. Overcome with sadness, Mousouris said: "A museum is the major repository of history and represents the identity of a people so that even the smallest object must not be moved or interfered with. The removal of objects from a museum is an attack on the soul and spirit of the nation. The destruction of these works is an irreversible disaster, and their theft and looting are an unforgivable betrayal of the people." He made an immediate decision to throw a lifeline to the museum by pledging the financial support of the United Nations and the cooperation of the U.N. Office for the Coordination of Humanitarian Affairs (UNOCHA), the only U.N. organization still active in Kabul. The other agencies had already transferred to Islamabad, Pakistan.

In 1995, the museum's repository was provided with steel doors and a zinc roof covering. The windows were bricked up as protection against bullets, rockets, and other projectiles. Attempts were made to prevent snow and rainwater from penetrating the storerooms, using such locally available materials as clay-straw mortar. The Society for the Preservation of Afghanistan's Cultural Heritage (SPACH) was established in the same year by Nancy Hatch Dupree, to assist the museum in cataloguing the remaining objects, training staff, publicizing the plight of Afghanistan heritage, and recovering stolen items. During that winter a team was brought in to rescue the collections from the upper galleries of the museum from the rubble. About 3,000 pieces, in stone, terracotta, and metal, many of them damaged, were saved and placed in storage.

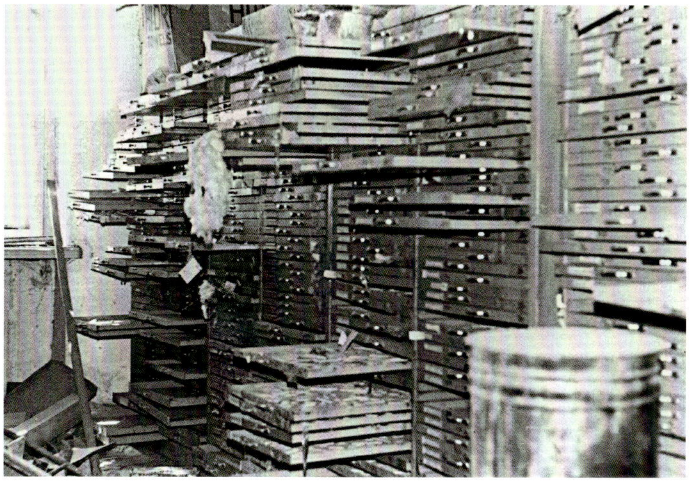

Fig. 2. Cabinets of the National Museum numismatic collection after looting

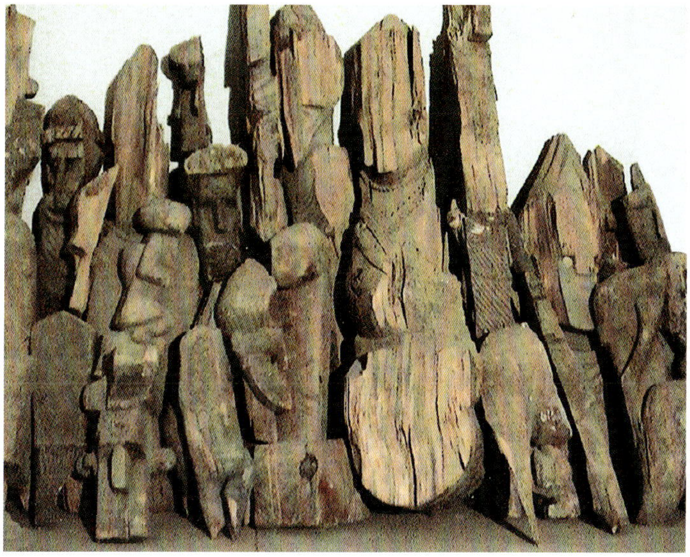

Fig. 3. Smashed and cut-up Nuristani wooden sculptures from the National Museum

Needless to say, the region was still chaotic, and even in 1995 the museum storerooms were again rifled and artifacts senselessly smashed. The museum had neither water nor electricity, and work trying to pick up the pieces was carried out using kerosene lamps after the generator was stolen. Nothing was sacred: heavy stone sculptures were stolen; Nuristani wooden statues were cut up for firewood (fig. 3); and the museum world missed the return of its staff.

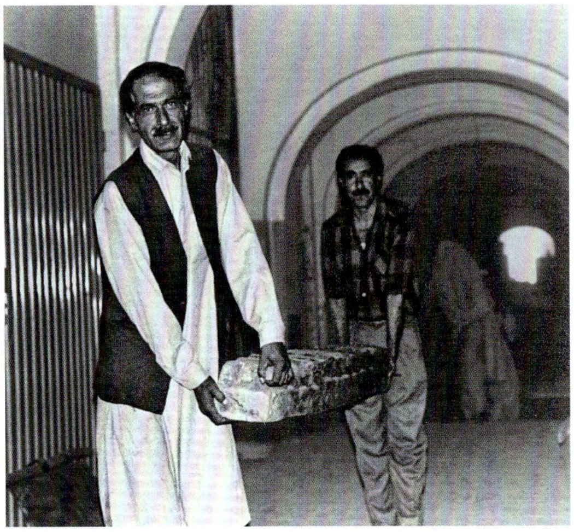

Fig. 4. Transfer of objects from the National Museum to the Kabul Hotel in 1996

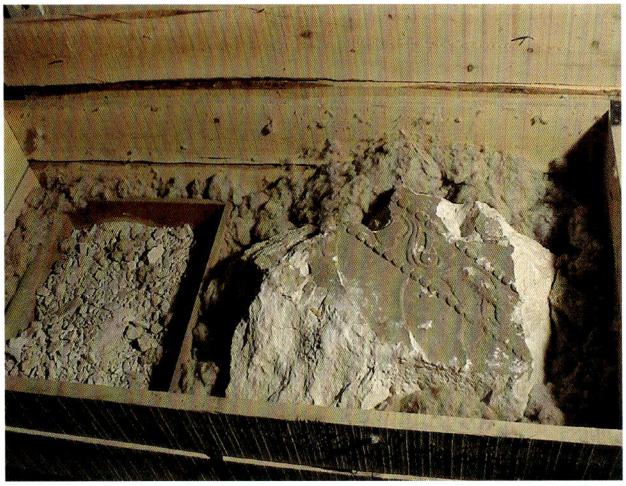

Fig. 5. Smashed remains of statue of Kushan ruler Kanishka (2nd century A.D.) after its destruction

Finally in 1996, a new order, the Taliban, brought a semblance of peace to the country. The Ministry of Information and Culture decided to remove the remainder of the works from the National Museum. Special committees were established to implement the project, dealing with record keeping, restoration, photography, packing, checking, transportation, and administration. A coordinating committee was also set up. Personnel from the National Museum and the Archaeological Institute of Afghanistan staffed these committees. With the assistance of the National Security Forces, they managed to complete their task within six months. They worked in the storerooms by torchlight in an atmosphere choked with dust. The exhaustion could be seen on their faces. Many staffers developed allergies and had to cover their faces and mouths with masks. A total of seventy people were engaged in the work of recording, photographing, and packing the works, some of which were then transferred to the Kabul Hotel in the center of the city (fig. 4). In September 1996 more than 500 crates were transferred and the newly installed Taliban government locked the museum once again—this time for two years. Museum staff members were forced to take other employment, some never returning to the museum or to Afghanistan.

In 1998, plans were made to continue the inventory, and the crates in the Kabul Hotel were transferred to the ground floor of the Ministry of Information and Culture. Museum personnel began the daunting task of sifting through the rubble of walls and broken artifacts at the National Museum. However, bombs still fell in Kabul, and work only began in late May 1999. A skeletal staff was all that was left, and the inventory begun in 1996 listed less than 4,000 objects—a fraction of the 100,000 plus objects before the destruction.

Amazingly, the museum masterpieces secretly held in the ministry and the bank vault were untouched. These storerooms included items from Surkh Kotal, Bamiyan, terracottas from Hadda, sculptures from Fondukistan, items from Rooms 10 and 13 at Begram, premier works from Aï Khanum, a selection of the finest coins, and the Tillya Tepe gold. In July 2000 a ministry commission privately confirmed that the

Tillya Tepe strong boxes had their seals intact. However, even though Mullah Omar issued an edict protecting the museum collections and making illegal smuggling of artifacts punishable by law, it was not time to reveal publicly this news about the museum's masterpieces.

At the beginning of 2001 the National Museum was faced with a further disaster as the Taliban decided that all images of humans, or idols, must be destroyed. A special group was charged with this task. They destroyed about 2,500 works of art in the National Museum (see fig. 5). They targeted the National Gallery of Art and the archives of Afghan films. In March 2001 they dynamited the giant Buddha statues at Bamiyan. These barbaric acts, which filled the heart of every decent Afghan with anger, represented an irreplaceable loss. Terrible damage was caused at every archaeological site in the country. Neither the coming generations of Afghans nor human history will forget this era of tyranny and destruction.

Regime change came once again after the overthrow of the Taliban by Afghan and international forces in late 2001, which was followed by restructuring and rebuilding all over Afghanistan. The population of Kabul swelled to more than five million people—ten times what it had been before the war—and Darulaman, where the museum is located, became an integral part of the city. The first step was to put a new roof on the museum and restart the inventory. International aid poured into the ministry for the museum. SPACH initiated training courses in English and computers, and by 2002 had started coordinating repairs at the National Museum. Conservation of the wood sculpture was aided by Austrians, and in 2004 the museum opened (fig. 6). Its first new exhibition was of Nuristani wood sculptures (fig. 7). These objects were painstakingly restored after having been desecrated and chopped up during the time of chaos at the museum (see fig. 3). Specialists from the Musée Guimet, Paris, assisted in the conservation of smashed terracotta and stone

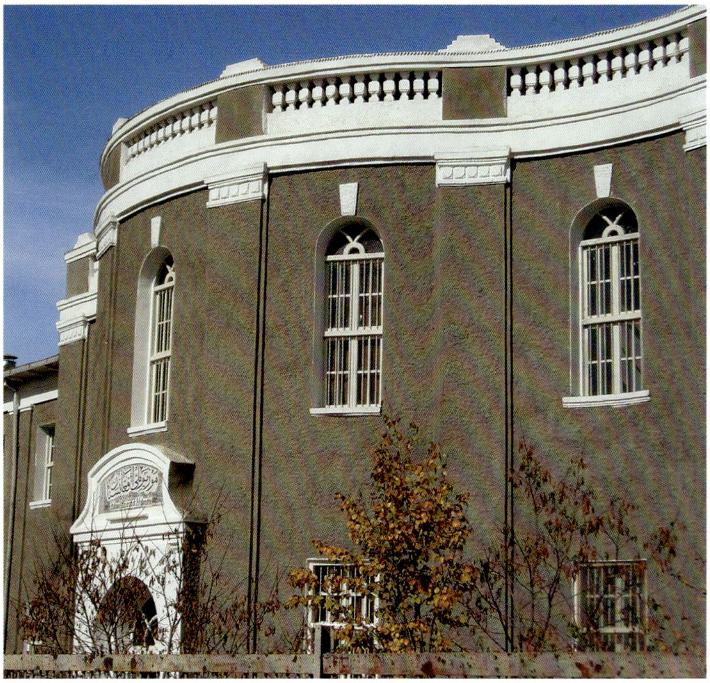

Fig. 6. Repaired exterior of the National Museum

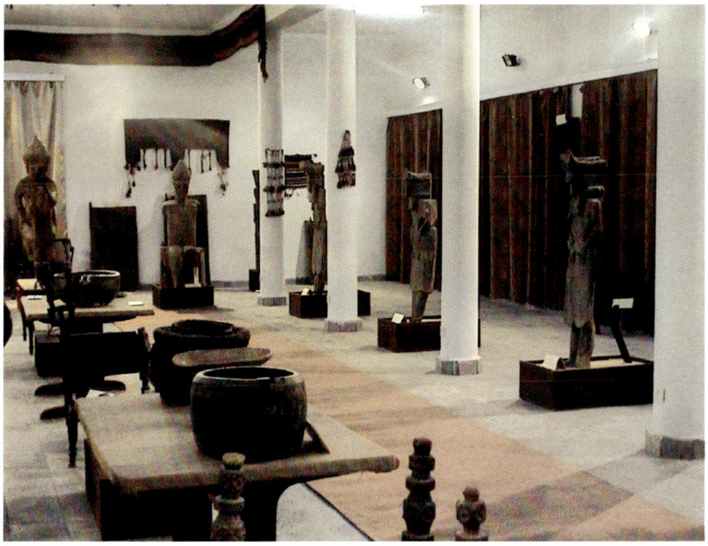

Fig. 7. Restored Nuristani wooden sculptures on exhibit in the National Museum

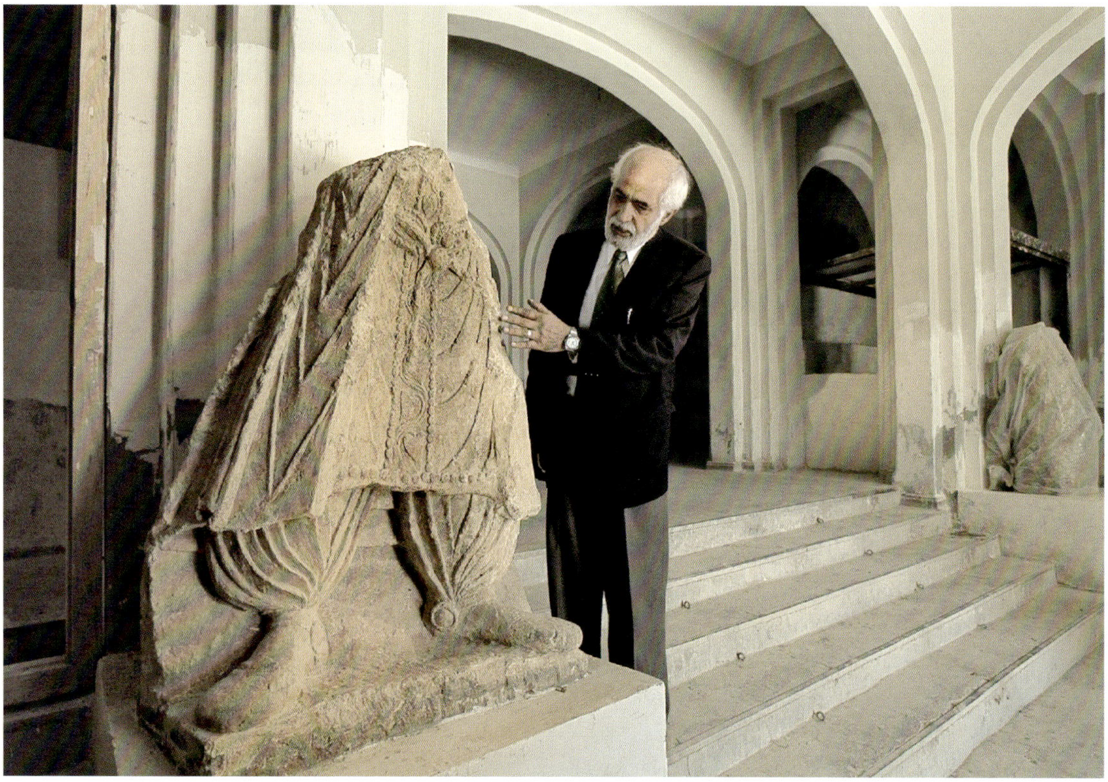

Fig. 8. Omara Khan Massoudi inspecting restored statue of Kanishka

sculpture, most notably the statue of Kanishka (fig. 8; see also fig. 5). Even the ceramic storage depot was renovated with foreign assistance.

In 2003, the Ministry of Information and Culture decided to institute a systematic inventory of the "hidden masterpieces" from the bank vault and from the ministry collections. It would be the first time these collections were assessed since they were placed in storage in 1988. With assistance from the National Geographic Society (NGS), the inventory began in the spring of 2004, after a museum committee was established to create the inventory format. Then, a method of quickly assessing the collections in a non-museum environment had to be developed. Finally, key staff had to be located—some of whom were missing after years of civil war. The NGS team brought a "mobile inventory lab" consisting of laptops, scanners, digital cameras, and first-aid conservations supplies. The Afghan government gave the legal authorization to open the seals of the crates. The first collection opened was the Tillya Tepe Bactrian gold—held in six safes. Professor Viktor Sarianidi was brought in to authenticate the finds. It was a tense moment when the first safe was finally opened, in the presence of the Minister of Information and Culture, but it revealed the finds from Tillya Tepe. Professor Sarianidi was able to verify that these were the original objects from his excavations and not copies or fakes (fig. 9; see Hickman essay, fig. 1). Then the day-to-day task of inventory began. The team, consisting of members of the

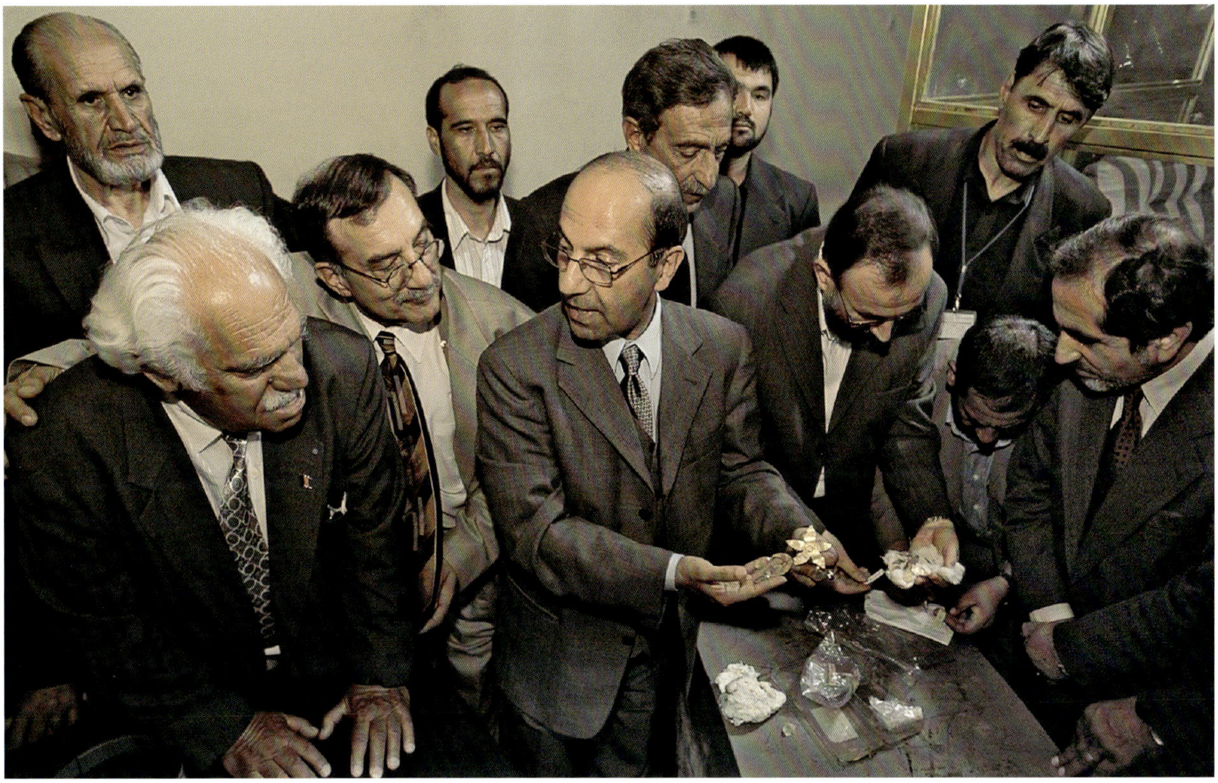

Fig. 9. Minister of Information and Culture Sayeed Makhdoom Raheen turning toward Viktor Sarianidi, as the inventory team opens the first safe of Bactrian gold in the bank vault, Kabul, 2004

museum, the Institute of Archaeology, the National Bank, the Attorney General's office, along with Carla Grissmann (formerly of SPACH) and Fredrik Hiebert (of NGS), worked for three months at a time, first on the palace collections, then on the ministry collections (fig. 10). By early 2006, the inventory of the hidden treasures was complete. As we had hoped, these treasures were safe and fully accounted for, thanks to their secret safekeeping during all those long, difficult years of war and changes of administration.

The next step was to inform the public of these finds, an equally daunting task. First, the news was shared with members of parliament. The ministry and the president's office embraced the idea of creating an international touring exhibition of a selection of

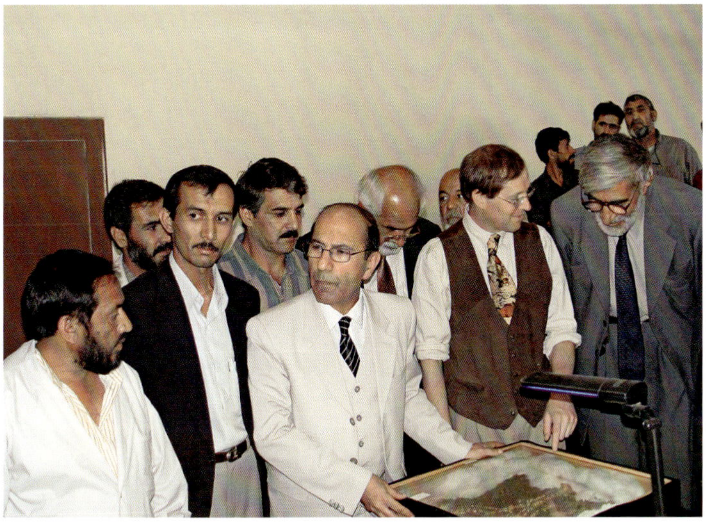

Fig. 10. Beginning of inventory of museum collections held in the presidential palace and the ministry, 2004

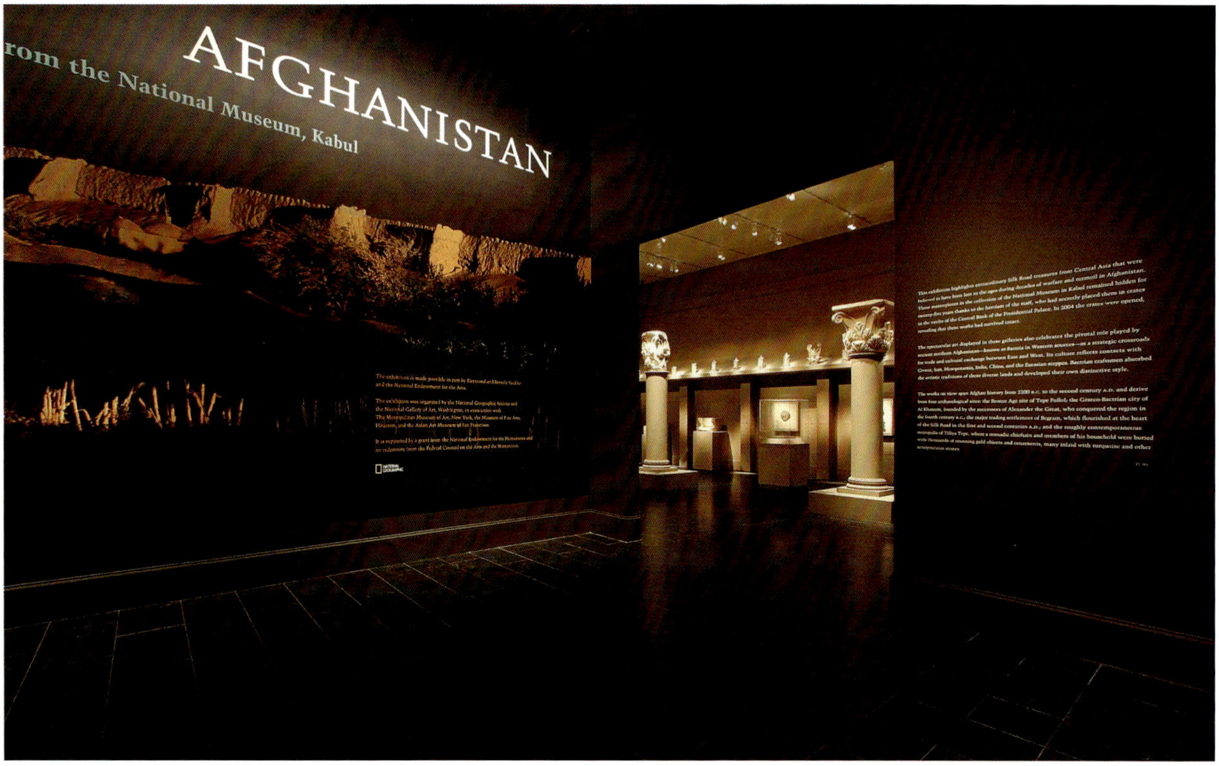

Fig. 11. Opening of the traveling exhibition "Afghanistan: Hidden Treasures from the National Museum, Kabul" at The Metropolitan Museum of Art, 2009

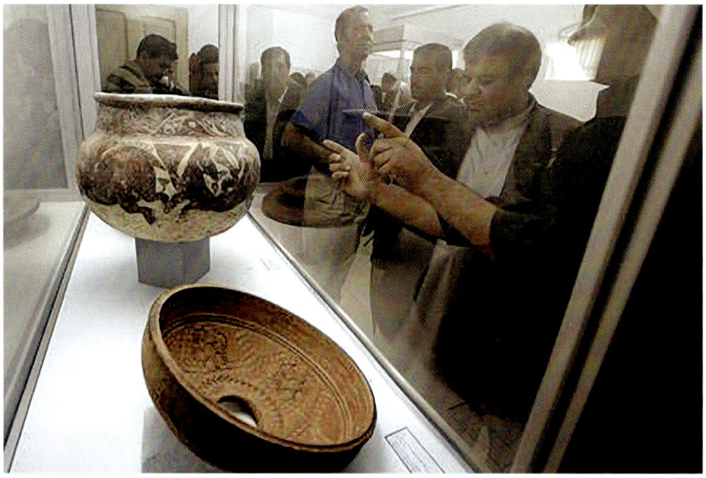

Fig. 12. Exhibition at the National Museum, Kabul, of Afghan artifacts seized in London and repatriated, 2009

these objects to show the world a different perspective on Afghans—people who persevered in the face of chaos and saved their cultural heritage.

The objects that had been crated since 1988 were in remarkably good condition: ancient ivories intact, and even fragile 2,000-year-old glass was in good condition. But in order to be exhibited, they required cleaning and conservation. The Musée Guimet, Paris, stepped up to the challenge with an offer to conserve 324 of the most iconic objects from four important archaeological sites: Tepe Fullol, Aï Khanum, Begram, and Tillya Tepe.

With the unanimous agreement of the Afghan parliament, a military transport plane brought these treasures to Paris, where what seemed like the entire conservation community turned its attention to the finds. The objects went on to be exhibited in Paris, Turin, and Amsterdam to throngs of people. They traveled to institutions in North America, to the National Gallery of Art in Washington D.C., the Asian Art Museum of San Francisco, The Museum of Fine Arts in Houston, The Metropolitan Museum of Art in New York (fig. 11), and the Museum of Civilizations in Ottawa, Canada. More than one million visitors saw the exhibition in 2009—offering both tangible evidence of the beauty and importance of ancient Afghanistan and of the compelling story of contemporary Afghans who had maintained these treasures for the entire world to see. The exhibition continues to circulate, most recently at the British Museum in London. In each of the museum venues, young Afghan museum staff were sent both as couriers and as museum professionals to gain experience in modern museum environments.

While the exhibition is touring abroad, museum personnel continue with staff training and additional inventory of newly added objects. These objects come both from new excavations in Afghanistan and from the return of looted Afghan antiquities that had been seized abroad. For example, in 2009 the National Geographic Society and the British Museum repatriated over 1,500 Afghan objects that had been seized at Heathrow airport. (See Hiebert essay, fig. 12.) These artifacts (fig. 12) were of special significance since they "replaced" similar objects that had previously been on display from the Bronze Age and from the Islamic period and that had been destroyed or stolen during the destruction of the museum building in Darulaman.

International collaboration is key to the future of the National Museum of Afghanistan. In September 2010, an international conference was held in Munich to organize assistance to the museum in coming years. The future lies in working together. Pledges were made to (1) upgrade the museum's security and its physical structure; (2) improve museum collections management through training and advanced storage facilities; (3) continue with exhibitions, education, and public access to the museum and Afghanistan history both within Afghanistan and abroad; (4) assist the museum in creating comprehensive digital collections management; (5) establish a sustainable financial basis for the museum; and (6) promote future publications, including web access, to allow more people to learn about Afghanistan's important cultures and artifacts. The National Museum of Afghanistan is ready to partner with our international colleagues to make these ideals into reality in the near future.

Fredrik T. Hiebert

The Bronze Age World of Afghanistan

Afghanistan's present borders were set in the 1890s by colonial governments desiring a buffer zone between Russia, Persia, and British India during the "Great Game." Ethnic groups on those borders were, and still are, divided among modern states, leading to the impression that Afghanistan is a contrived "nation." Yet, the archaeological and historical record suggests that this buffer zone had a similar footprint in the past (fig. 1)—approximately overlapping with modern Afghanistan. Here, it is argued that Afghanistan in the Bronze Age began a long-term pattern of elite centers of settlement and ceremony. Along with closely allied pastoral groups, these centers participated in flourishing exchange networks, which provided Afghanistan with a Bronze Age identity.

To the Persians and Greeks, Afghanistan was a series of separate regions sewn together, to which they provided individual names: extensive agricultural oases to the north (Bactria); mountains rich in mineral wealth (Parapamisadai); alluvial plains in the west (Aria); and river valleys and deserts in the east (Arachosia). Geography is the background fabric for these regions: the Hindu Kush forms a rugged mountainous center surrounded on three sides by harsh deserts. The mountains, rather than creating barriers, attracted populations because of mineral deposits of copper, gold, stone, and tin, while their well-watered foothills and valleys allowed agriculture and pastoralism to flourish. The valleys leading into the mountains act like highways for migrations, commerce, and exchange. Neither the Persians nor the Greeks referred to these regions as a single entity, but the archaeological evidence suggests that they represented a vibrant region of interaction, a melting-pot culture, linked by social and economic relationships that have left few historical traces.[1]

The earlier existence of this distinct regional identity can be demonstrated only by archaeology, as there are no local texts or outside historical records to document it; furthermore, the scholarly bias against regarding contact zones as unique phenomena mitigates against such an identity for ancient Afghanistan. Traditional core-focused analytical approaches see large-scale riverine societies as centers, and everything else as peripheral. In addition, the nature of ancient Afghanistan is difficult to discern due to the slow accumulation of knowledge about its Bronze Age society because of a hiatus in field research for the last thirty years and the recent loss of archaeological data from looting.

Bronze Age occupations in Central Asia, whether they are substantial cities or small cave sites, can be identified immediately by their characteristic ceramics. Warwick Ball recorded over 1,500 known archaeological sites in Afghanistan proper, of which fewer than fifty are categorized as Bronze Age.[2] For several reasons this figure considerably under represents the true number of archaeological sites in Afghanistan. First, large regions of Afghanistan have not been systematically explored; second, war and political chaos have prevented investigation of the known sites within Afghanistan; and third, rampant looting of sites of all periods—including hundreds of prehistoric sites—has forever destroyed much of the context of the occupational history of

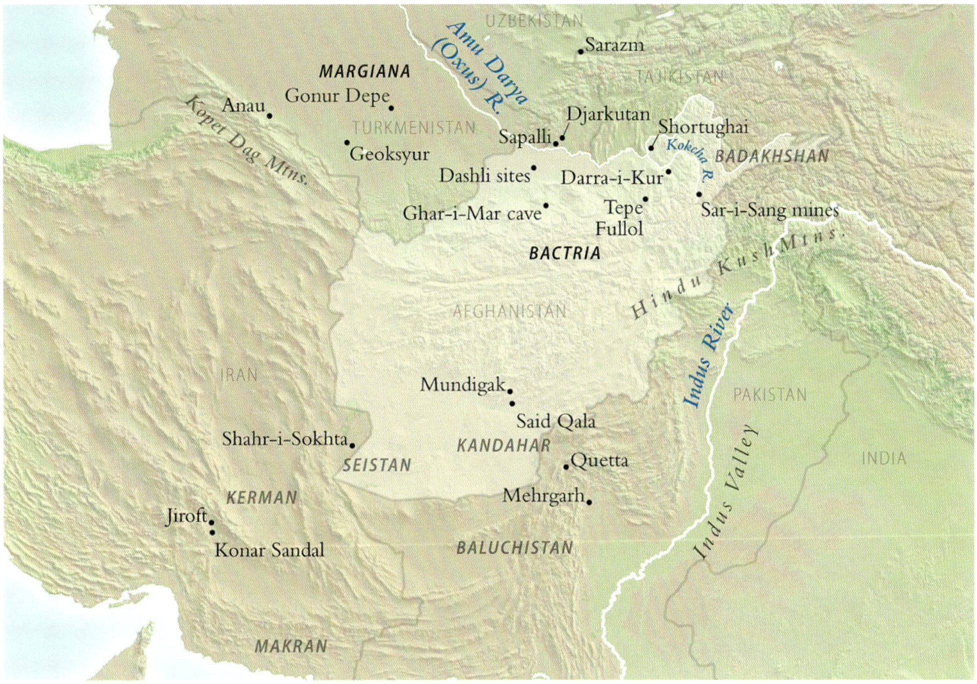

Fig. 1. Map of Bronze Age sites of Afghanistan and surrounding regions

Afghanistan. For these reasons, many of the best-documented sites that reveal the nature of Bronze Age Afghanistan lie just outside of the proper borders of Afghanistan, in eastern Iran, Turkmenistan, Uzbekistan, and Pakistan.

The Neolithic origins of settlement in this region are known primarily from sites on the periphery of Afghanistan, as village life was clearly established as early as the seventh millennium B.C. on all sides of Afghanistan's mountainous massif. At the beginning of the third millennium B.C., during the Early Bronze Age, interaction across the vast regions of mountains and desert can be discerned in the form of exchanged products and the sharing of styles and technologies. These similarities in material culture at many sites imply a community of trade and interaction across Afghanistan.

History of Research

Research on Afghanistan's Bronze Age origins is a work in progress, one that is best understood in the historical context of discovery. Raphael Pumpelly was the first scholar who looked at Central Asia (including northern Afghanistan) as a possible cradle of ancient civilization.[3] A geologist, long interested in the relationship between environment and civilization, he focused his attention late in life on the area, looking for traces of early settlement in oasis regions that, though once fertile, are now arid. He was the originator of the "propinquity" theory of the origins of civilization—the theory later championed by V. Gordon Childe—suggesting that the shrinking subsistence resources in the regions of these oases forced humans to settle and adopt agriculture. His excavations at Anau in Turkmenistan in 1904 established, for the

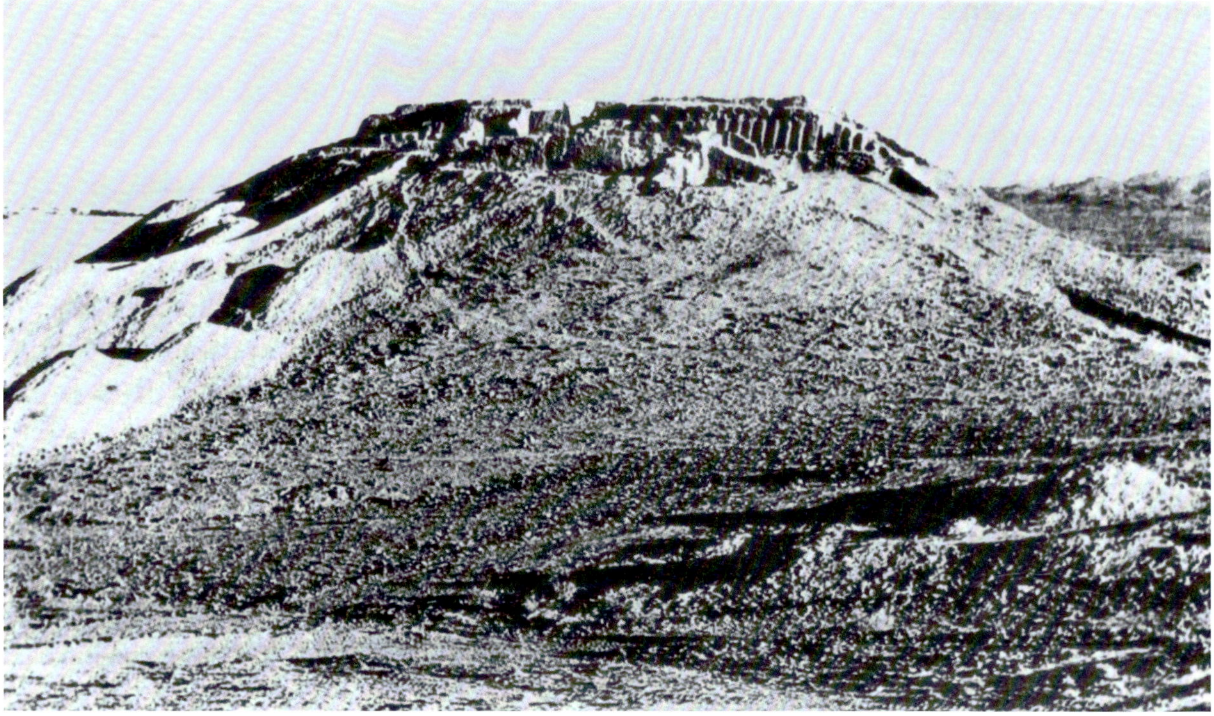

Fig. 2. Mundigak, site A, with a view of the palace

first time, antiquity comparable with that of western Iran.[4] In particular, Pumpelly was struck by the parallels between Susa and Anau. Working almost in a vacuum, Pumpelly initially devised a chronology based on rates of sedimentation that, in retrospect, were far too old. He corrected his estimates in a reexamination of the data[5]—but by this time his hypothesis and data were dismissed by other archaeologists more inclined to see Central Asia as simply a peripheral anomaly.

Early Soviet archaeologists also tended to dismiss Pumpelly's work, suggesting that he was a spy in disguise or that his methodology was too crude to merit consideration.[6] Ironically, it was a Russian botanist, Nikolai Vavilov, who became fascinated with the idea, based on modern genetic variation, that early forms of wheat and barley could have been transformed into better varieties in the area of Afghanistan. Vavilov led several expeditions to Afghanistan in the 1920s before disappearing in Stalinist purges.[7]

In 1922, Alfred Foucher, a specialist in Indian studies, was invited by King Amanullah to visit the recently independent Afghanistan. Within months, Foucher signed a convention granting the French a thirty-year monopoly on archaeological investigations in Afghanistan.[8] Foucher stayed in Afghanistan until 1925, excavating at the classical site of Bactra and setting the agenda of the Délégation Archéologique Française en Afghanistan (DAFA) to concentrate on historic sites until the 1950s.

Despite this focus on later periods, the connections between prehistoric sites in northeastern Iran and Baluchistan (on either side of Afghanistan) were pointed out by Stuart Piggott,[9] thereby alluding to the possibility of a rich prehistory along the foothills of Afghanistan. Soon afterward, this possibility was confirmed in Baluchistan by Walter Fairservis' surveys near Quetta,[10] the Seistan survey of Beatrice De Cardi,[11] and, most clearly, in the excavations of Jean-Marie Casal at Mundigak in the Kandahar region.[12] At Mundigak, DAFA investigated a towering stratified site (fig. 2) that spanned some 3,000 years, from the beginning of the fourth to the second millennium B.C. Five major cultural phases were identified: I–III, representing the development of a small village, which grew into a massive Bronze Age fortified center in phases IV–V (fig. 3). Casal's report tended to focus on the connections with Indus Valley sites, but there was no doubt that the local cultures, though distinct, also had links with eastern Iran, Central Asia, and Baluchistan.

By the mid-1950s, Afghanistan opened its doors to archaeologists from other countries, and interest grew in prehistoric investigations. Small-scale excavations followed on the success of Mundigak, including Louis Dupree's work at cave sites in the northeast of Afghanistan.[13] At the Ghar-i-Mar cave and at Darra-i-Kur, respectively, Early Bronze Age and Late Bronze Age pottery typical of sedentary agriculturalists was found in a transitional zone far from any settlement.[14] Equally, discoveries of Bronze Age stone ritual items by George Dales in Seistan[15] and Jim Shaffer's work at Said Qala in Afghan Baluchistan[16] pointed to a culture of communication and long-distance exchange during the Bronze Age.

Perhaps most emblematic of this exchange was a set of silver and gold vessels found in 1966 near Tepe Fullol in northeastern Afghanistan (fig. 4).[17] While the vessels were part of a chance find made by a farmer, they undoubtedly came from an elite prehistoric burial. Decorated with repoussé motifs common to Mesopotamia, the Indus, and the Bronze Age of Central Asia, the five gold and seven silver vessels were unlike any others previously found in Afghanistan. Controversy surrounded scholarly estimates of their dates, which included suggestions of later parallels with Marlik and Babylonian art of the twelfth century B.C. or of Mesopotamian parallels dating to the late third millennium. Still others, pointing to similarities of the geometric designs with earlier pottery, suggested an early third millennium date.[18]

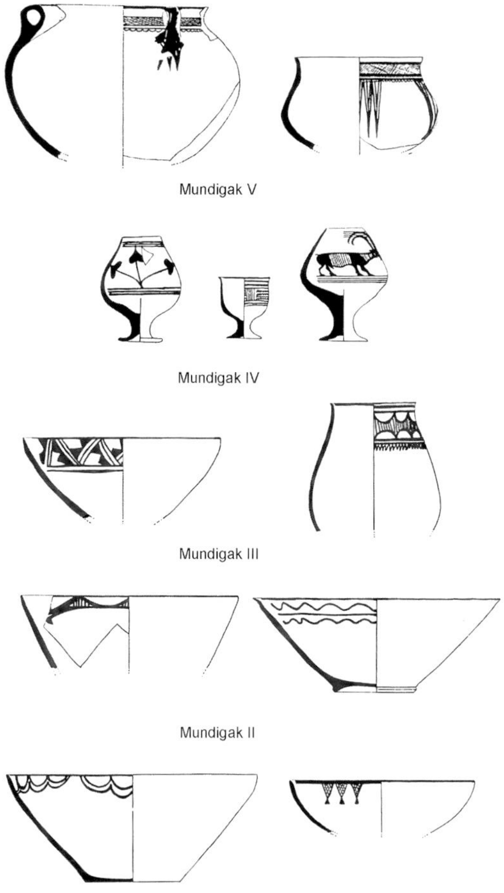

Fig. 3. Mundigak pottery. Periods I, II: Chalcolithic, black-painted buff/red wheel-finished ware; Periods III, IV: Bronze Age black-and-red-painted buff fast-wheel ware; Period V: Iron Age red-painted handmade ware

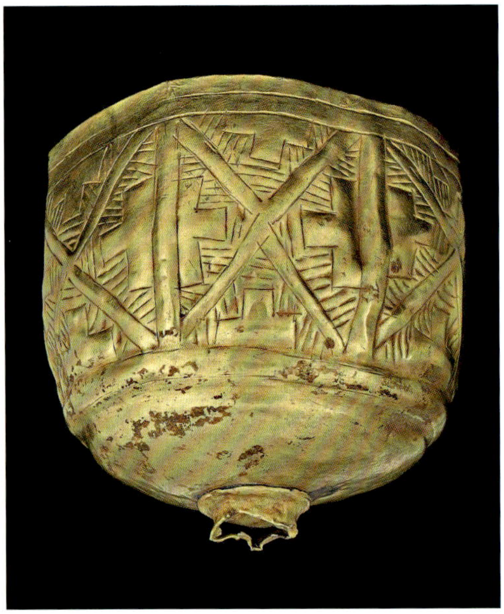

(a)

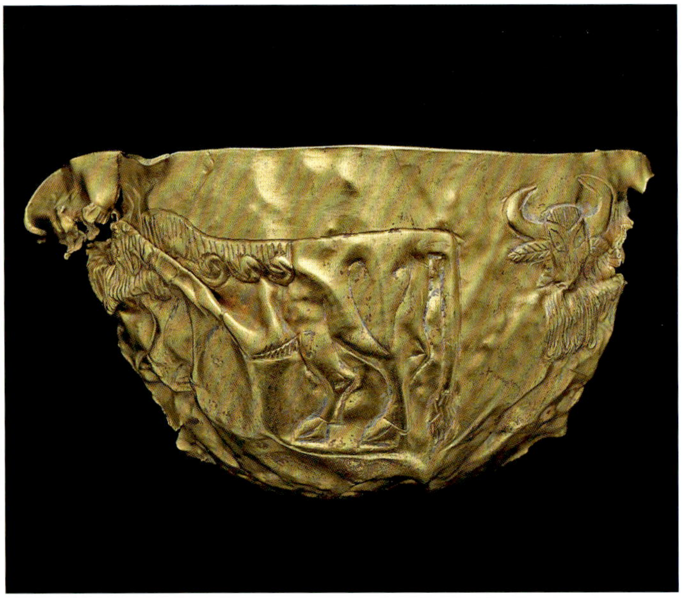

(b)

Fig. 4. Silver and gold finds from Tepe Fullol, ca. 2200–1900 B.C.: (a) goblet with geometric motif, D. 9.9 cm; (b) fragment of a gold bowl with bearded bulls, H. 14.9 cm; and (c) bowl fragments with boar, largest H. 11.6 cm. National Museum of Afghanistan, Kabul (04.29.1, 04.29.5, 04.29.3)

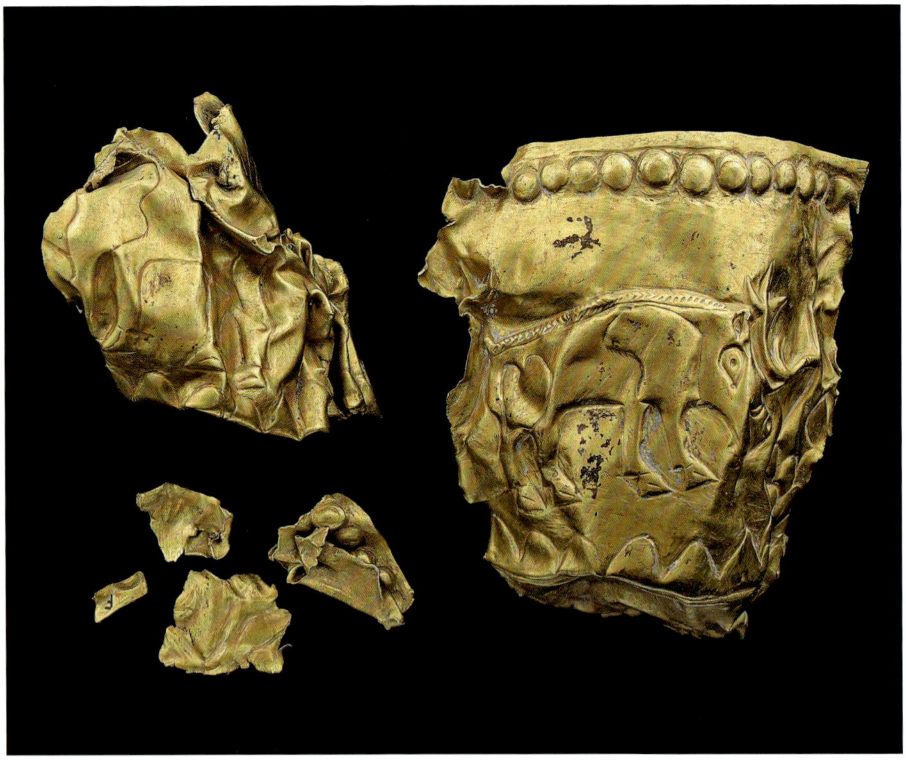

(c)

Shortly after the discovery of the Fullol hoard, Georgina Herrmann authored the first extensive survey of the trade in lapis lazuli, one of the hallmark products of the mineral wealth of Afghanistan. She demonstrated the importance of the Sar-i-Sang mines (fig. 5) in long-distance trade to Mesopotamia and Egypt as early as 3500 B.C.[19] As seen in the overall assemblage of artifacts from the Bronze Age in the exhibition "Afghanistan: Hidden Treasures from the National Museum, Kabul," brilliant blue lapis lazuli was not a preferred stone for inlay in Afghanistan or its near neighbors, where light blue-green turquoise or black and white marble from the Baluchistan and Makran regions was favored. This fact suggests a mechanism of trade and resource acquisition for semiprecious stones (and probably metals) from region to region in Afghanistan during the Bronze Age, which accounts for the mixing of Near Eastern, Central Asian, and Indus Valley iconography throughout Afghanistan.

Aside from research at Sar-i-Sang and Fullol in the mid-1960s, most of the important archaeological discoveries pertaining to the Bronze Age were made just outside of the modern border of Afghanistan. Excavations at Geoksyur in Turkmenistan and at Shahr-i-Sokhta in Seistan both showed surprising similarities with Quetta and Mundigak in Baluchistan during the Early Bronze Age. Later, massive Soviet research at the sites of Djarkutan and Sapalli in southern Uzbekistan (northern Bactria) uncovered large fortified citadels or small towns with highly planned architecture and a very high level of craft production.[20] The similarity of the Bronze Age Bactrian material culture to that of the desert oasis of Margiana in Turkmenistan led Viktor Sarianidi to name this the Bactrian–Margiana Archaeological Complex (BMAC).[21]

The significance of the BMAC was confirmed when Sarianidi located similar clusters of Bronze Age settlements in the oases of Farukhabad, Dashli, and Daulatabad in southern Bactria near Akcha, in Afghanistan. Sarianidi's excavations at Dashli 1 and Dashli 3 revealed architectural compounds almost similar to those in northern Bactria and in Margiana (figs. 6, 7). Other aspects of the material culture—elegant, unpainted

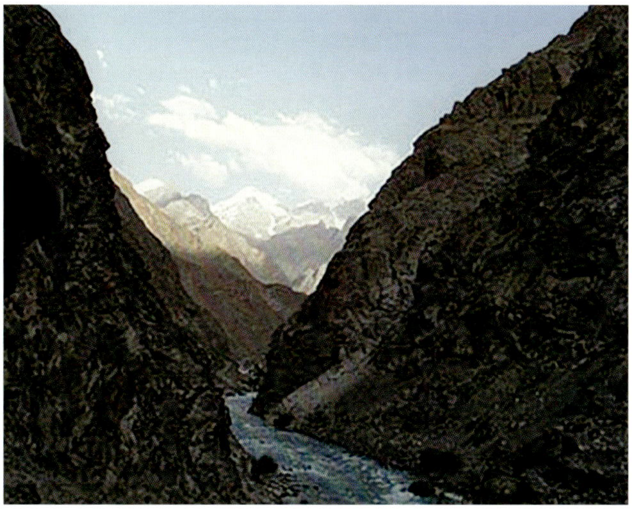

Fig. 5. Sar-i-Sang mines, northern Afghanistan

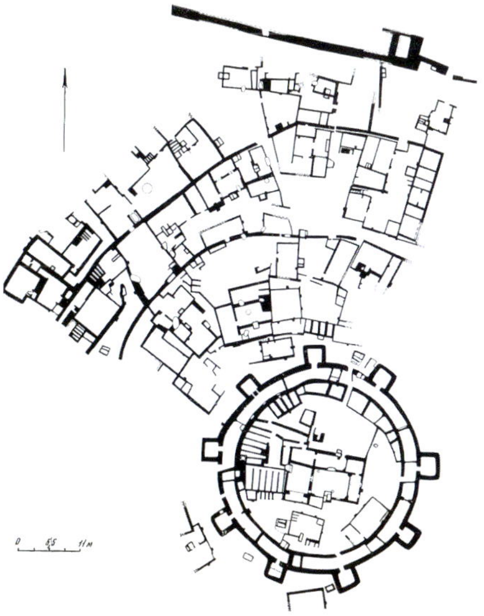

Fig. 6. Plan of Dashli 3 temple

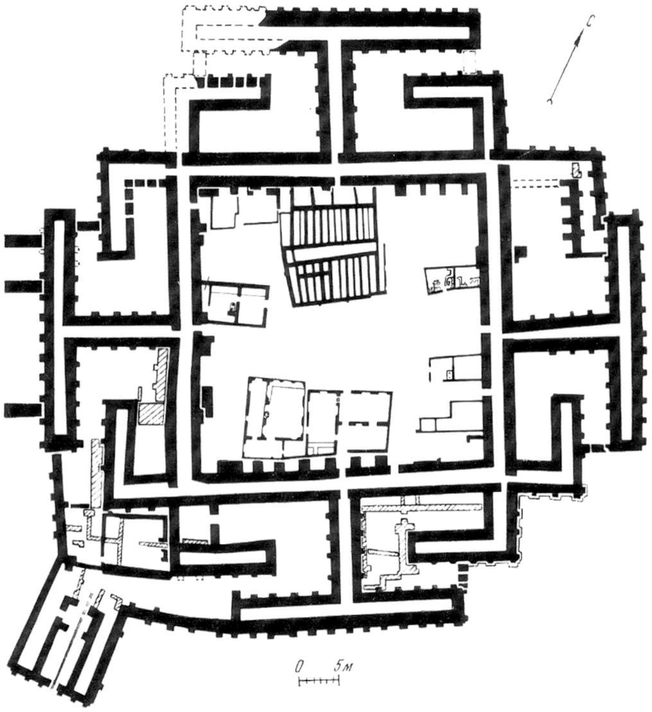

Fig. 7. Plan of Dashli 3 palace

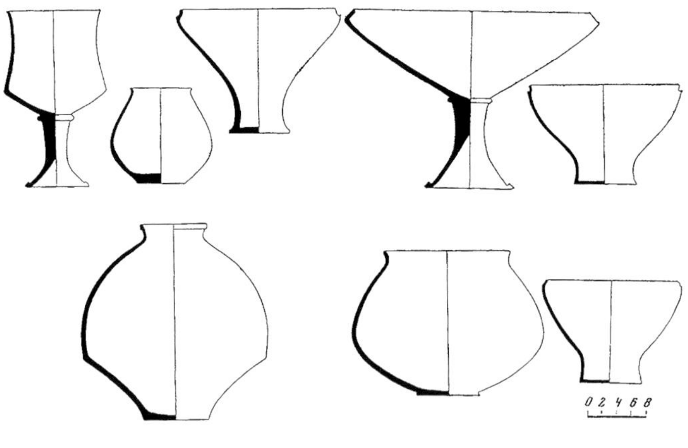

Fig. 8. Dashli ceramics

fast-wheel pottery (fig. 8) and large numbers of objects made locally from imported stone and metal (fig. 9)—indicated that the BMAC was as much at home in Afghanistan as it was across the Amu Darya in Uzbekistan and Turkmenistan.[22] One major difference between Bronze Age Bactria and Bronze Age Margiana, however, is the lack of terracotta figurines in the Bactrian sites. This absence is likely due to a chronological difference between the two regions, with such figurines being in the earlier levels in Margiana, probably derived from a Kopet Dag prototype.[23]

Equally, it was no surprise when DAFA archaeologists surveyed the deltaic plain between the Kokcha and the Amu Darya in northeastern Afghanistan and found an array of Bronze Age settlements.[24] Again, the material culture of these sites was very similar to that of southern and northern Bactria, leading these scholars to dub this the "eastern Bactrian" plain. A surprise came from the excavations at nearby Shortughai—a large mounded site with two citadels, revealing occupation stretching from 2800 to 2000 B.C.[25] The two earlier phases had ceramics (fig. 10) and other materials so stylistically similar to the Indus that the excavator considered it to have been an enclave of the Indus civilization in northern Afghanistan—a gateway community, close to the lapis lazuli mines of Sar-i-Sang.

Excavations in Afghanistan, including at Shortughai, were cut short in 1979 by political disruptions, and no systematic excavations of Bronze Age sites have since been conducted in Afghanistan. However, vast amounts of artifacts from illegal excavations at Bronze Age sites have appeared on the market in Kabul (fig. 11). An entire monograph has been devoted to the small finds—bronzes, stone vessels, stone ritual objects, and pottery that came primarily from looted cemeteries in northern Afghanistan.[26] Sarianidi compiled an amazing array of Bronze Age Bactrian-style seals from the Kabul market, which also revealed important iconographic differences from those

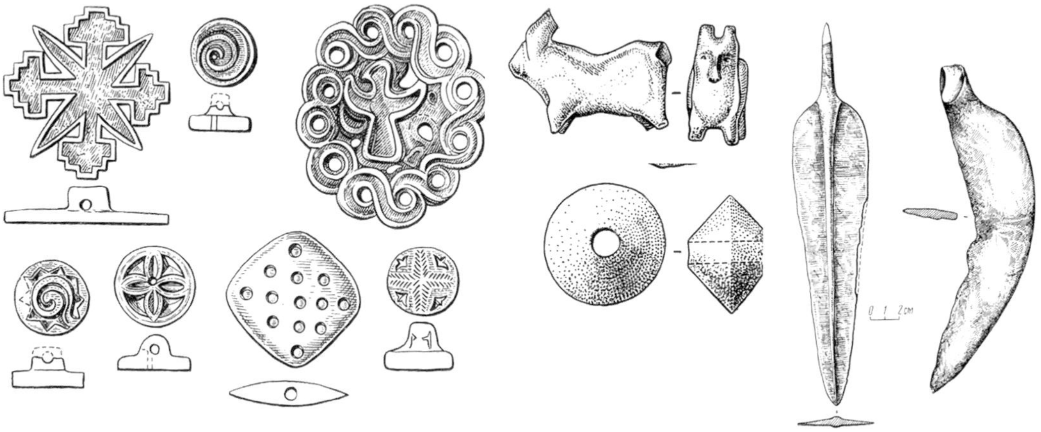

Fig. 9. Dashli small finds

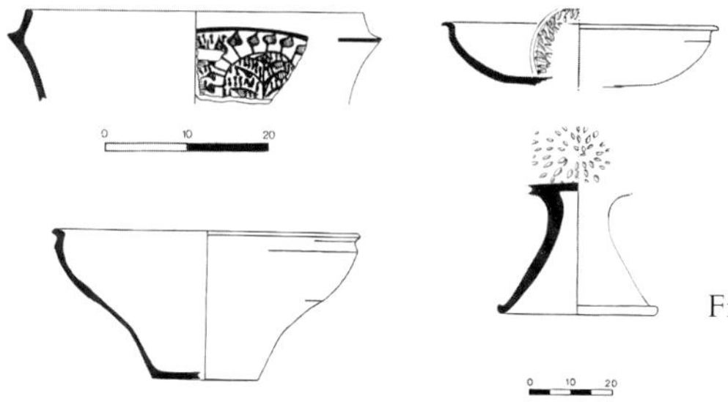

Fig. 10. Shortughai: Indus-related ceramics

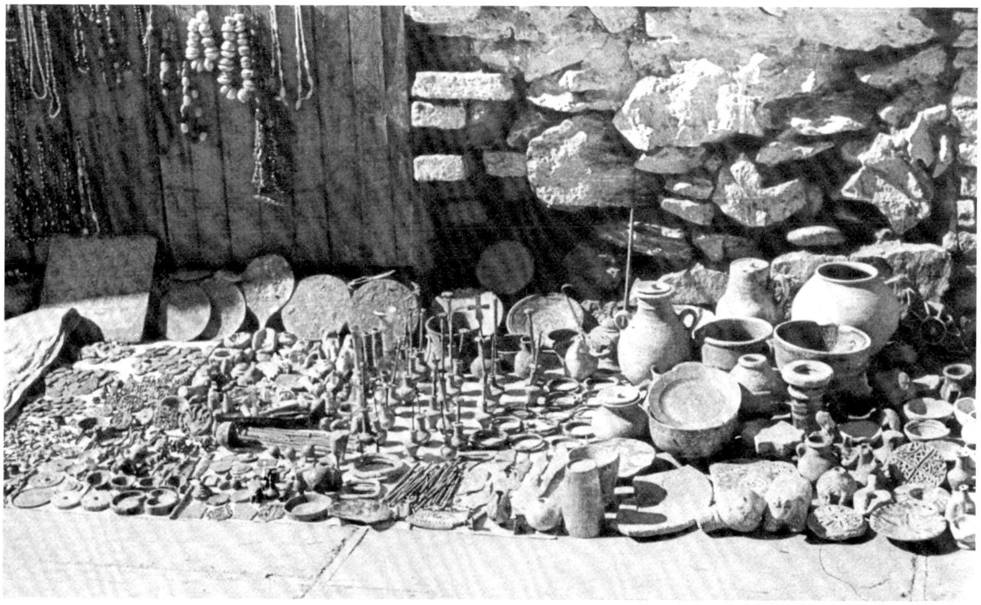

Fig. 11. Outdoor market in Kabul, displaying Bronze Age objects from illegal excavations

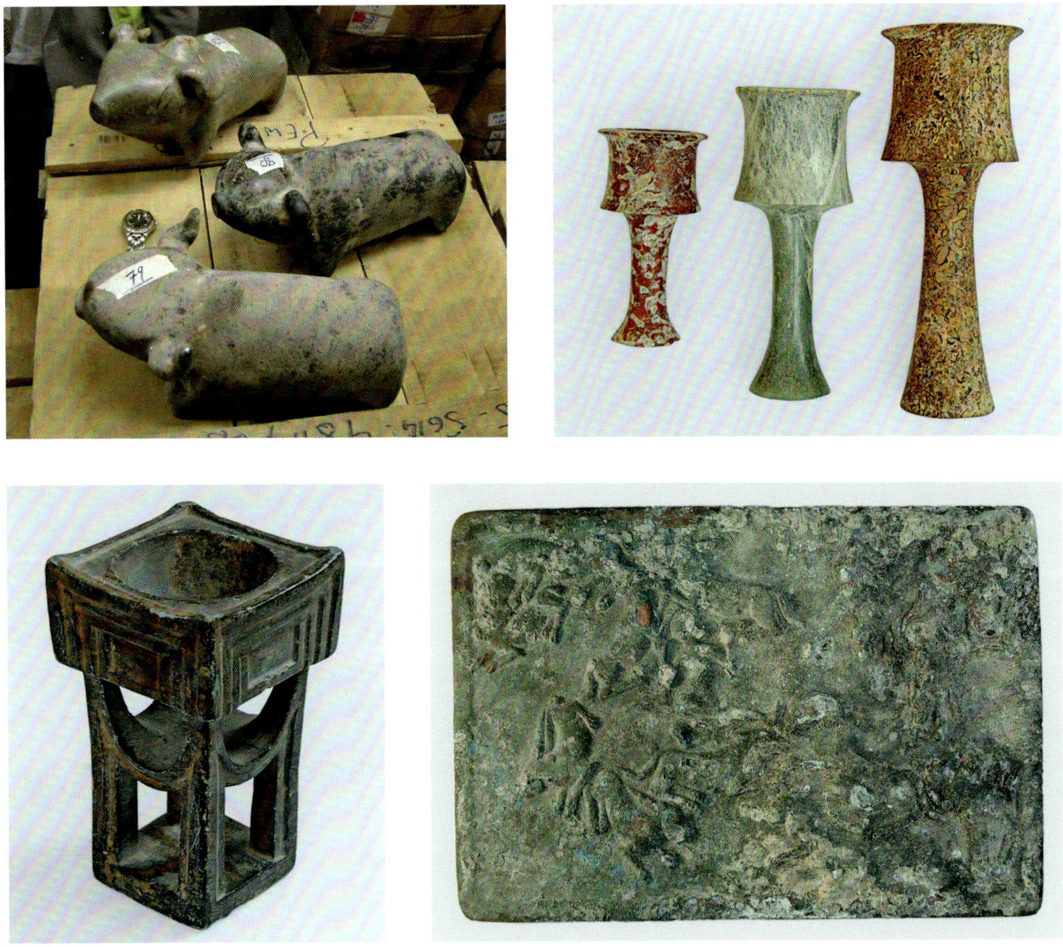

Fig. 12. Clockwise from top left: Bronze Age zoomorphic sculptures, stone footed cups, copper-alloy plaque with a narrative scene of human and animal combat, and steatite incense burner. These objects, from looted sites in Afghanistan, were seized at Heathrow Airport, London, and repatriated in 2009.

found in Turkmenistan and in Bactria.[27] With the chaos in Afghanistan, Sarianidi moved his excavations to Turkmenistan, focusing on the major settlement of Gonur Depe, north of Merv in Margiana. The excavation of many elite burials at Gonur showed objects with important iconographic connections, both with the Indus and with Iran and Mesopotamia in good archaeological context, providing us with a sad glimpse of what must have been major Bronze Age cemeteries at the now-looted sites in northern Afghanistan (fig. 12).[28]

The discovery in the last decade of third and second millennium settlements and burials from eastern Iran provides the latest piece in the Bronze Age Afghanistan puzzle. In the region of Jiroft, dozens of archaeological sites have recently been mapped and new excavations initiated, shedding light on settlement and social complexity on the western border of Afghanistan. First identified from an array of finely carved chlorite bowls and Bronze Age pottery looted from burials,[29] sites in the Jiroft region show striking similarities with the small sites of Seistan and Kerman in southern Iran, while including aspects of iconography and pottery style similar to Shahr-i-Sokhta and Mundigak as well.[30]

Conclusion

What is the impact of this accumulated information on our understanding of Bronze Age Afghanistan? We now have a more or less comprehensive chronology for the era from radiocarbon dating of sites surrounding Afghanistan (fig. 13): data from stratified sites in Turkmenistan (Anau and Gonur) and Baluchistan (Mehrgarh), and data from the excavations at Konar Sandal (Jiroft region). It appears that there are three variants of Afghan culture reflected in the historic past: western Afghanistan and eastern Iran; eastern Afghanistan and South Asia; and northern Afghanistan and Central Asia. We can clearly see that pattern emerging already in the Early Bronze Age, by 2900 B.C.

Dramatic geography clearly played a strong role in Afghanistan's settlement history through time, the Bronze Age being no exception: settlements were located in

		Shar-i Sokhta	Namazga	Margiana	S. Bactria Uzbekistan	N. Bactria	E. Bactria	Pastoral cave stations N. Afghanistan	Deh Morasi	Said Qala	Mundigak	Mehrgarh	Harappa
IRON AGE	1200												
	1300												
	1400												
	1500		Iron 1	Yaz I	Bustan	Tillya tepe I		Aq Kupruk I, II			Mundigak V		
BRONZE AGE	1600												
	1700												
	1800	SS IV	NMG VI	Togolok	Djarkutan	Dashli	Shortughai IV	Darra-i-Kur					
	1900						Shortughai III	Fullol				Sibri	Jukhar
	2000				Sapalli								Late Mature Harappen
	2100			Gonur								Nausharo IIIc	
	2200						Shortughai II						
	2300	SS III	NMG V				Shortughai I					Mehrgarh VIII	Harappen 3C
	2400												Harappen 3B
	2500												Harappen 3A
	2600	SS II	NMG IV										
	2700								Deh Morasi IV		Mundigak IV	Mehrgarh VII	
	2800								Deh Morasi				
	2900								Deh Morasi II	Said Qala II			
	3000		NMG III		Sarazm			Ghar-i-Asp	Deh Morasi I	Said Qala III	Mundigak III	Mehrgarh VI	Early Harappen
CHALCOLITHIC	3100	SS I								Said Qala II	Mundigak II		
	3200		NMG II								Mundigak I		
	3300												
	3400											Mehrgarh V	Hakra
	3500		NMG I										
	3600												
	3700		Anau IA										

Fig. 13. Chronological chart of early cultures in Afghanistan

desert oases and along fertile foothill regions on the margins between the mountains and the deserts. In contrast, smaller-scale sites in the valleys reflect the remains of a more mobile adaptation of herders, traders, and migrants. Louis Dupree's excavations of cave deposits of ceramics at Ghar-i-Mar (Early Bronze Age) and Darra-i-Kur (Late Bronze Age) in northeastern Afghanistan shed rare light on the otherwise archaeologically invisible connections between sedentary sites and the locations of many transient and special purpose campsites in less productive regions. Similar "mountain" strategies have been proposed for cultural expansion in Kazakhstan and Margiana.[31]

It is just outside the borders of modern Afghanistan that we can contextualize the earliest "identity" for Afghanistan. The settlement of this region had at its origin a Near Eastern economy based on herding sheep and goats and on farming wheat and barley. Agricultural villages were established along the foothills of the Kopet Dag, north of Iran, by the seventh millennium B.C. (at Djeitun in Turkmenistan) and at about the same time along the foothill flanks of Baluchistan (at Mehrgarh in Pakistan). These early villages shared features of the Near Eastern productive economy, as well as traditions of mud-brick dwellings, painted pottery, and the use of terracotta figurines as ritual objects. These villages thrived in the fertile lowlands, but the mountains, with rare mineral wealth of copper and stone, attracted these people. The quest for resources likely drove expanded interaction in the fourth millennium B.C. and set the stage for the establishment of a distinctive Bronze Age pattern in Afghanistan. By 3300 B.C., a new level of interaction can be detected across Afghanistan in the exchange of commodities and in similarities of styles and technologies of production from eastern to western Afghanistan and north to the foothills of northern Afghanistan, Turkmenistan, and Uzbekistan. The Early Bronze Age sites mark the trade routes across the valleys and mountain passes of Afghanistan, providing evidence of a network of exchange and occupation between the settled sites along the foothills.

From our present perspective, we believe that the emergence of stratified societies in the foothill sites led to competition for the resources of the mountainous center of Afghanistan. By the end of the third millennium B.C., entire colonies from one region appear to manage the extraction of valuable and symbolically significant minerals. Sarazm, colonized from the Kopet Dag, and Shortughai, from the Indus, attest to the importance of these resources. Also, by the end of the third millennium B.C., fortified cities encircled the mountainous Hindu Kush of central Afghanistan, but such cities as Mundigak, Shar-i-Sokhta, and Shortughai represent just one aspect of the Bronze Age pattern. These urban sites are small compared to counterparts in Mesopotamia and India, and appear instead to be central places of ceremony, power, and the production of luxury goods related to a wider network of population beyond the urban area. This dispersed population formed a continuous cultural network of settlements following agricultural and pastoral lifeways in different places.

By the late third millennium large-scale irrigation made oasis life possible for larger populations. The architectural and ceramic traditions, deriving directly both from the earlier South Asian world as represented at Mundigak and from the Central Asian and Iranian spheres, form a distinctive culture in the desert oases. Ironically, these large-scale irrigation-based oases, with poor access to stone and metal but with high agricultural potential, were driven to form relations with areas at great distances, creating regional networks across what is now modern Afghanistan. By the end of the Bronze Age, this system thrived, despite global climate change that made rainfall agriculture even more risky, setting the stage for the end of urban cultures and the rise of a new social system in the Iron Age. Such a crisis, from the point of view of declining urban centers, may have provided an ideal opportunity for the expansion of pastoral herders, who could disperse across wide landscapes. This shift in influence and power to more mobile populations is a familiar pattern across the arid and rugged landscape of Central Asia and Afghanistan.

1. *Afghanistan* 2008, p. 55.
2. Ball 1982, vol. 2, fig. 58.
3. Pumpelly 1903.
4. Pumpelly 1908, p. 179.
5. Pumpelly 1918, pp. 801–14.
6. Bartol'd 1996 (1907), p. 142; Masson 1956, p. 292.
7. Vavilov 1951, p. XI; Miller 1956, pp. 96–105.
8. Fenet 2010.
9. Piggott 1950, p. 192.
10. Fairservis 1956, p. 359.
11. De Cardi 1951, pp. 63–67.
12. Casal 1961, p. 258.
13. Dupree 1972, pp. 25, 81–82.
14. Dupree and Kolb 1972.
15. Dales 1977.
16. Shaffer 1971.
17. Tosi and Wardak 1972.
18. Hiebert 2003, p. 73, fig. 6.14.
19. Herrmann 1968.
20. Askarov 1977.
21. Sarianidi 1977, p. 33.
22. Sarianidi 1986, pp. 89–298.
23. Hiebert 1994, p. 167, fig. 10.2.
24. Gardin and Lyonnet 1978–79.
25. Francfort 1989.
26. Pottier 1984.
27. Sarianidi 1998.
28. Sarianidi 2002.
29. Majidzadeh 2003.
30. Majidzadeh 2008.
31. Frachetti 2008.

Chronology: Western, Central, and East Asia after Alexander

(based on chronologies in Bopearachchi 1991, p. 453, table 5, and Invernizzi ed, pp. 24–25, 29–39; all dates are approximate)

MESOPOTAMIA | IRAN | BACTRIA | GANDHARA

ACHAEMENIDS (550–330BC)

ALEXANDER THE GREAT (330–323BC)

SELEUCIDS (312–141BC)

MESOPOTAMIA

312–281 Seleucus I Nicator
281–261 Antiochus I Soter
261–246 Antiochus II
246–225 Seleucus II
225–223 Seleucus III
223–187 Antiochus III the Great
187–175 Seleucus IV
175–164 Antiochus IV
164–162 Antiochus V
162–150 Demetrius I
145–139 Demetrius II

PARTHIANS

IRAN

PARTHIANS (247BC–AD224)

247–211BC Arsaces I
211–191 Arsaces II
191–176 Phriapatius
176–171 Phraates I
171–138 Mithridates I
138–127 Phraates II
127–124 Artabanus I
124–88 Mithridates II
90–80 Orodes I
70–57 Phraates III
57–38 Orodes II
38–2 Phraates IV
AD10–38 Artabanus II
40–51 Gotarzes II
51–78 Vologases I
78–80 Vologases II
78–105 Pacorus II
105–147 Vologases III/109–129 Osroes I
147–191 Vologases IV
191–208 Vologases V
216–224 Artabanus IV

BACTRIA

GRAECO-BACTRIANS (256–130BC)

256–248 Diodotus I
248–235 Diodotus II
230–200 Euthydemus I
200–190 Demetrius I
185–170 Antimachus I
175–170 Demetrius II
170–145 Eucratides I
145–140 Eucratides II
145–140 Plato
145–130 Heliocles

SAKA/YUEZHI INVASIONS

145BC Fall of Aï Khanum
after 130BC five Yuezhi yabgu

50BC–AD50 Pulagid kings
1–30 Heraios

KUSHAN (AD30–320)

30–80 Kujula Kadphises
80–95 Vima Taktu
95–127 Vima Kadphises
127–140 Kanishka I
140–160 Vasishka
160–190 Huvishka
190–230 Vasudeva

GANDHARA

INDO-GREEKS (190–70B

190–180 Agathocles
180–160 Apollodotus I
165–155 Antimachus II
155–130 Menander I
130–125 queen Agathoclei
95–90 Amyntas

SAKA/YUEZHI

90–70 Hermaios

INDO-SCYTHIA

INDO-PARTHIA (50BC–AD30)

AD20–46 Gondoph

ROMAN EMPIRE

27BC–AD14 Augustus
14–37 Tiberius
41–54 Claudius
54–68 Nero
69–79 Vespasian
98–117 Trajan
117–138 Hadrian
138–161 Antoninus Pius
161—180 Marcus Aurelius
193–211 Septimius Severus
211–217 Caracalla
217–218 Macrinus
218–222 Elagabalus
222–235 Severus Alexander

SASANIANS (AD224–651)

HEPHTHALITES (AD450–565)

NORTH–CENTRAL INDIA

MAURYA (321–185 BC)

321–297 Chandragupta

273–232 Ashoka

SHUNGA (185–73BC)

185–149 Pushyamitra Shunga

116–83 Bhagavata

IS (ca. 90BC)

BC–AD30)

90BC Maues

57–35 Azes I

C–AD20 Azes II

GUPTA (AD321–500)

SOUTH INDIA

SATAVAHANA (2nd cent. BC–AD300)

EASTERN CENTRAL ASIA (NOMADIC CONFEDERATIONS)

SAKA

(known archaeologically from the 8th cent. BC; moved into western Central Asia 2nd cent. BC)

YUEZHI

(ca. 4th–3rd cent. BC; moved into western Central Asia 2nd cent. BC)

XIONGNU (3rd cent. BC–AD 1st cent.)

(presence in Xinjiang in the 1st cent. AD)

209BC Modu Chanyu

XIANBEI (1st cent. BC–AD 3rd cent.)

141–181 Tanshihuai

CHINA

WARRING STATES (475–221BC)

QIN (221–206BC)

WESTERN HAN (209BC–AD9)

206–195 Gaodi

180–157 Wendi

156–141 Jingdi

141–86 Wudi

80–75 Zhaodi

73–49 Xuandi

48–33 Yuandi

32–3 Chengdi

EASTERN HAN (AD25–220)

25–57 Guangwudi

57–75 Mingdi

76–88 Zhangdi

89–105 Hedi

107–125 Andi

126–144 Shundi

147–167 Huandi

168–189 Lingdi

189–220 Xiandi

THREE KINGDOMS (AD220–265)

WESTERN JIN (AD265–318)

SIXTEEN KINGDOMS (AD304–439)

Later Yan (Murong Xianbei) AD384–409

Southern Yan (Murong Xianbei) AD384–407

Northern Yan (Murong Xianbei) AD407–436

NORTHERN WEI (AD386–534)

TUOBA XIANBEI

KOREA

THREE KINGDOMS

GOGURYEO (37BC–AD668)

BAEKJE (18BC–AD668)

GAYA CONFEDERATION (42BC–AD562)

SILLA (57BC–AD668)

Frank L. Holt

Coins: "The Great Guides of the Historian"

In 1843, the Reverend Joseph Wolff (1795–1862) set off on a perilous journey to rescue two British officers being tortured within the infamous "Bug Pit" of Bukhara.[1] The heroic mission failed. Colonel Charles Stoddart and Captain Arthur Conolly were beheaded, and the Emir of Bukhara threatened Wolff with the same gruesome fate for meddling in his affairs. Poor Reverend Wolff endured many hours of interrogation before his eventual release. Among other things, his captors demanded to know how the British people could tolerate a female ruler; how fast a steamship could travel; how many witches inhabited Europe; and why the English took such an extraordinary interest in old coins.[2] Joseph Wolff's answer to this last question shows a remarkable grasp of numismatics, even under duress:

> I explained that their value in the eyes of Englishmen arose from the circumstance that coins were looked upon as the very backbone on which the frame of history is supported. That without them we could not ascertain the duration of the world, dynasties of kings, and national events. That they were the great guides of the historian in determining his eras, and formed a metallic history of the earth.[3]

Indeed, in the two decades before Wolff's incarceration, the atmosphere created by the "Great Game" in Central Asia had inspired foreigners to scour the countryside from Bukhara to Peshawar in search of ancient coins. The import of their discoveries would not be superseded until the excavations celebrated in the "Hidden Treasures" exhibition. Captain Conolly, whom Wolff could not rescue, is actually credited with coining the term "Great Game" long before Rudyard Kipling made it famous, and he took up numismatics while spying in Central Asia under the punning name "Khan Ali."[4]

What Coins Reveal About Graeco-Bactrian Rulers

Before the Great Game, scholars knew almost nothing about the history, geography, and monuments of ancient Central Asia. They understood only that Alexander the Great had invaded and colonized the region in the late fourth century B.C., and that his successor Seleucus did the same. Scholars knew that Greek settlers remained on the eastern frontier for another 200 years or so, carving out an independent kingdom called Bactria. From a few fragmentary ancient sources, the names of just seven Greek kings of Bactria could be gleaned: Diodotus I and his son Diodotus II, Euthydemus and his son Demetrius, followed by Eucratides the Great, Menander, and Apollodotus. Little else was known beyond their names, until one or two of the coins minted by these monarchs began to show up in collections from Central Asia. As late as 1820, only four Bactrian coins were known, attesting to the reigns of two of these kings (Euthydemus and Eucratides), plus a third (Heliocles) who is otherwise unrecorded in ancient literature. By the time Reverend Wolff explained the importance of numismatics to the Emir of Bukhara, the coins numbered in the tens of thousands—so many in fact, that unwanted bronze duplicates were simply melted down to make cannons for local militias.[5] Soon, the reigns of all seven recorded kings of Bactria

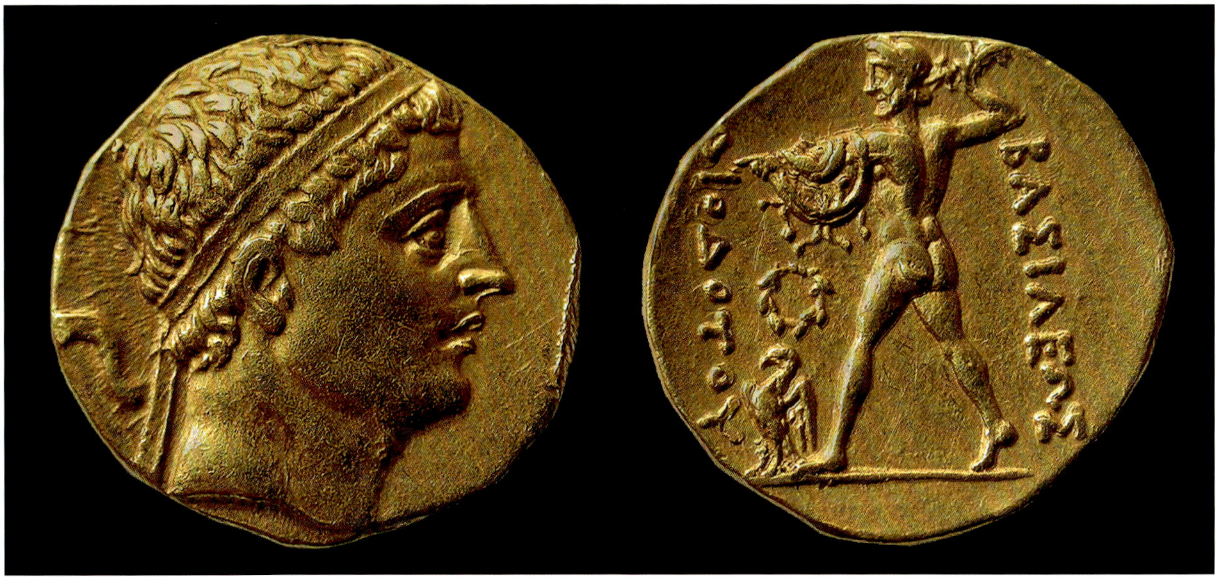

Fig. 1. Gold stater of Diodotus II, founder of Bactrian kingdom (obverse and reverse)

could be reconstructed through coins, not to mention the dozens of other sovereigns whose existence came as a total surprise—eventually forty-three rulers altogether, including a few queens. (See Chronology, pp. 28–29, and Table, p. 39.)

True to Reverend Wolff's remarks, ancient coins remain the very backbone on which the frame of Central Asian history has been built. Fortunately for us, these coins were carefully designed to tell us as much as possible about the people who minted them. Hard currency was an ancient monarch's primary means of mass communication: each coin was like a tiny disk of information technology, crammed with data that a ruler wished to record and disseminate. These traveling disks, recording names, royal titles, honorific epithets, family portraiture, the insignia of power, and the images and attributes of patron deities, were encoded with messages. For instance, the founders of the independent kingdom of Bactria (Diodotus I and II) relate to us numismatically a compelling history of how they broke free of Seleucid power (fig. 1).[6] The founder of the next Bactrian dynasty, Euthydemus I, has bequeathed through his coinage a veritable photo album of his long reign.[7] Year by year, royal coins trace the aging of the king (fig. 2), from youth to

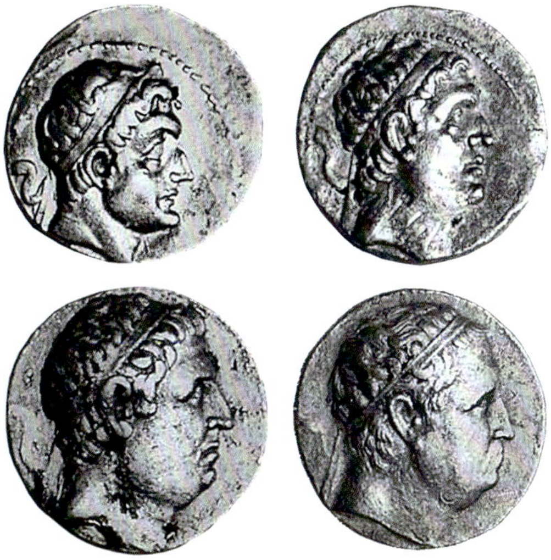

Fig. 2. Silver tetradrachms of Euthydemus I, showing the aging of the king (all obverse), from youth (top left) to old age (bottom right)

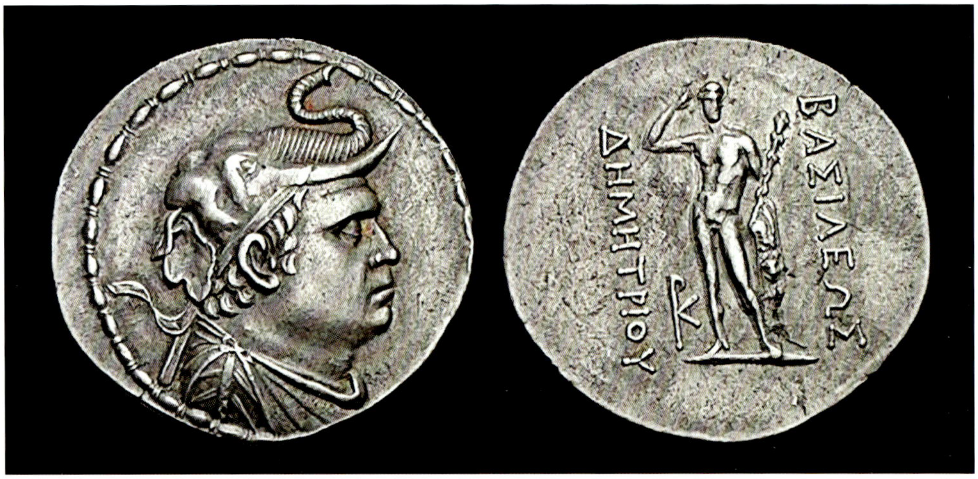

Fig. 3. Silver tetradrachm of Demetrius I, with headgear showing the extension of the king's authority into India (obverse) and the figure of Heracles (reverse)

hoary old age. The longevity of Euthydemus finally secured the independence of Bactria once and for all, in spite of a punitive invasion by Antiochus the Great of Seleucid Syria.[8]

On the coins of Demetrius and Eucratides, the regalia of power include not only their diadems (distinctive ribbons tied around the head of each Greek king), but also more and more elaborate paraphernalia.[9] Demetrius' eye-catching headgear, the scalp of an Asian elephant, signifies the spread of his authority into India (fig. 3, obverse). Eucratides appears "dressed to kill" in his ornate cavalry helmet adorned with the horns and ears of a bull; he even brandishes a spear at his enemies (fig. 4). As for names, titles, and epithets, the coins of Menander (ca. 155–130 B.C.) tell us that he proclaimed himself a savior (fig. 5, obverse). He became the only Bactrian king celebrated in Indian literature, where he is acclaimed as a convert to Buddhism. Other rulers styled themselves the Conqueror, the Invincible, the Do-Gooder, and the Just. Numismatists have even found a Bactrian king named Plato, who declared himself God Manifest on Earth, as well as a queen Agathocleia (ca. 130–125 B.C.), who is called the God-Nourisher, perhaps alluding to her son Strato as the god-king she nurtured. The divinities worshipped in Bactria include the familiar array of Greek gods and goddesses: thundering Zeus for the Diodotids (fig. 1, reverse), mighty Heracles for Euthydemus and Demetrius (fig. 3, reverse), the galloping Dioscuri for Eucratides (see figs. 7, 8, reverse, and 13), and war-like Athena for Menander (fig. 5, reverse). Sometimes, the coins feature deities that are decidedly non-Greek, such as the avatars of Vishnu found

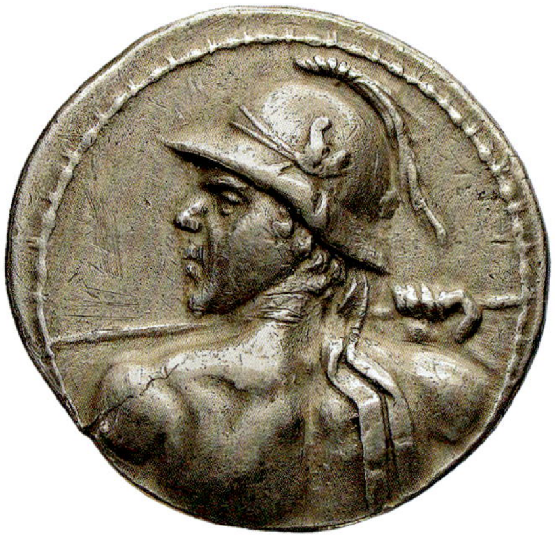

Fig. 4. Silver tetradrachm of Eucratides I (obverse)

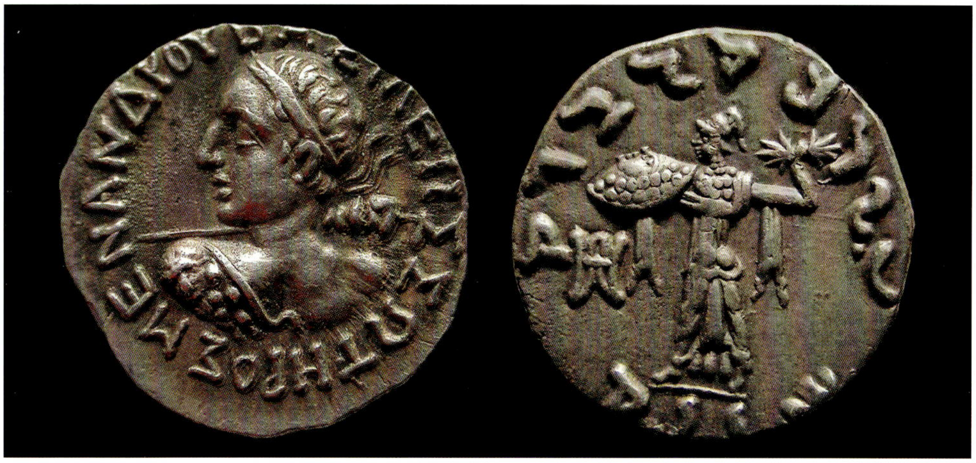

Fig. 5. Silver bilingual drachm of Menander I as "Savior" (obverse) and depiction of Athena (reverse)

on a square silver coin minted by Agathocles the Just.[10]

Nothing captures the diversity of ancient Bactrian culture quite like its coins. Agathocles, for example, was among those rulers who first struck bilingual coins, translating the Greek inscription on one side of his coinage into Brahmi, or into Kharosthi on the other. Like little Rosetta stones, the bilingual coinages of Bactria facilitated the decipherment of early Indian scripts by dedicated scholars, such as James Prinsep, a contemporary of Reverend Wolff.[11] Agathocles also experimented with the use of nickel for coinages, which put him centuries ahead of his time, and he furthermore produced an unprecedented series of silver coins to commemorate his royal predecessors in Bactria. Replicating the coin types of earlier monarchs, Agathocles added to his commemorations a grammatical construction called a genitive absolute that clarified his responsibility for this remarkable reissue of an older-styled currency. Agathocles stretched this numismatic tribute all the way back to Alexander the Great.[12]

Meanwhile, on another special issue commemorating his parents (fig. 6), Eucratides does us the great favor of identifying them:

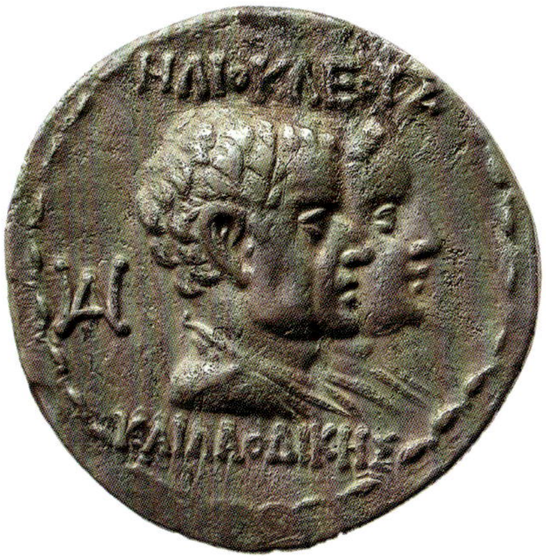

Fig. 6. Silver tetradrachm of Eucratides I commemorating his parents, Heliocles and Laodice (reverse)

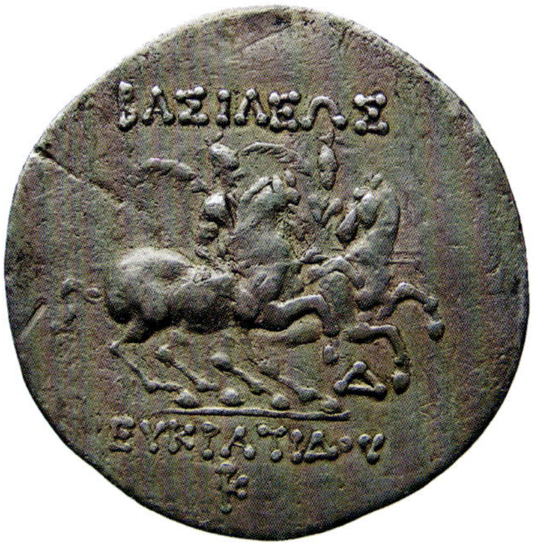

Fig. 7. Silver tetradrachm of Eucratides I, issued before he became "Great" (*Megas*) (reverse)

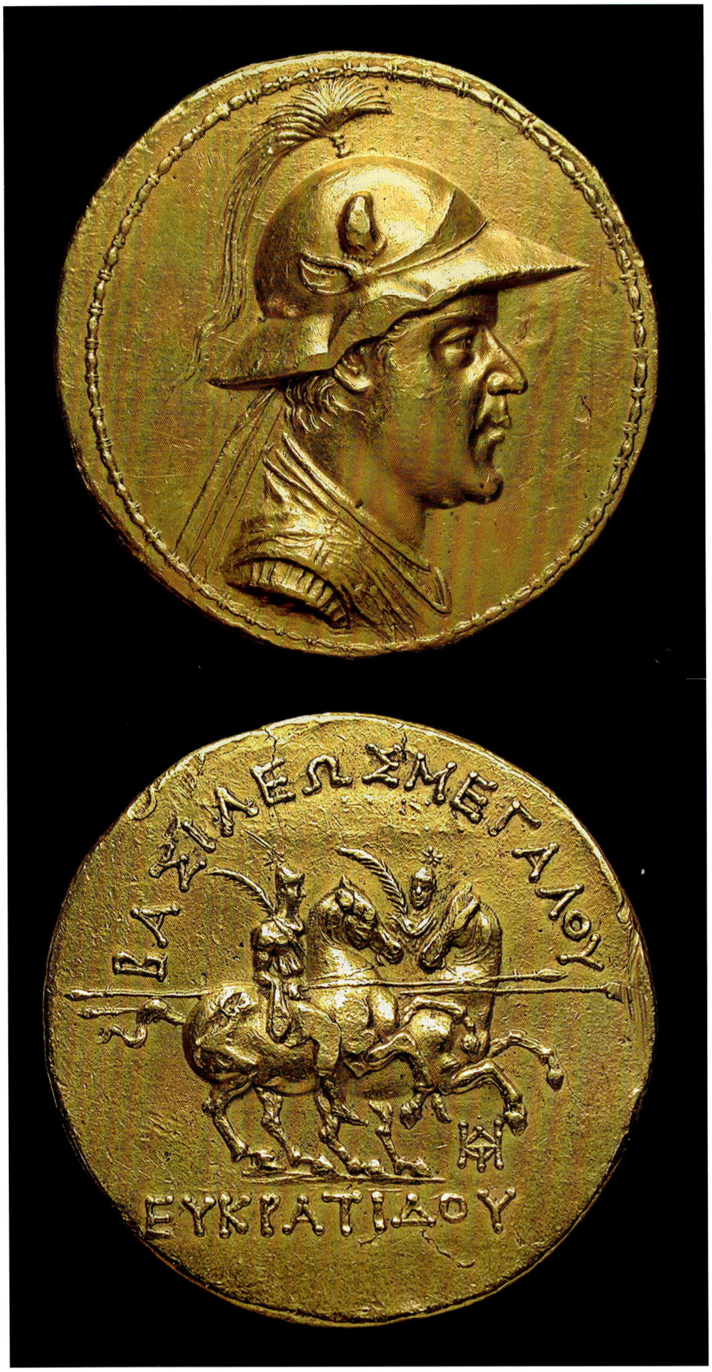

Fig. 8. Gold 20-stater of Eucratides I (obverse and reverse)

Heliocles (apparently a commoner without a diadem) and his mother Laodice (apparently royal, because she wears one).[13] Without the coin, this important bit of family history would be otherwise lost forever, and it makes it all but certain that the mysterious Heliocles the Just was Eucratides' son, named in typical Greek fashion after his grandfather, husband of Laodice. Coins also inform us that Eucratides was not always called "great" (*megas*), but that he began his reign as simply "king" (fig. 7). He added the more exalted title sometime during his reign, and scholars can actually determine when he did so because of a blatant case of numismatic envy. Timarchus, a contemporary king in far-away Babylon, copied every detail of Eucratides' stylish coinage (fig. 8), right down to the epithet (fig. 9). Since the brief reign of Timarchus can be securely dated, we can be certain that Eucratides became Eucratides the Great King shortly before 161 B.C., when his coin type was plagiarized.[14] Years later, in about 145 B.C., this Great King Eucratides was apparently the last ruler of the impressive city at Aï Khanum. Paul Bernard's excavations there turned up no coins of Eucratides' son and successor, Heliocles the Just; the famous Kunduz treasure, however, found west of the city, contained more coins of Heliocles than of any other king. This find proves that Heliocles' coins (fig. 10) circulated in Bactria after the fall of Aï Khanum, but not before.[15] The coins thus establish some of the key chronological markers for Central Asian archaeology.

We are indeed fortunate in the coins of ancient Bactria, for while no other history depends so much on numismatic evidence, no other kingdom experimented so boldly in the design of its currency. Eucratides the Great went so far as to produce the largest gold coin of antiquity, a piece of mega-money twenty times the size of a normal Greek stater (fig. 8).[16] A later Bactrian king, Amyntas the Conqueror (ca. 95–90 B.C.), minted the largest silver coins in the ancient world, which were (perhaps not

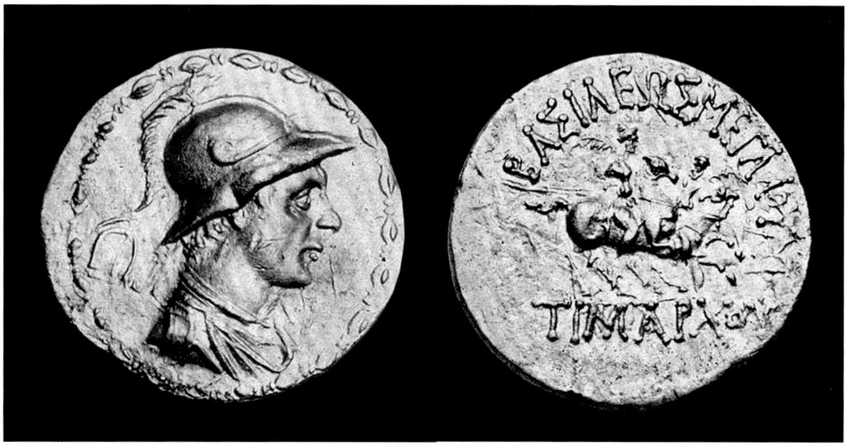

Fig. 9. Silver tetradrachm of Timarchus imitating Eucratides (obverse and reverse)

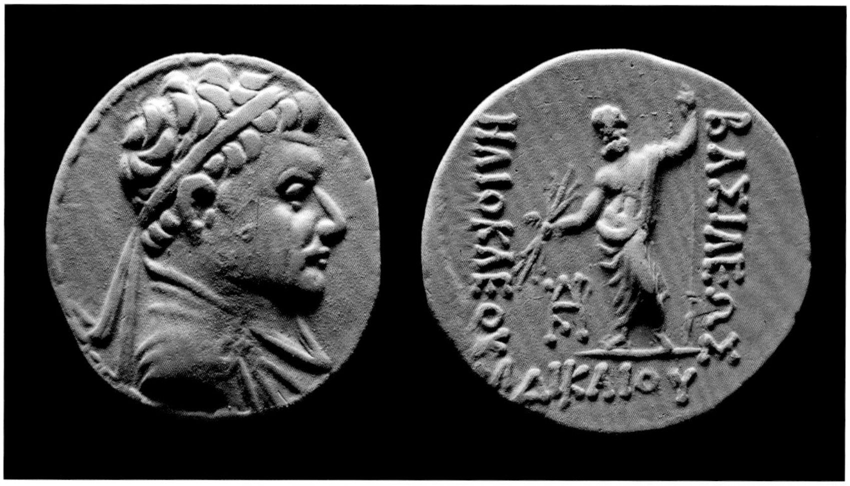

Fig. 10. Silver tetradrachm of Heliocles (obverse and reverse)

coincidentally) twenty times the size of a standard Greek drachm (fig. 11).[17] Beyond royal ego, these artifacts may have served some special pecuniary purpose, such as hefty payments to foreign powers (akin to Danegeld?) or grandiose service awards following some military victory.

What Coins Reveal About Their Creators

Money of this sort could hardly have circulated widely among commoners for daily transactions, any more than most of us carry around large bank notes today. While these huge coins represent the world of wealthy, powerful elites in ancient Bactria, they also reflect another, humbler stratum of society that we might call "sub-historic," existing below the threshold of recorded history. I refer to the anonymous, heretofore invisible, artisan class that labored in the mints of the rich and famous. In ways that Reverend Wolff never imagined, a new approach to coins that I call Cognitive Numismatics takes us inside these mints, and even inside the minds of the workers there. Cognitive Numismatics, like its cousin Cognitive Archaeology, asks how material objects might illuminate the patterns of thought that shaped them. How

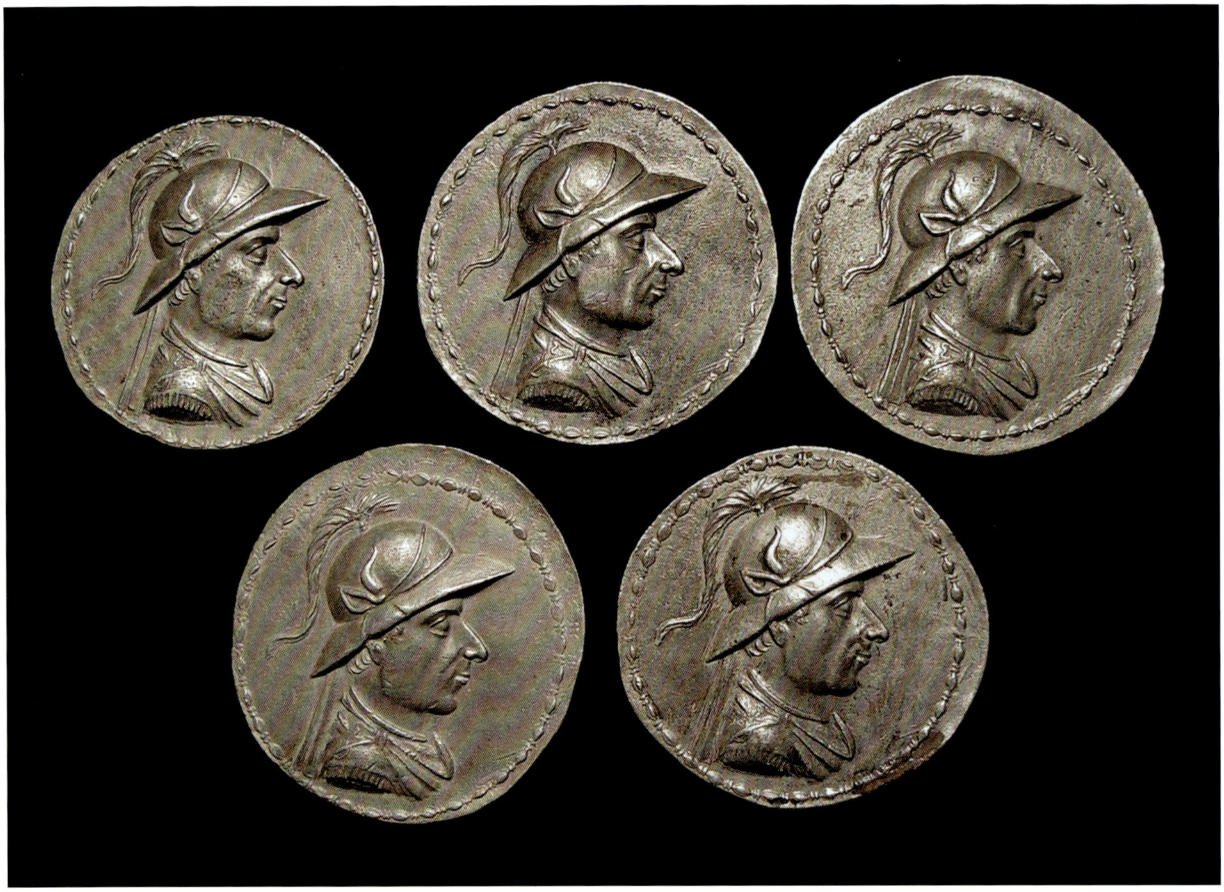

Fig. 11. Silver double-decadrachms of Amyntas (obverse, above, and reverse, opposite)

did ancient craftsmen plan out a complex task or respond to new challenges in the workplace? Let's take a look at the next phase of numismatic discovery.

Most ancient coins were made by hammering a blank piece of pre-weighed metal, called a flan, between two carved dies. The lower die is called the obverse (or heads), and the upper die the reverse (tails). Workers had to engrave each of these two dies in mirror image. Thus, to produce the dies for any coin, the die-cutter took up his tools and carved everything backward, including the inscription. By careful study, we can look over the shoulders of these artisans to determine how they planned and executed this task. We can tell from the finished product that die-cutters did not blindly copy an already reversed model as so much gibberish. Instead, they were thinking out each word in Greek, as one would in English, engraving the text backward from its beginning, as though spelling it out from right to left (producing a coin to be read left to right). Thus, the ends of words, not the beginnings, sometimes fall out of alignment on a die, which occurs if the artisan knows (or believes he knows) the language, not if the worker is replicating a string of meaningless symbols set before him.[18]

The ancient die-cutter must pay some attention to spacing as well as spelling. He must be able to anticipate how the different design elements of his dies will translate into

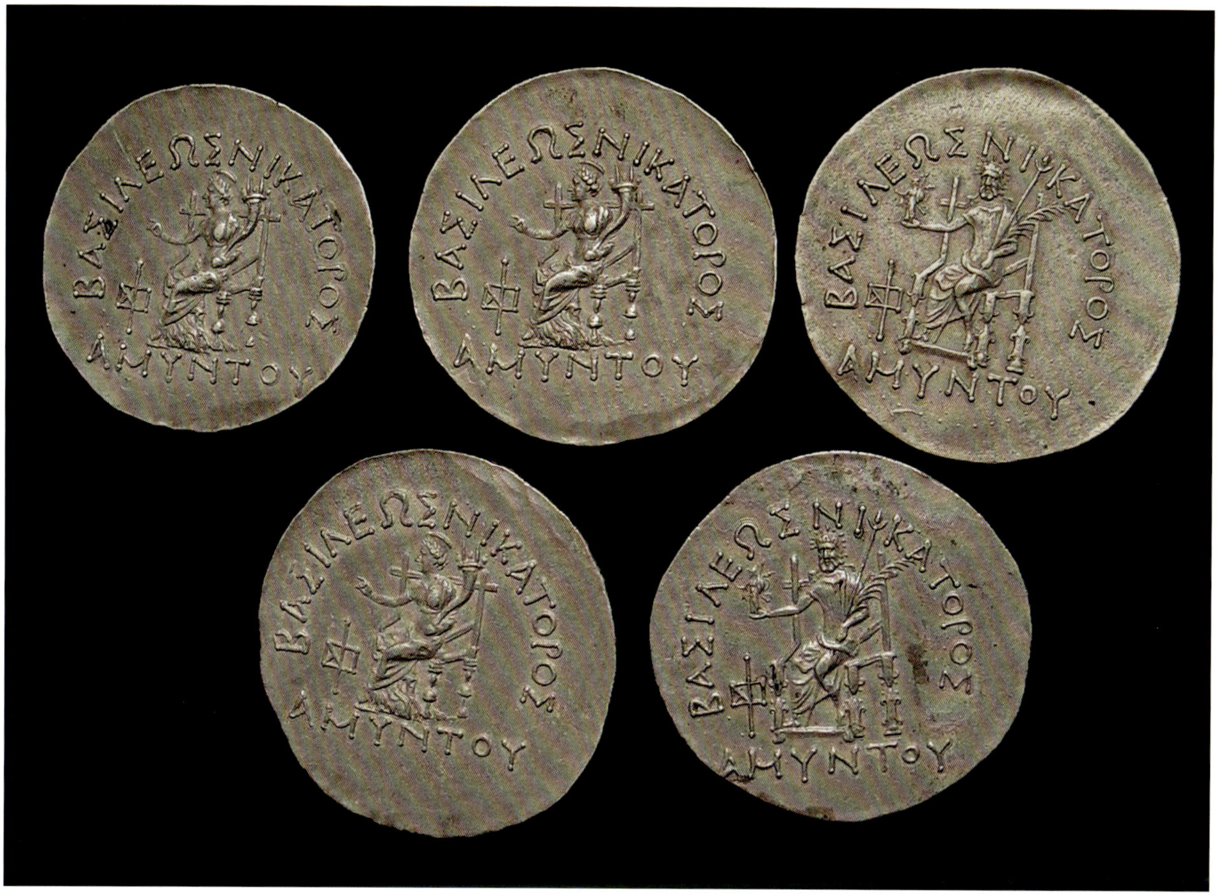

a coin. We can therefore notice on many coins the telltale signs of advance planning, usually in the form of small guide dots drilled into the die. These can be used for individual letters and/or for the inscription as a whole, and for the monogram. The larger-than-normal coins of Eucratides and Amyntas reveal these dots quite clearly (see figs. 8, 11, and 12). From these material expressions of an ancient thought process, we discern that the mind of the man who created the latter coins was fastidious and focused; the former was indecisive and careless. Amyntas' die-cutter had firmly in mind a finished product that required a semi-circular arrangement of letters for the royal title and epithet. To achieve this, he first devised a universal template for his dies, probably in the form of a simple punch that transferred to each new reverse die a set of two concentric circles of guide dots. This arrangement of dots appears on all the reverse dies for this series, and the dots extend into the exergue, where they are not needed for the king's name, which is engraved horizontally.[19] Guide dots, even where none are actually necessary, show that indeed the universal template was step one in the engraving process, or *chaîne opératoire*. Next, within the inner circle of dots, the engraver neatly framed the coin type (the image of a deity enthroned; fig. 11, reverse). Finally, he cut (backward) the upper inscription, ΒΑΣΙΛΕΩΣ ΝΙΚΑΤΟΡΟΣ, within the

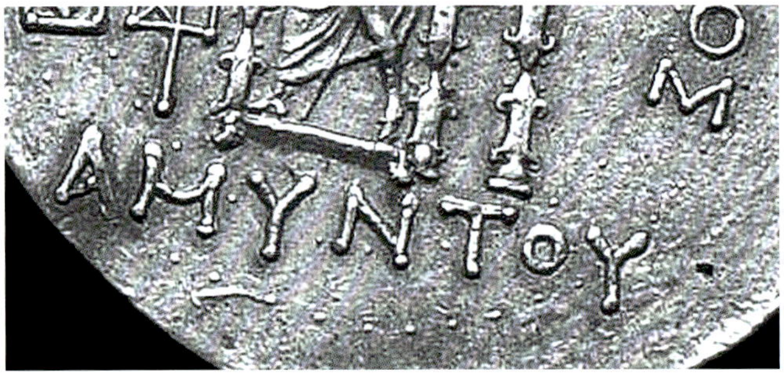

Fig. 12. Silver double-decadrachm of Amyntas (detail of fig. 11, reverse) showing guide dots

arc of concentric circles, and the lower inscription, ΑΜΥΝΤΟΥ, straight across. The strokes forming each letter (except, of course, for omicrons) were guided by a separate set of deeper dots. It is obvious that the spacing of the text accommodates the already-engraved type (at the tip of Zeus' scepter, for example) and not the other way around; this *chaîne opératoire* is evident on many Bactrian coins where the letters must squeeze into available spaces after the type has been finished (fig. 13).

As we spy over the shoulder of the artisan who made the dies for Eucratides' twenty-stater coin (fig. 8), we observe a very different pattern of thought and behavior. This worker seems not to have begun his commission with an appropriate "cognitive map" since he clearly had to erase part of his work and start again. Traces of this debacle can still be observed on the reverse. The die-cutter finished the Dioscuri design and began cutting the upper inscription, ΒΑΣΙΛΕΩΣ ΜΕΓΑΛΟΥ, aligned straight across *before* he realized that it would not fit properly. He therefore chiseled out his first attempt and substituted a less crowded, arched alignment (fig. 8, reverse). He did not bother to remove all telltale traces of his changes, and he had no intention of starting completely fresh with a new die after already carving the horsemen type on this one. What can we say about this unknown man who erred badly at one end of the *chaîne opératoire*, after which he did not care to make it completely right at the other end of the process? Given the extraordinary size of this coin, it can hardly be imagined that it would not be eyed closely—perhaps by the king himself. Thus, the lack of foresight on this special project seems startling. Was the engraver careless, overworked, pre-occupied, or indifferent? Was he an ancient free spirit given to trial and error even on the weightiest of royal commissions?

Some scholars have theorized that this engraver was the first to make a Eucratides die after the king added the title "Great" and, therefore, did not anticipate the requirements for these extra letters.[20] Even this circumstance would not reflect well on an artisan who failed to sketch out or measure his design prior to cutting. This simple procedure would have exposed the proverbial corner into which this die-cutter was painting himself. Fresh numismatic evidence shows, furthermore, that this engraver was not the first or only worker to deal with the expanded text; tetradrachms of Eucratides with the entire inscription engraved horizontally have come to light (fig. 13).[21] Had the engraver of the twenty-stater die

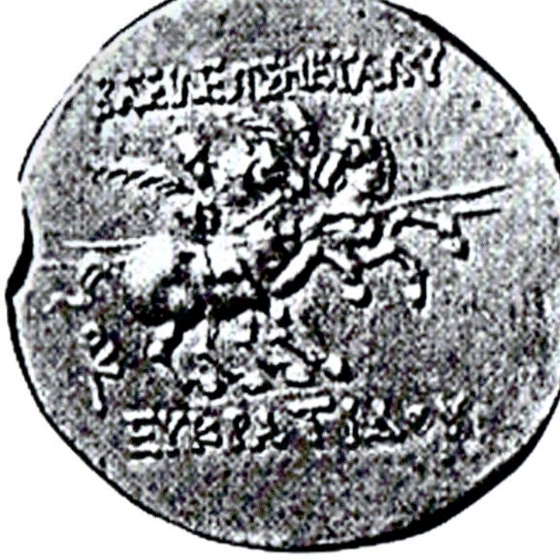

Fig. 13. Silver tetradrachm of Eucratides I (reverse)

not seen and noticed the crowding of letters on these circulating varieties? Whatever the case, he was having a bad day when he made the mistakes still visible on the ancient world's grandest coin.

We might infer that some official gave the kingdom's biggest task to an incompetent or lazy worker, which speaks poorly of a supervisor at the mint, in addition to the engraver himself. Dare we instead argue that artistic standards were slipping, even on a commission as important as this one? For his part, Anatole Chabouillet insisted that the obverse and reverse of Eucratides' huge gold coin had to be the products of different engravers because one side is vastly inferior to the other, and thus presumably a Greek could not have made it.[22] This chauvinistic suggestion does not help at all, particularly since Chabouillet considered the reverse (the side with the inscription!) to be the work of a gifted Greek artist, and the obverse the poor scratchings of a non-Greek native of Bactria.

What Cognitive Numismatics Reveals About Hellenistic Bactria

Cognitive Numismatics invites us to take a less "aesthetic" approach, one that considers working conditions as well as workers' talents. We ask, for instance, what the rate of error was on inscribed dies in Bactria as a whole and seek to explain those errors. This broader view reveals that our die-cutter was not the only mint worker to make mistakes. At times, engravers in Bactria so garbled their work that they actually misspelled their king's name, a mistake overlooked or ignored as coins from their dies passed into circulation. Even a common word like ΒΑΣΙΛΕΩΣ (king), routinely found on nearly every Bactrian coin, could be horribly blundered.[23] Was this mere carelessness, or was it the inability to recognize and rectify carelessness due to a growing incompetence in the Greek language? The practice noted earlier, of engraving the Greek as though spelling out each word, does not support the idea of non–Greek-speaking die-cutters, but were they suddenly spelling poorly for some reason? Do these deviations from expected norms mean that Greek education and culture were suddenly breaking down in Bactria?

Quantifiable errors within Greek inscriptions (as opposed to judgments about an artist's ethnicity) can enlighten us. My earlier study of engraving errors on Bactrian coins has uncovered an interesting pattern in these mental lapses.[24] The basic statistics drawn from a controlled group of specimens appear in the table below.

Table:
The Incidence of Error on Coin Dies

King	Inscribed Dies	Error Dies	% Flawed
Diodotus I/II	31	0	0
Euthydemus I	160	11	7
Demetrius I	18	0	0
Euthydemus II	9	0	0
Agathocles	18	0	0
Apollodotus	1	0	0
Antimachus	20	3	15
Demetrius II	44	4	9
Eucratides I/II	263	11	4
Fall of Aï Khanum (ca. 145 B.C.)			
Plato	10	0	0
Heliocles I	180	34	19

Overall, the Greek vocabulary engraved on coins remained quite small and repetitive, yet the rate of error increased notably before the fall of Aï Khanum and the death of Eucratides, therefore, before the troubled reign of his successor, Heliocles, a reign that heretofore has been associated with the first real signs of decline in Hellenistic Bactria. Was the kingdom already becoming somehow less Greek before Eucratides' time, or do other factors explain the errors?

The employment of non-Greek artisans unable to master even a few Greek words is possible, but the treasury records from Aï Khanum demonstrate that workers with non-Greek names managed the Greek language with no apparent difficulty. I suggest instead a significant change, not in the ethnicity or education of the workers, but in their working conditions. This change impacted peoples' ability or inclination to produce pristine dies. In other words, even before the abandonment of Aï Khanum, there was a period of stress and change in Bactria that adversely affected the anonymous workers in the mints. Their attention occasionally strayed from the planning of perfect dies or from the engraving of perfect Greek, and the same lack of attention led to less rigorous control of the work. The high incidence of error on the coinage of Euthydemus I offers confirmation here, for during his troubled reign we know that Bactria was invaded and besieged by Antiochus the Great of Syria. Political and military conditions may occasionally have made the workers less careful, but not necessarily less Greek.

Scholars sometimes argue that Bactria remained a strong Hellenistic state right up to the day that the nomads arrived, as evidenced by its immaculate coinage. The eminent historian Sir William Tarn stated flatly that "the Greek coinage of Bactria remained fine to the end, and then the great Bactrian artists vanished from the world."[25] He envisioned a sudden, stark, violent line of demarcation between a Greek Bactria and a barbarian Bactria. Tarn imagined an event not unlike a cultural holocaust, whereas the coins suggest a process more akin to the transformation of the late Roman Empire. Quantifiable errors on the coins betoken a build-up of serious strains within the workforce, a period of increased production demands, lax supervision, less apprenticeship training, and perhaps major external distractions leading up to the nomadic incursions. Those invasions may be the consequence rather than the cause of Bactria's so-called collapse. The same circumstances that eventually prompted the Greeks to abandon Aï Khanum may have already led the lowly workers in royal mints to abandon the highest standards of their craft. That conclusion appears to be one new, but significant, insight offered by Cognitive Numismatics.

Two hundred years ago, Reverend Joseph Wolff looked to numismatics as the backbone of Bactrian history. Today, we have added the brains of anonymous ancient workers to that impressive anatomy. For the public that flocked to the exhibition of extraordinary artifacts recovered from Afghanistan, the coins that were largely absent there must not be forgotten. They are absolutely essential for any understanding of Bactria, from the basics of its languages and chronology to the minds of its monarchs and mint workers. In a land otherwise lost to us, coins remain the great guides of the historian.

1. Wolff 1845. Wolff, who had met Conolly at Cawnpore in 1833, volunteered in 1843 to search for him after the latter had gone, in turn, to search for Captain Stoddart. Wolff himself only survived the emir's wrath through the timely intervention of the Shah of Persia.
2. Ibid., p. 224.
3. Ibid.
4. Conolly 1834. On the fruits of Conolly's numismatic explorations, see the notice about him published in the *Journal of the Asiatic Society of Bengal* 3 (1834): 246–47.
5. See, for example, Longpérier 1839.
6. Holt 1999b.
7. The coins help us to distinguish this king from a second, homonymous, ruler. See Holt 2000.

8. Holt 1981.
9. Technical details and photographs of the Bactrian and Indo-Greek coins may be found in Bopearachchi 1991.
10. Even a well-known deity, such as Poseidon, might pose a conundrum on Bactrian coins: see Holt 2005.
11. Prinsep 1835.
12. Holt 1984a.
13. First reported and studied by Prinsep 1838.
14. Bopearachchi 1998.
15. Bernard 1985, pp. 97–105.
16. First published by Chabouillet 1867. This coin remains unique.
17. The five known examples of this type all derive from a single major hoard. See Curiel and Fussman 1965.
18. See, for example, Classical Numismatic Group auction 39 (September 1996), no. 859.
19. This interpretation differs from the one offered in Bopearachchi 1991, p. 102.
20. For example, ibid., p. 69.
21. Bopearachchi 1995.
22. Chabouillet 1867, pp. 389–90.
23. There are over 40 such errors evident among the coins in Curiel and Fussman 1965.
24. Holt 1999a.
25. See Holt 1984b, p. 301.

Paul Bernard

Aï Khanum: A Greek Colony in Post-Alexandrian Central Asia, or How to Be Greek in an Oriental Milieu

Before entering the heart of my subject, which concerns the reaction of Greek settlers to the Central Asian environment to which they were exposed in the last two or three centuries B.C., I would like to call to mind some basic background material.

The existence of Greek kingdoms in Central Asia and northwestern India after Alexander's conquests had been known for a long time from a few fragmentary texts from Greek and Latin classical sources and from allusions in contemporary Chinese chronicles and later Indian texts. These texts inform us that two kingdoms were formed as a result of Alexander's conquests in the eastern part of the Achaemenid empire, where he settled the first colonists. The one we call the Graeco-Bactrian kingdom is located north of the Hindu Kush, mainly in the provinces of Bactria and Sogdiana; the other is the Indo-Greek kingdom to the south of it. We also know that, for fifty years after Alexander's death, these territories became part of the Seleucid Syrian kingdom founded by Seleucus I, one of Alexander's commanders, who, together with his immediate successors, gave a new impulse to colonization. About 250 B.C., these colonies declared their independence, which they maintained until they were submerged by nomadic invasions between 145 B.C. and the beginning of the first century B.C.[1]

The material vestiges of these Greek colonies had long been sought in vain by French archaeologists, beginning as early as 1923–25. An American mission from the University of Pennsylvania led by Rodney S. Young, the future excavator of Gordion, had even joined this search.[2] It was only in 1964 that the French archaeological mission discovered, at the site of Aï Khanum in eastern Bactria, the ruins of a huge Greek town,[3] which it started excavating, under my direction, from 1965 to 1978 (fig. 1). The remains of the monuments we discovered, which had been destroyed and pillaged about 145 B.C. by nomadic invaders,[4] were completely pillaged a second time, together with most of the unexcavated parts of the site, in the 1990s, during the last years of the Afghan civil war (fig. 2).[5]

The city we unearthed, founded probably around 300 B.C., was built at the confluence of the Oxus and the Kokcha rivers. The upper town, situated on a flat hill, dominated the lower town, where the main monuments were concentrated. These included the massive ramparts of sun-dried bricks;[6] the main street; the palace in the middle of the lower town, with the funerary monument of the founder, a commander of Seleucus I; a theater; a gymnasium; the main temple of the city; the arsenal;[7] the residential quarters at the confluence of the rivers; and, outside the ramparts, a large patrician house and another temple (figs. 3, 4).[8]

It would be of great interest to assess, even approximately, the number of the city's inhabitants, but reliable criteria are missing.

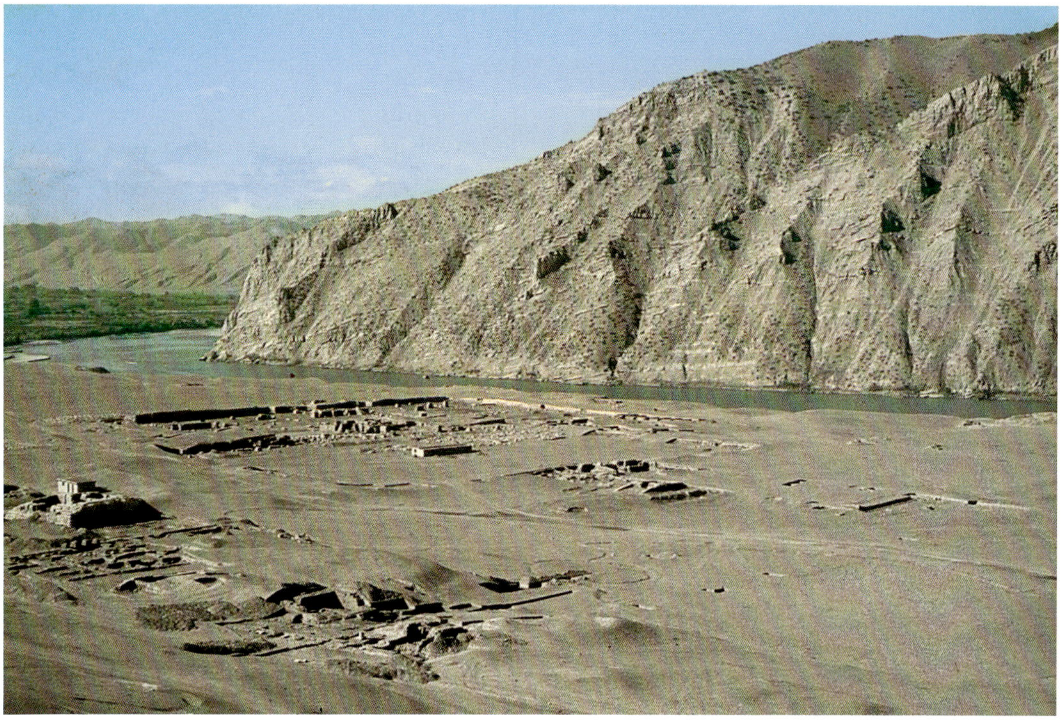

Fig. 1. Aï Khanum. Lower town at the end of excavations in 1978

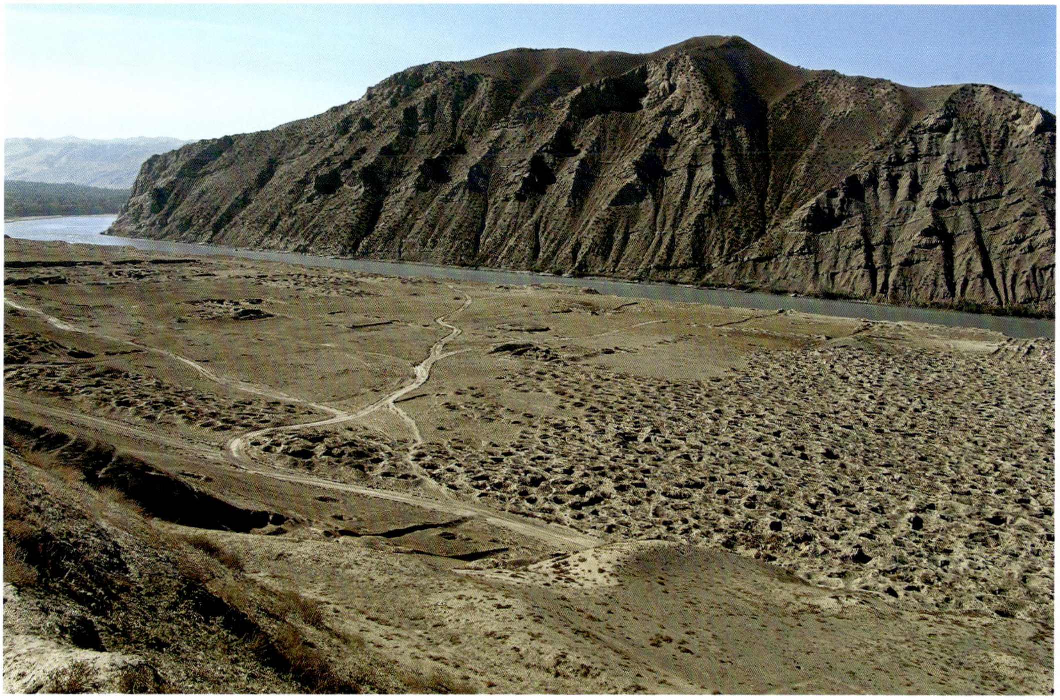

Fig. 2. Aï Khanum after the pillaging of the 1990s

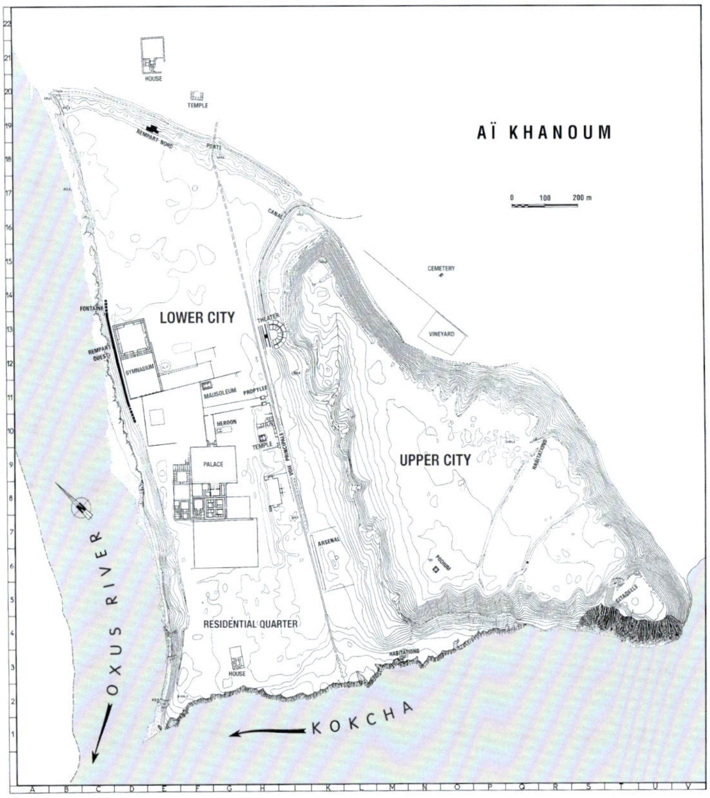

Fig. 3. Map of Aï Khanum at the end of excavations in 1978

We know that the northern section of the lower town was never built up; that the three or four thousand seats in the theater, too many for the male public of the city, were probably meant to accommodate the Greek spectators of the whole province; that the residential houses in the southern quarter were fewer than fifty; and that the humbler dwellings formed small groups scattered in different locations. One also cannot completely trust the huge dimensions of the public buildings, for they were visibly dictated by the state's desire to use architecture as a statement of power. Aï Khanum gives the impression of having been primarily a center of political and administrative power, rather sparsely populated, mostly by colonists. In proportion to the native population, I would say that the Greek settlers in the entire Graeco-Bactrian kingdom must have been more numerous than the British were in India, but certainly less numerous than the French in Algeria. The survival of the Graeco-Bactrian kingdom, whatever its military superiority, was made possible only

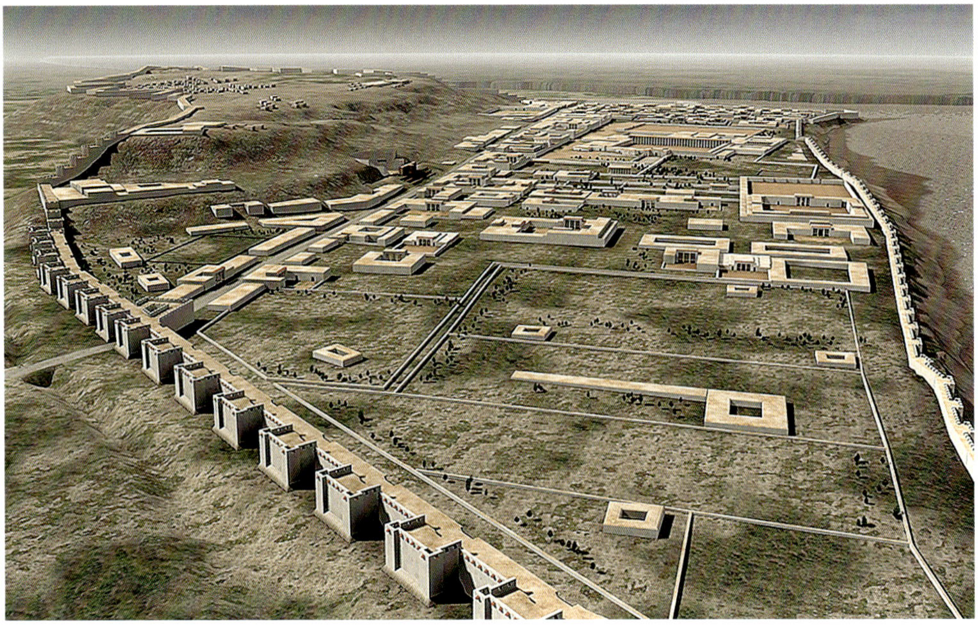

Fig. 4. 3-D reconstruction of Aï Khanum from the north by G. Lecuyot and O. Ishizawa

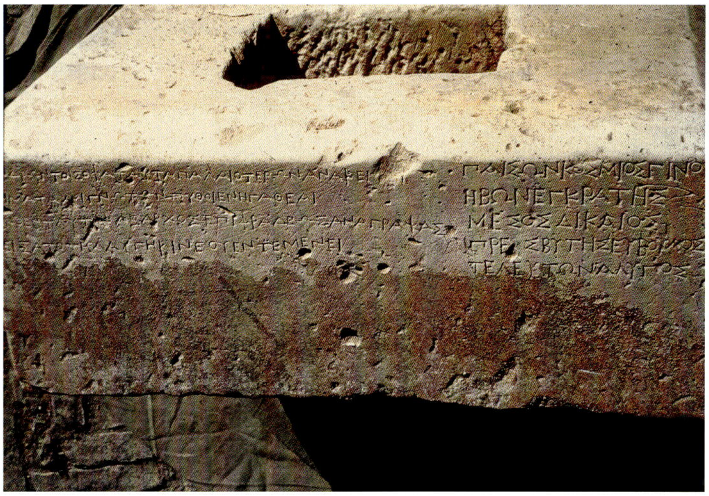

Fig. 5. Base of *Heröon* of Kineas with dedication by Clearchos (left) and last five Delphic maxims (right). Aï Khanum, beginning of 3rd century B.C. Limestone, 28 × 65.5 × 46.5 cm. National Museum of Afghanistan, Kabul (05.42.13)

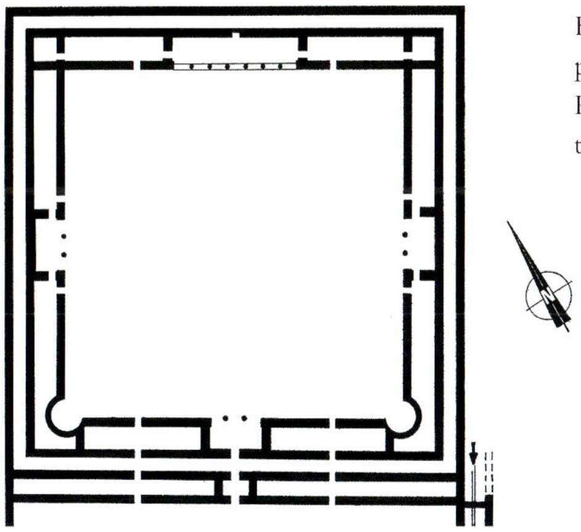

Fig. 6. Plan of northern part of gymnasium at Aï Khanum, dedicated to teaching

because the local Bactrian elite was willing to collaborate with the colonists, as had previously been the case in the sixth century B.C., when it had made common cause with the Persian conquerors. We perhaps have a sign of this collaboration in the names of the administrators of the palace treasury, some that are typically Bactrian, such as Oxubazes and Oxeboakes, alongside those of Greeks, even if the positions the former occupy are not of the highest rank.

Although inscriptions are not plentiful, those that have been found show that the settlers continued to speak and write Greek correctly, and even to compose poetry, during the two hundred and fifty years of residence in Central Asia and northwestern India.[9] They include tags handwritten in ink on ceramic vessels in the treasury of the palace, reporting the date and the quantity of stored goods;[10] a receipt for payment and a contract (?) on parchment;[11] and literary manuscripts, one of which could be identified as part of a philosophical treatise by Aristotle, despite the disintegration of the parchment and papyrus support, leaving nothing but an imprint of the ink on clods of earth.[12] There are also inscriptions on stone, one of which has gained wide renown (fig. 5). It commemorates the dedication by a certain Clearchos, perhaps a philosopher and disciple of Aristotle, of the 150 maxims of wisdom ascribed to the famed Seven Sages of Greece and dedicated by them to the god Apollo in the sanctuary of Delphi. The last of these maxims, which set forth the ideal virtues of the Greek man, has been preserved: "When a child, have good manners; when a young man, control thy passions; in middle age be just; in old age give good advice; die without regret."[13] One unique and still unpublished document is written in ink on a sherd with the same Aramaic alphabet as was used by the scribes of the Achaemenid administration. It testifies to the existence of a written language of eastern Iranian origin, perhaps related to that of the Parthians.[14] Its use was very limited in the Bactrian population, at a time when the Bactrians had not yet learned to write their own Iranian language with the Greek alphabet.

Though vigilant in maintaining the purity of their language, the settlers were much more open to the local culture in the field of architecture. For those buildings destined to enshrine specifically Greek institutions that had no equivalent outside of Greece, the architects naturally chose Greek models. Such was the case with the gymnasium (fig. 6), the function of which was both athletic

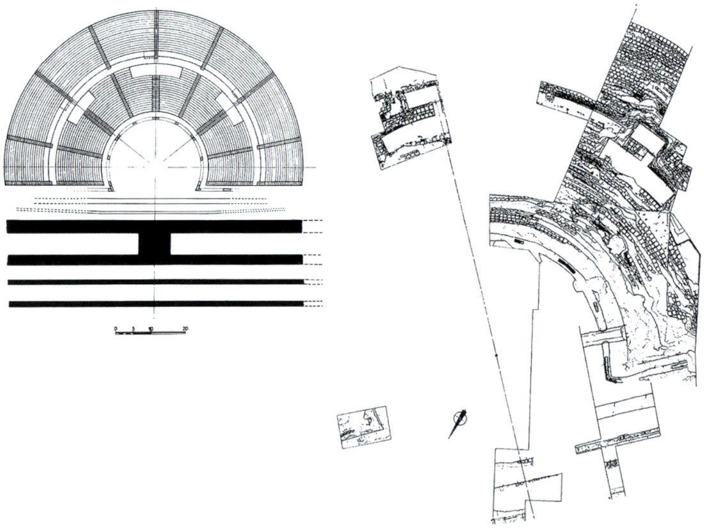

Fig. 7. Plan of the theater at Aï Khanum

and academic and which took the conventional form of a vast courtyard bordered by colonnaded porticoes and lecture rooms.[15] The theater was also modeled on Greek precedents, with around thirty-five rows of stepped seats forming a semicircular fan above the orchestra and the proscenium (figs. 7, 8).[16] Another symbol, and not the least important, of the Greek urban legacy was the custom of honoring the city's founder—a certain Kineas, probably a trusted officer of Seleucus I—by placing his tomb in the heart of the city[17] and not outside the ramparts, the normal place for burials. It was in this sacred enclosure that Clearchos had the Delphic maxims engraved on a stele and its base, to exemplify the unifying principles of the civic body (see fig. 5).

Likewise, the stone columns bordering the courtyards of the main public buildings, such as the palace (fig. 9),[18] the gymnasium,[19] and even surrounding a mausoleum,[20] have capitals of the three classical orders: Doric,[21] Ionic,[22] and Corinthian (fig. 10, left),[23] even if the canon was tampered with in one of the

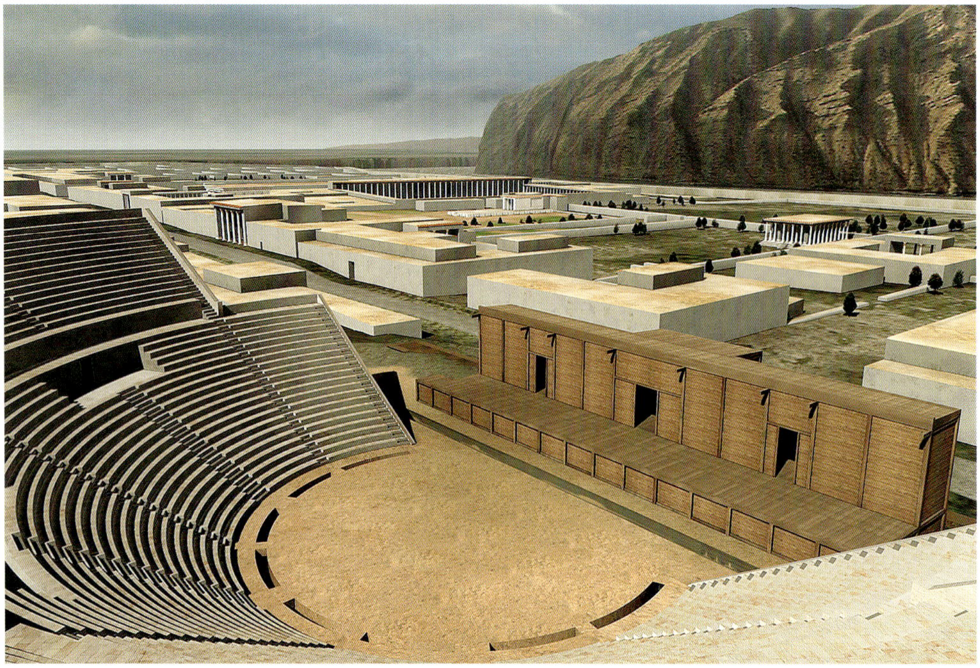

Fig. 8. 3-D reconstruction of the lower town of Aï Khanum, with theater and palace (far left), by G. Lecuyot and O. Ishizawa

two types of this last order. The same may be said of the terracotta antefixes decorating the edges of the roofs. There, next to the traditional Greek palmette, we find strange compositions, totally foreign to the Greek repertoire, combining animal and vegetal motifs (fig. 10, right).[24]

But architecture at Aï Khanum is also the field where the Greeks, freeing themselves from their own traditions, experimented most boldly with eastern forms and conceptions. When they built the palace, the Graeco-Bactrian architects, failing to find in classical architecture any credible forerunner, sought their inspiration in the most recent Near Eastern traditions, those of the Neo-Babylonian[25] and Persian Achaemenid palaces. It is particularly from the palace of Darius the Great at Susa[26] that they borrowed the conception of grouping together, within an all-encompassing wall, units serving different functions—political, administrative, economic,[27] and residential—each self-contained, with occasional courtyards, the circulation being effected by a labyrinth

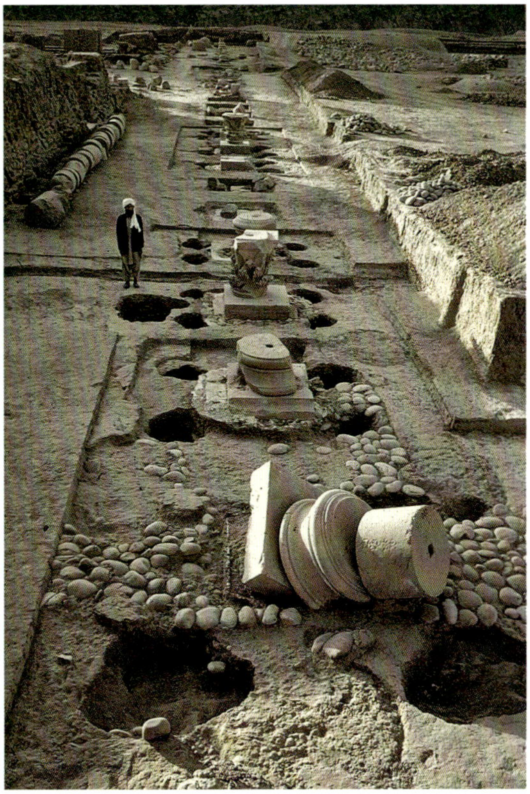

Fig. 9. Vestiges of southern colonnade of main courtyard of the palace at Aï Khanum

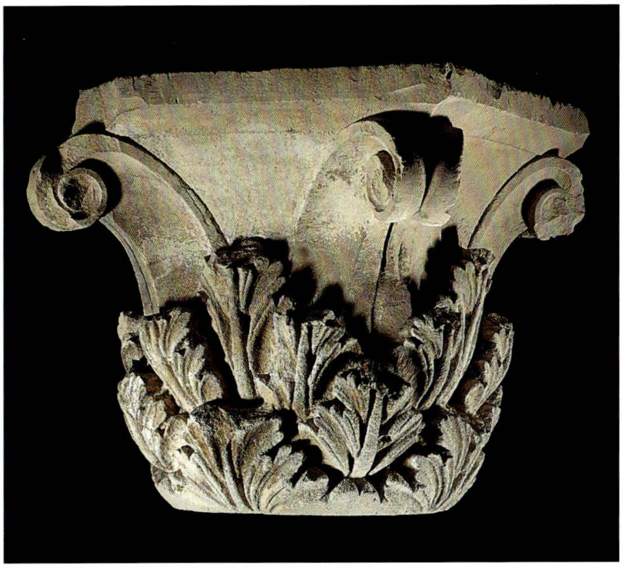

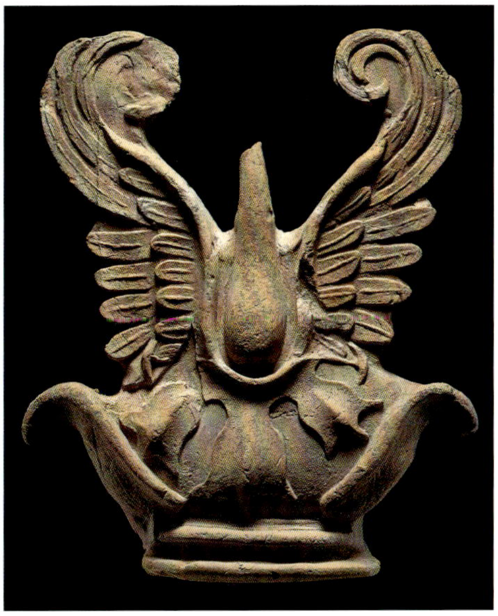

Fig. 10. Corinthian capital (left), Greek type. Aï Khanum, Citadel, before 145 B.C. Limestone, H. 74 cm, D. 90 cm. Winged antefix (right), Graeco-Oriental style. Aï Khanum, Palace, main entrance, 3rd century B.C. Terracotta, H. 55 cm. National Museum of Afghanistan, Kabul (06.42.640; 05.42.84/1)

of corridors. The palace at Aï Khanum, its colossal dimensions (350 × 250 m) reflecting the same assertion of imperial grandeur as the palaces of the Persian kings, introduces into this kind of plan a clarity of composition lacking in the latter (fig. 11). It imposes an almost obsessive predilection for symmetry and an insistence on a clear division of space that fosters the multiplication of long, wide corridors.[28] The Greek builders embraced the local construction techniques, best suited to the country, of walls made of unbaked bricks and flat roofs. The ubiquitous earth floors were covered, in oriental fashion, by rugs. In this strongly eastern context a few courtyards with their stone columned porticoes, crowned by Doric and Corinthian capitals, emerged as islands of Greek atmosphere.

The rupture with the Greek tradition was even more striking in domestic architecture, varying the basic plan of the Greek house, one that was a series of rooms set around an inner courtyard. At Aï Khanum the central space was reserved for the main living and reception room of the master of the house, while the other rooms and service areas were disposed around it, but at the same time separated from it by a surrounding corridor (fig. 12).[29] The courtyard became a forecourt with privileged access from the living room through a porch with two columns. The residential units in the palace follow the same pattern. This radical change was not sudden, but was rather the result of a progressive evolution that reached its final stage in the last fifty years of the city. This new feature, which makes use of an eastern construction unit consisting of a room surrounded by a corridor, appears to be the architectural expression of a stricter hierarchy in the family community, expressing the increased importance of the master of the house.

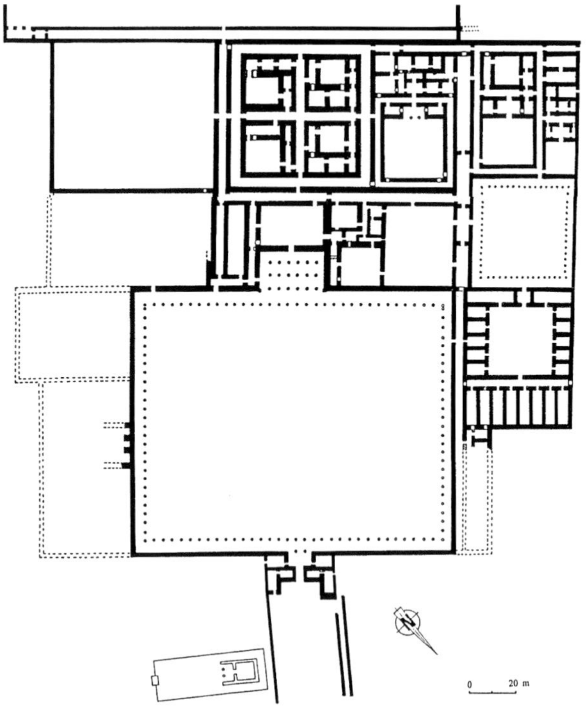

Fig. 11. Plan of palace at Aï Khanum

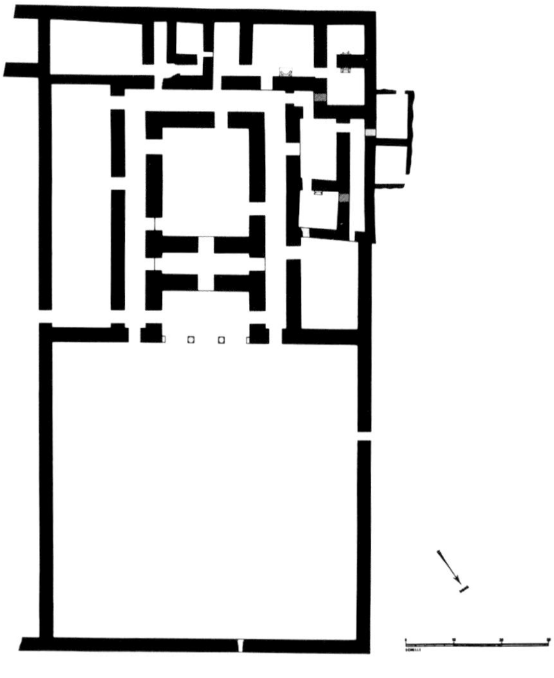

Fig. 12. Plan of private house in residential area of Aï Khanum near Kokcha River

No less innovative and certainly more surprising is the religious architecture.[30] Instead of the typical rectangular plan of Greek temples with their enveloping stone colonnades, double-sloped roofs, and pediments, the main temple of the city, which stood on the main street, not far from the palace, was a compact building of sun-dried bricks on a twenty meter–square ground plan, set on a high (1.5 m) three-stepped podium (fig. 13).[31] Inside, a wide vestibule preceded a smaller cult room containing the cult statue, flanked by two narrow sacristies on either side. The plan, the raised podium, the whitewashed exterior walls of brick masonry forming a decoration of indented niches, and the flat roof are all features that recall certain religious buildings of the east, from Mesopotamia[32] to Central Asia. It was nevertheless a Greek god who was worshipped in this non-Greek building, to wit Zeus, the supreme deity of the Greek pantheon. The symbol of this divinity, a winged lightning bolt, was delicately carved on the Greek sandal of one of the marble feet, which, with some fingers from the hands, is practically all that has survived of his acrolithic cult statue (fig. 14).[33] The best way to reconcile the Greek aspects of the god with the unmistakably eastern character of the building is to presuppose a syncretic deity of mixed Graeco-Iranian parentage, such as Zeus–Mithra, who is depicted with a Persian cap and a halo of rays on the coinage of certain late Greek kings of the first century B.C. (Amyntas,[34] Hermaios[35]) who reigned in northwestern India. In such temples, where the Greek settlers enshrined their gods, the oriental architecture helped the local populations to recognize in them their own deities. The Temple with Indented Niches in Aï Khanum undoubtedly provided the Bactrian population of the surrounding plain[36] with a place to practice its own religious creeds inside the city of the colonists. No less astonishing is that the two other sanctuaries discovered were also of a non-Greek type. One, close in conception to the Temple with Indented Niches, has a triple

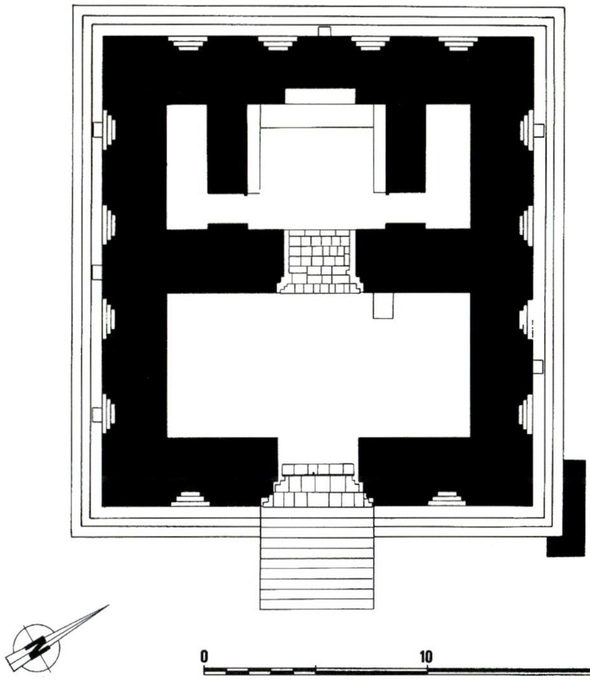

Fig. 13. Plan of Temple with Indented Niches at Aï Khanum

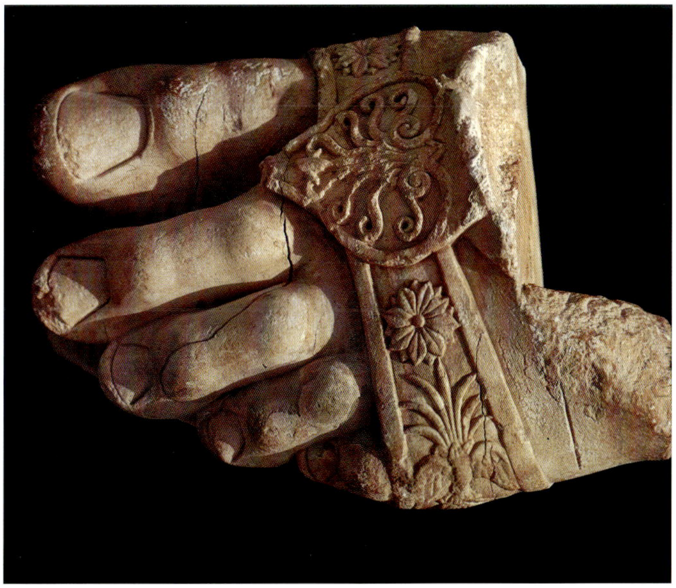

Fig. 14. Left foot of cult statue. Aï Khanum, Temple with Indented Niches, first half of 2nd century B.C. Marble, L. 27 cm. Formerly National Museum of Afghanistan, Kabul

cult room and an open-air foreground instead of a vestibule;[37] the other is a monumental stepped altar in the open air on top of the acropolis[38]—therefore reminiscent of the religious monuments of the Persians who, as recorded by Greek historians, worshipped their gods, without representing them in human form, on elevated places in the open air.

In the field of figurative arts, the settlers chose not to be imaginative and, contrary to what we have just seen, stubbornly held on to their national traditions. Their artists, as skilled as their western counterparts (judging from the wonderful fragment that survives from the statue of Zeus in the Temple with Indented Niches), were satisfied to repeat the forms and styles that had been favored in the western world when the colonists left. They strove to perpetuate what they knew best: the tradition of the second phase of classicism of the fourth century B.C. A statuette of a young athlete, crowned with a leafy wreath—perhaps an ex-voto commemorating a victory in a gymnastic competition—is a perfect example of the Greek mastery of anatomy (fig. 15).[39] Another is the portrait of an ephebe on his funerary stele, wearing the typical Macedonian long cloak wrapped around his left arm, while the broad-brimmed hat, the petasos, hangs from his neck down his back. The long flowing hair, unusual for a Greek, probably denotes a local Bactrian fashion.[40] A typically Greek "Hermaic pillar" exhibits a remarkably sensitive portrait carved with an alert hand (fig. 16).[41] It bears the bust of an old man draped in a cloak, his left hand clenching a metallic rod now lost, the insignia of his function as gymnasiarch or director of the gymnasium where the statue was found. Two heads from statues of almost human proportions (fig. 17), one modeled in unbaked clay,[42] the other one in stucco,[43] bear testimony to the long and illustrious line of descendants that these modeling techniques, introduced into Central Asia by Graeco-Bactrian and Indo-Greek artists, were destined to produce. One has only to think of the myriads of modeled statues of Gandharan art. The royal coinage of the Graeco-Bactrian and Indo-Greek dynasties—minted in gold, silver, and bronze, with the forceful portraits of their kings on the main side and the representation of the Greek pantheon on the other (see Holt

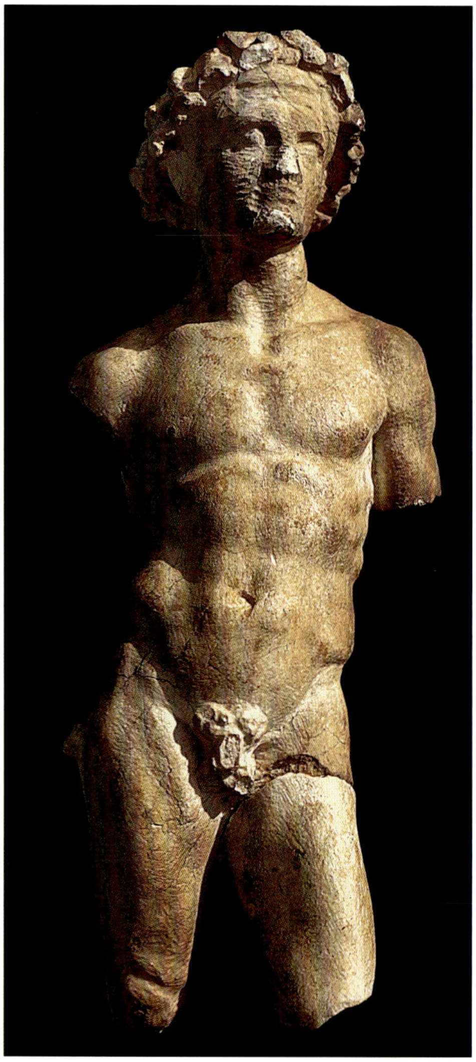

Fig. 15. Statuette of young athlete (?) with crown of foliage. Aï Khanum, Temple with Indented Niches, before 145 B.C. Limestone, H. 35 cm. National Museum of Afghanistan, Kabul

essay)—is another branch, the easternmost, of Greek numismatics with almost no oriental influence.[44]

None of the statues from Aï Khanum would have been out of place in the excavations of any Greek archaeological site from the fourth century B.C. Nor would they have been especially prized in that context, as much as they are, rightly, by us today, as the improbable children of a brief episode of Greek expansion in a foreign culture far to the east of the Mediterranean, three thousand miles from home. As much as we admire the untiring creativity and the powerful originality of the architects of Aï Khanum, blending western and eastern traditions to make something new, we must resist the temptation to regret that its artists were mainly imitators of the late classical tradition and that their productions—covering Bactria from the years 300 to 150 B.C., at a time when the western world was experiencing a fantastic renewal of artistic creation—leave us with a feeling of "déjà vu." How can we explain this difference of creativity between the architects and the artists in the Neo-Hellenism of Bactria?

The grandiose monuments of the Near East, namely of Achaemenid architecture, which were to be encountered throughout the Persian empire from Asia Minor to Iran and Bactria, presented the colonial architects with a challenge to create forms better adapted to their new needs and to their lifestyle as masters of an empire. But the aesthetics of their artists had nothing in common with the artificially archaic and repetitive sculptural decoration of these same Achaemenid monuments, which, from their point of view, looked antiquated, and they turned away from it. Just as the Greek settlers cherished their national language and preserved it intact, so, too, did they perpetuate Greek scientific knowledge as exemplified, for instance, by one of their sundials, a unicum among ancient astronomical instruments, which embodies a feat of stunning scientific originality (fig. 18).[45] It also came naturally to them

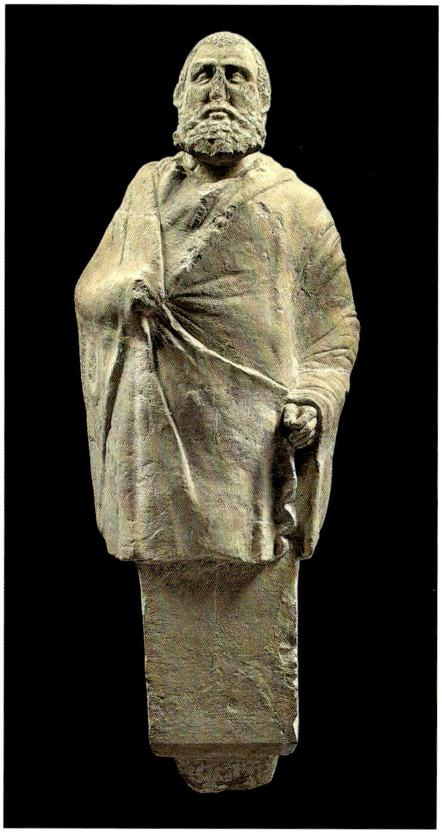

Fig. 16. "Hermaic pillar" with bust of an old man. Aï Khanum, gymnasium, first half of 2nd century B.C. Limestone, H. 77 cm. National Museum of Afghanistan, Kabul (05.42.14)

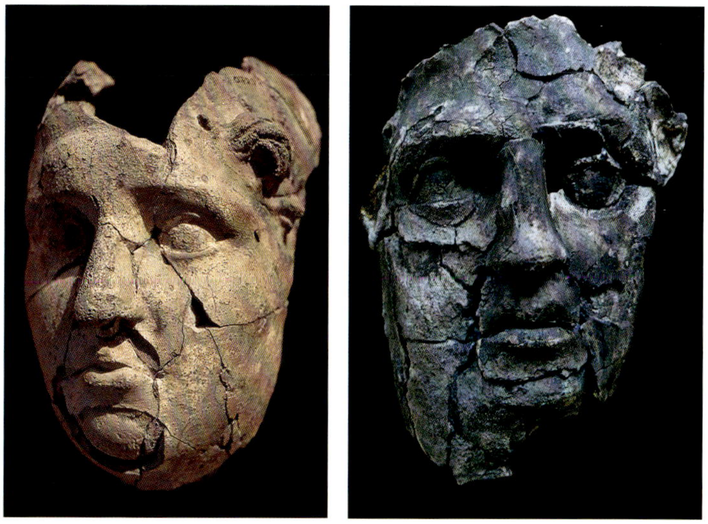

Fig. 17. Head (left) of a woman (?) from the Temple with Indented Niches. Unbaked clay, 21 × 15 cm. Head (right) of a man, stucco, H. 25 cm. Aï Khanum, before 145 B.C. National Museum of Afghanistan, Kabul (05.42.74)

to cherish the arts that embellished the cities of the homeland they had left and that defined their national identity. It is not the traditionalism of Graeco-Bactrian visual art that requires an explanation, but rather the radical changes, inspired by local building traditions and their own predilection for imperial greatness, that transformed Greek models into a new type of Graeco-Oriental architecture.

The final destiny of the Greek colonies is a kind of judgment pronounced by history on the Hellenic episode in Central Asia. As might be expected, the Greek language did not last long after nomadic invaders snatched power from the colonists in the first century B.C. But the Greek alphabet survived even after the Arab conquest in the eighth century A.D., being used for centuries to write the Bactrian language, which up to the time of Greek settlement had existed only as a spoken language. Of the remarkable Graeco-Bactrian architecture, only the decorative Corinthian capital and base were to survive. It was the most deeply ingrained Greek tradition of the late classical period, reverently fostered by the Graeco-Bactrian artists, that left the deepest imprint on the local cultures, surviving down to the Islamic conquest: namely, a wealth of iconographic motifs and, above all, a conception of the visual arts as a challenge to nature through imitation, rather than a conception of art as a vehicle for personal expressiveness. It was from an artistic tradition fertilized by the Hellenism of the Greek kingdoms of Central Asia and northwestern India that emerged the splendid flowering of Gandharan Buddhist art.

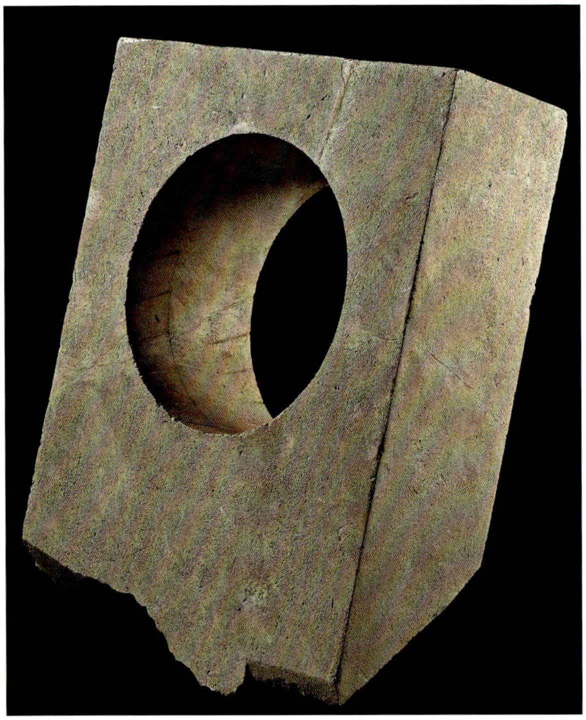

Fig. 18. Sundial of unique type. Aï Khanum, gymnasium, before 145 B.C. Limestone, 44.5 × 34.5 cm. National Museum of Afghanistan, Kabul (05.42.55)

1. The history of the Greek Hellenistic kingdoms in Central Asia and of the textual tradition on which it is based has been masterfully analyzed by W.W. Tarn (see Tarn 1938; updated, Holt 1984b). For further research based on new numismatic finds and excavations, see also Narain 1957; Bernard 1985; Bopearachchi 1991; Sherwin-White and Kuhrt 1993; Lerner 2003–4; and Widemann 2009. For the Chinese texts, see Thierry 2005.
2. Young 1955. The American archaeologist opened a trial trench on the southern rampart, the results of which are today fully appreciated after subsequent excavations conducted by the French Archaeological Delegation in Afghanistan beginning in 2004. See Bernard, Besenval, and Marquis 2006; Besenval and Marquis 2008.
3. The site was visited for the first time in 1838 by the English explorer John Wood (see Wood 1841), and again in 1926 by the French archaeologist Jules Barthoux (Tarzi 1996). Both suspected the presence of a large ancient town, but lacked any clue for dating it. Afterward, the site sank into oblivion. For the events leading to its rediscovery in 1964 and the planning and conduct of the archaeological exploration from 1965 to 1978, see Bernard 2009.
4. Bernard 1987a; Rapin 1992, pp. 287–94; Martinez-Sève 2010.
5. Bernard 2001; Bernard, Besenval, and Marquis 2006.
6. Leriche 1986.

7. Frantz Grenet in Bernard et al. 1980, pp. 51–63.
8. For general presentations, see, for instance, Bernard 1982 and Bernard 2009 as well as Afghanistan 2008, pp. 81–129 (P. Bernard). The author of this article feels responsible only for the French version of the catalogue of the exhibition at the Musée des Arts Asiatiques–Guimet, Paris: *Afghanistan, les trésors retrouvés. Collections du musée national de Kaboul*, edited by Pierre Cambon (Paris: RMN, 2006), pp. 55–67, 262–70; and for the English version of the catalogue of the British Museum exhibition, Afghanistan 2011, pp. 81–129.
9. Rougemont 2012, nos. 97–150. See also Canali De Rossi 2004, nos. 322–386; Merkelbach and Stauber 2005, nos. 102–103.
10. Rapin 1992, pp. 95–114; Afghanistan 2008, pp. 109–10, nos. 10–11; Rougemont 2012, nos. 99–120.
11. Rea, Senior, and Hollis 1994 (also Rougemont 2012, no. 92); Clarysse and Thompson 2007 (also Rougemont 2012, no. 93). These two documents are chance finds from Bactria.
12. Rapin 1992, pp. 115–23.
13. Dedication: Ἀνδρῶν τοι σοφὰ ταῦτα παλαιοτέρων ἀνάκει[τα]ι / ῥήματα ἀριγνώτων Πυθοῖ ἐν ἠγαθέαι / ἔνθεν ταῦτ[α] Κλέαρχος ἐπιφραδέως ἀναγράψας / εἵσατο τηλαυγῆ Κινέου ἐν τεμένει.
Delphic maxim: Παῖς ὢν κόσμιος γίνου, / ἡβῶν ἐγκρατής, / μέσος δίκαιος, / πρεσβύτης εὔβουλος, / τελευτῶν ἄλυπος.
L. Robert in Bernard et al. 1973, pp. 211–37; Canali De Rossi 2004, nos. 382–384; Merkelbach and Stauber 2005, no. 103; Afghanistan 2008, nos. 28–29; Rougemont 2012, no. 97 a, b, c.
14. Bernard 1971, p. 432; Rapin 1992, pp. 105, 111–13, 304 (28), pls. 57 and 111 (28). I am grateful to Professor V. A. Livshits, of the Oriental Institute of Saint Petersburg, for the identification of the language and for a first tentative decipherment.
15. Veuve 1987; Afghanistan 2008, nos. 30–33; Bernard 2009, pp. 43–44.
16. Bernard 1976, pp. 314–22; Bernard 1978, pp. 429–41; Afghanistan 2008, no. 33; Bernard 2009, pp. 44–45.
17. Bernard et al. 1973, pp. 85–104; Bernard 2009, pp. 47–49, fig. 15.
18. Bernard et al. 1973; P. Garczynski in Bernard et al. 1980, pp. 39–43.
19. Veuve 1987.
20. H.-P. Francfort and J.-C. Liger in Bernard et al. 1976, pp. 25–45; Bernard 2009, p. 49, fig. 16.
21. P. Garczynski in Bernard et al. 1980, pp. 19–42, pl. XXXIII c; Veuve 1987, pp. 25–26, pl. 13 a, 18.
22. Bernard 1969, pp. 349–52, figs. 24–25 (wooden Ionic capital from the Temple with Indented Niches); H.-P. Francfort and J.-C. Liger in Bernard et al. 1976, pp. 36–37, pl. XIV (2) (funerary monument).
23. Bernard 1968; Bernard et al. 1973, pls. 23, 37 (pseudo-Corinthian); Afghanistan 2008, p. 80 (Corinthian), pp. 120–21, no. 24 (pseudo-Corinthian).
24. Bernard et al. 1973, pls. 100–102; Afghanistan 2008, nos. 25–27 (with garbled text; rather see Afghanistan 2011, nos. 25–27).
25. Downey 1988.
26. Perrot 2010.
27. For the treasury and the work carried out there, see Rapin 1992; Afghanistan 2008, pp. 88–89, 107–10.
28. Bernard et al. 1973; Bernard 1976; Bernard 1981; Bernard 2009, pp. 41–43.
29. Lecuyot 1993; Bernard 2009, pp. 46–47. Lecuyot has prepared the publication, soon to appear, of the monuments of domestic architecture.
30. Bernard 1990.
31. Bernard 2009, pp. 49–51. For the finds, see Francfort 1984; Afghanistan 2008, pp. 111–19, nos. 12–23.
32. Downey 1988.
33. Bernard 1969, pp. 338–41, figs. 15–16. On the technique of the acrolithic statues in Central Asia and Gandhara, see Bopearachchi 2007.
34. Bopearachchi 1991, pp. 299–305, pls. 45–46. On the Amyntas silver coinage (95–90 B.C.), only a discrete crown of rays distinguishes the enthroned Zeus from his Greek counterpart, but on bronze coins the god has a more eastern aspect, wearing a Phrygian cap encircled by a halo of conspicuous rays: Bopearachchi 1991, pl. 47, series 14–15.
35. The same remarks (see previous note) apply to the Hermaios coinage. See Bopearachchi 1991, pls. 52–54; for the god with the Phrygian cap and the crown of long rays, see pl. 54, series 9. On Zeus-Mithra, see Grenet 1991; Grenet 2001.
36. The plain of Aï Khanum was, from the Achaemenid period, well irrigated by canals dispensing the water from the Kokcha River and was thus densely populated: Gentelle 1978; Gentelle 1989; Lyonnet 1997; Gardin 1998.
37. Bernard 2009, p. 51.
38. Ibid., fig. 19.
39. Bernard 1969, pp. 341–44, figs. 17–18.
40. Bernard 1972, pp. 623–25, fig. 13; Afghanistan 2008, pp. 99–100, 129, no. 34.
41. Veuve 1987, pp. 91–93, pls. 52–53 (P. Bernard); Afghanistan 2008, pp. 126–127, no. 32.
42. Bernard 1969, p. 344, fig. 19; Afghanistan 2008, p. 111, no. 12.
43. Bernard 1969, p. 344, fig. 20.
44. Bopearachchi 1991; Afghanistan 2008, fig. on p. 103 (incorrectly oriented; rather see Afghanistan 2011, fig. on p. 103 [gold medallion of Eucratides I]).
45. Veuve 1987, pp. 86–91, pls. 15, 51; Savoie 2007; Afghanistan 2008, pp. 125–26, nos. 30–31.

David Whitehouse

The Glass from Begram

The exhibition "Afghanistan: Hidden Treasures from the National Museum, Kabul," contained 18 of the roughly 180 glass vessels in the Begram treasure, a unique hoard of luxury objects from India, China, the Mediterranean, and elsewhere. Most visitors to the exhibition, including students of early glass, had never seen these 18 objects face to face, and the colloquium that accompanied the show in New York provided a wonderful opportunity to talk about them.[1]

In my lecture, I took issue with two statements in the catalogue of the exhibition.[2] According to the first statement, "there is virtually no reference material pertaining to the exact age of the Roman artifacts, more particularly the glassware";[3] the second statement maintains that "all the [chemical] analyses of glass from Begram show that they are solely classical Roman pieces."[4]

With respect, I disagree. Many of the glass objects from Begram have parallels from the Roman world that have been closely dated, while many other glasses have almost no parallels in the Roman world. Despite chemical analyses, I find it difficult to believe that the latter are "classical Roman pieces."

In what follows I begin with reviews of the glass objects described in the catalogue that, without doubt, are Roman and of the evidence for their date. I conclude with the objects that I think are very probably not Roman and offer a suggestion for reconciling their "Roman" chemistry with their "non-Roman" character.[5]

The Roman Objects and Their Date

Traditionally, shape and ornament apart, students of early glass describe objects first in terms of the techniques used to form them and then in terms of the techniques used to finish them. The earliest method of forming glass vessels, practiced principally in western Asia and Egypt, was the technique known as core-forming; other methods were casting, fusing, and slumping. Glassblowing was discovered on the Levantine coast of the Mediterranean in the first century B.C. By the beginning of the first century A.D., it had replaced core-forming, and in the course of that century it became the most common method of making vessels throughout the Roman Empire.

There are no core-formed objects at Begram, but two groups of glasses fall into the cast, fused, or slumped category: mosaic glass[6] and ribbed bowls.[7]

Five mosaic glass bowls were found at Begram. Of these, three are of colorless glass decorated with polychrome garlands.[8] A similar bowl was found in a tomb of the early first century A.D. at Taranto in southern Italy.[9] Another example is on display in the Greek and Roman galleries of the Metropolitan Museum,[10] and two more (from the Campana Collection, presumably found in Italy) are in the Louvre.[11] It is generally agreed that colorless mosaic glass bowls decorated with garlands were made in the Mediterranean region between the late first century B.C. and the early first century A.D.

The same provenance is almost certainly true for a dish formed by fusing slices of mosaic glass canes to form a disk, then slumping the disk over a mold (fig. 1).[12] Thousands of fragments of similar dishes and other vessels have been found at sites throughout the Roman world, most notably at Rome itself, and, residual fragments apart, the majority of those from datable contexts were deposited in the Augustan and Julio-Claudian periods (27 B.C.–A.D. 68).[13]

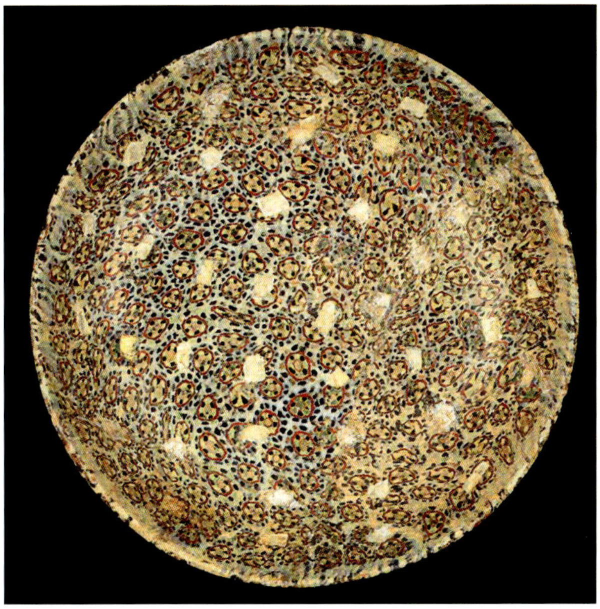

Fig. 1. "Millefiori" bowl. Begram, Room 10, 1st century A.D. Mosaic glass. H. 4 cm, D 17.7 cm. National Museum of Afghanistan, Kabul (04.1.55)

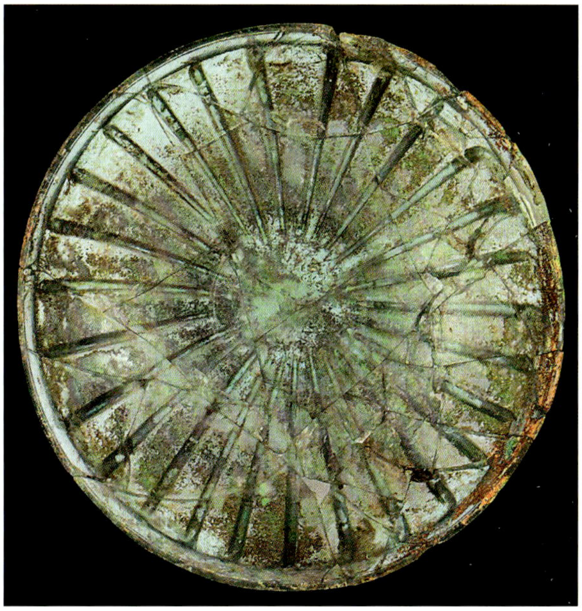

Fig. 2. Monochrome ribbed bowl. Begram, Room 10, 1st century A.D. Glass, H. 7 cm, D. 23.5 cm. National Museum of Afghanistan, Kabul (04.1.54)

Another vessel formed by slumping is a monochrome bowl decorated with pinched ribs (fig. 2).[14] Bowls of this type were common in all parts of the Roman Empire.[15] They appear to have originated in the Syro-Palestinian region in the early first century B.C. Vessels with uniform, evenly spaced ribs came into use in or just before the reign of Augustus (27 B.C.–A.D. 14). Later examples, such as eight bowls from a shop in Herculaneum, where they were awaiting buyers at the time of the city's destruction in A.D. 79, have short, rather irregular ribs. Monochrome ribbed bowls were made until the early years of the second century. The long, evenly spaced ribs on the bowl from Begram suggest that it was made no later than the early first century A.D. A second ribbed bowl from Begram (fig. 3) is made of brown and white mosaic glass.[16] It, too, has numerous Roman parallels of the early first century A.D.[17]

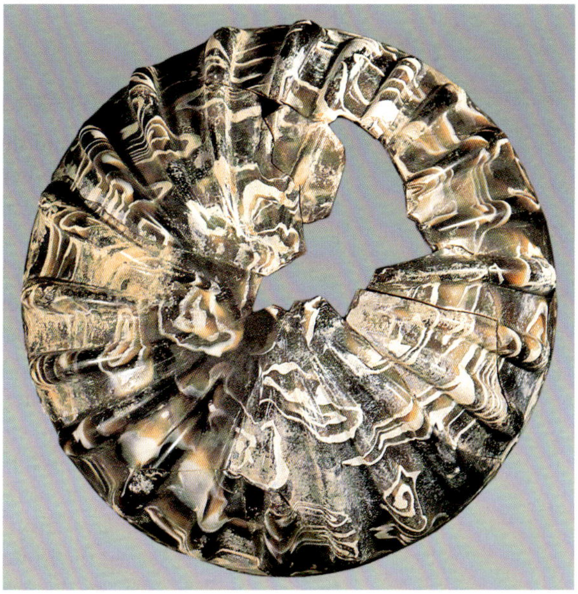

Fig. 3. Ribbed bowl. Begram, Room 10, 1st century A.D. Mosaic glass, D. 17.2 cm. National Museum of Afghanistan, Kabul (04.1.82)

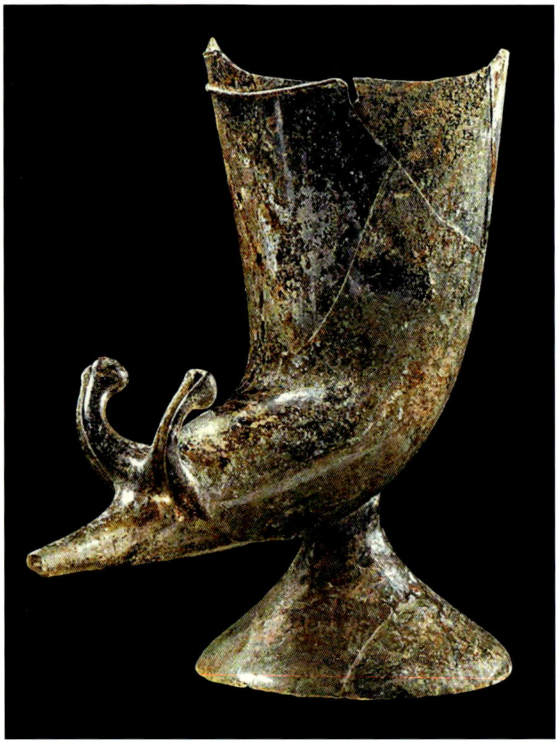

Fig. 4. Footed rhyton. Begram, Room 10, 1st century A.D. Blown glass, H. (surviving), 16.5 cm, D. 13.9 cm. National Museum of Afghanistan, Kabul (04.1.57)

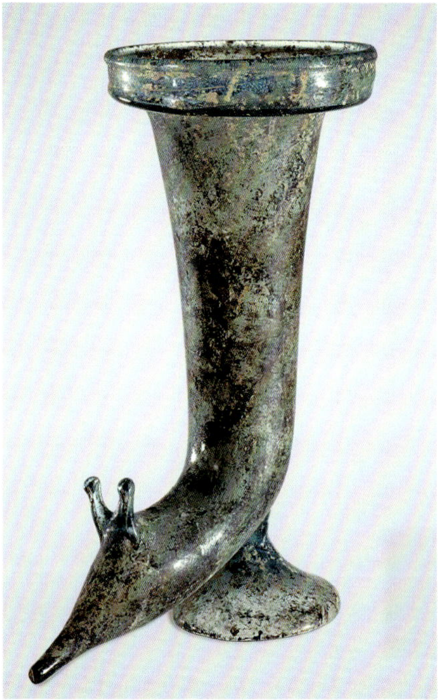

Fig. 5. Footed rhyton. Roman Empire, late 1st–early 2nd century A.D. Transparent pale bluish green glass, blown from two gathers, tooled, H. 21 cm. The Corning Museum of Glass, Corning, New York (87.1.2)

In short, the cast, fused, and slumped vessels from Begram were made between the late first century B.C. and the early to mid–first century A.D.

The exhibition included eight blown glass objects that are certainly or almost certainly Roman. In fact, the only one that gives me pause is the blue vase decorated with vertical ribs.[18] My hesitation—a brief one—derives from the absence of an exact parallel in the Roman world, although there are similar blown glass objects, usually identified as *carchesia* or *kantharoi*, from Pompeii, Rome, and other sites in the Roman Empire.[19] Precise parallels exist, on the other hand, for a drinking horn on a hollow conical foot (fig. 4).[20] Identical objects occur in the Roman world in contexts of the first century A.D. (fig. 5): an example from a cemetery on the Greek island of Siphnos was found in the same grave as a coin of Vespasian minted in A.D. 75, and a similar object appears in a wall painting at Herculaneum. The tips of these horns were perforated, and the wall painting shows the user holding a horn above his head and directing the contents into his mouth.[21] We shall never know, but it is interesting to wonder, whether the owner of the Begram horn knew how the Romans would have used it.

One of the Roman objects is very unusual: a pitcher decorated with a Dionysiac scene made of applied gold foil (fig. 6).[22] The scene has three figures: a maenad and two satyrs, each of whom brandishes a thyrsus. A second pitcher with a similar form is of deep purple glass—

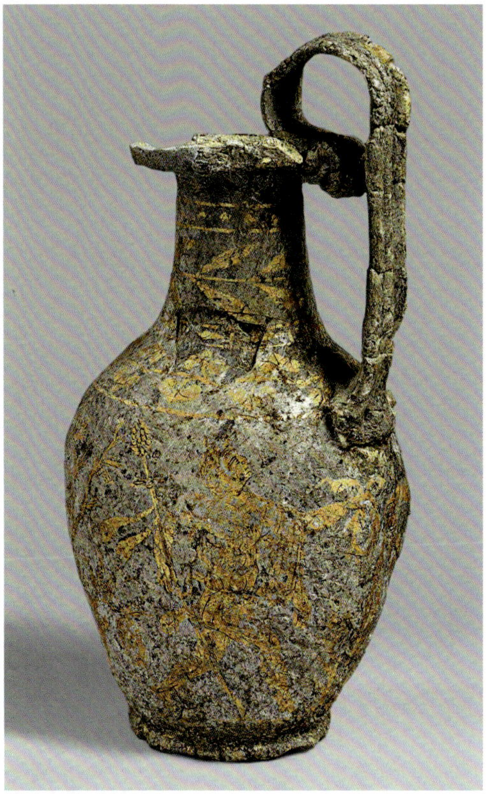

Fig. 6. Pitcher. Begram, Room 13, 1st century A.D. Glass, gold foil, H. 21.4 cm. National Museum of Afghanistan, Kabul (04.1.33)

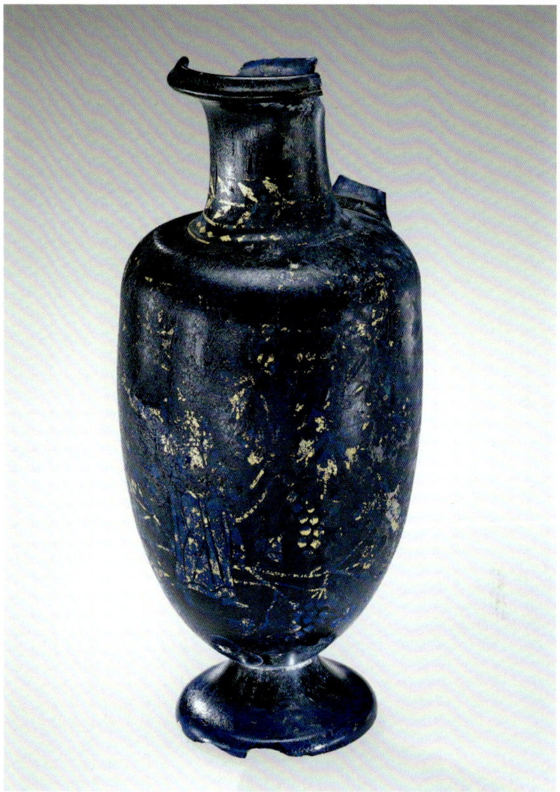

Fig. 7. Pitcher. Roman Empire. Translucent deep blue glass, blown, gilded, H. 21.5 cm. The Corning Museum of Glass, Corning, New York (70.1.3)

so deep that it appears to be black.[23] Presumably it was such glass, according to Pliny (*NH* 36.198), that was known as "opsian" because it resembled the mineral obsidian. A deep blue glass pitcher in the Corning Museum combines the use of gold foil with the form of the black pitcher (fig. 7).[24] Here, too, the scene is Dionysiac, with two figures. The shape of these vessels recalls early first-century jugs signed by Ennion[25] and silver vessels depicted in a wall painting from the tomb of Vestorius Priscus at Pompeii.[26]

Some of the most spectacular glasses from Begram have painted decoration carried out in vitreous enamel, sometimes accompanied by gilding (e.g., fig. 8).[27] These enameled glasses provide some of the strongest evidence for those who wish to date the Begram treasure to the second or third century A.D. They have been compared with painted vessels from graves at Pollwitten and Lübsow-Tunnehult in northern Europe, which are dated between A.D. 70 and the early third century. Michael Menninger, for example, places them between the mid-second and early third century and emphatically rules out an earlier date.[28] I am not so sure. Apart from the fact that the beginning of Menninger's chronological range for the Pollwitten and Lübsow-Tunnehult vessels is A.D. 70, recent finds from excavations in Egypt, at sites such as Quseir al-Qadim,

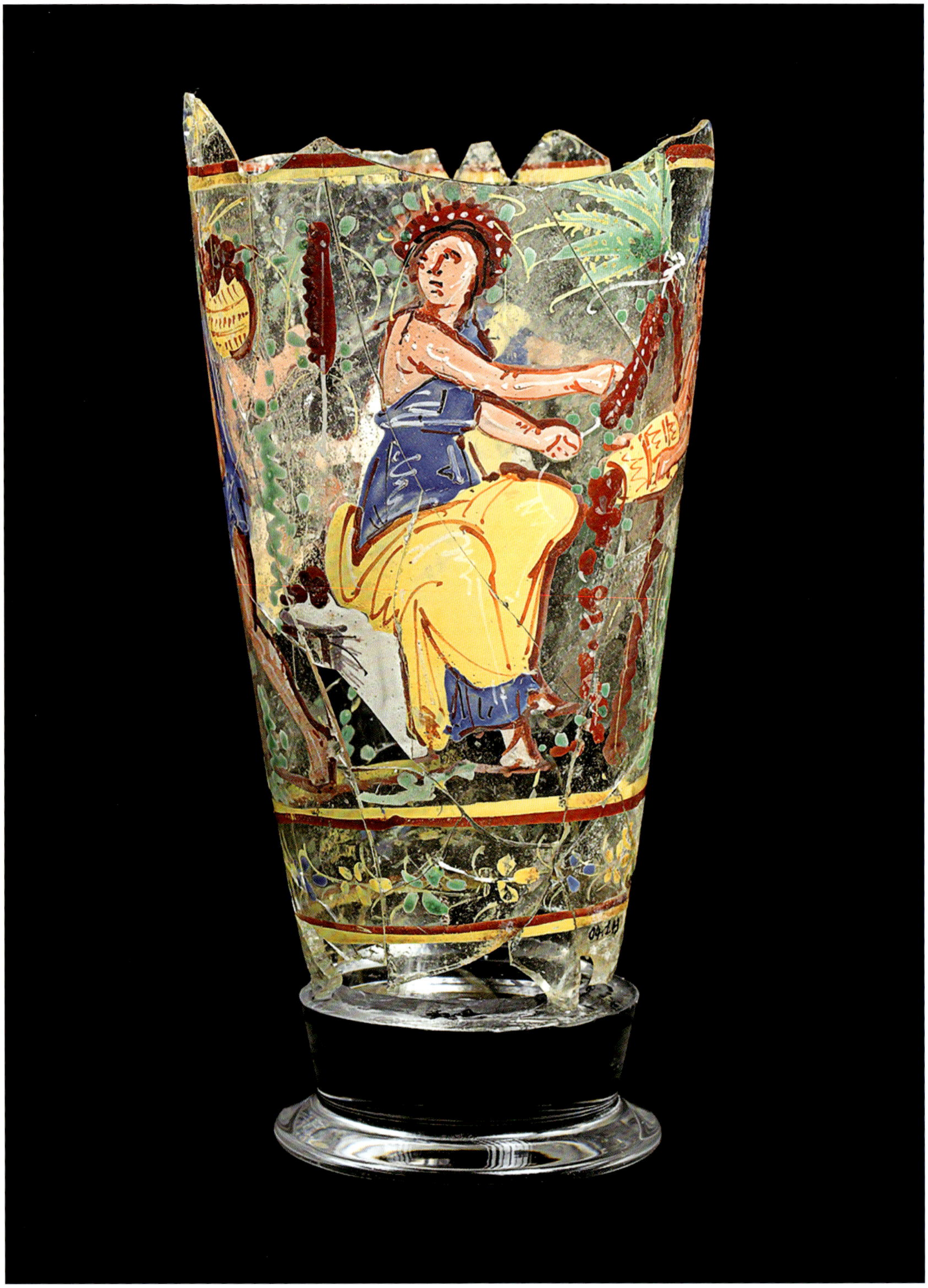

Fig. 8. Beaker depicting date-palm harvest. Begram, Room 10, 1st century A.D. Glass, enameled decoration and gilding, H. 12.6 cm, D. 8 cm. National Museum of Afghanistan, Kabul (04.1.43)

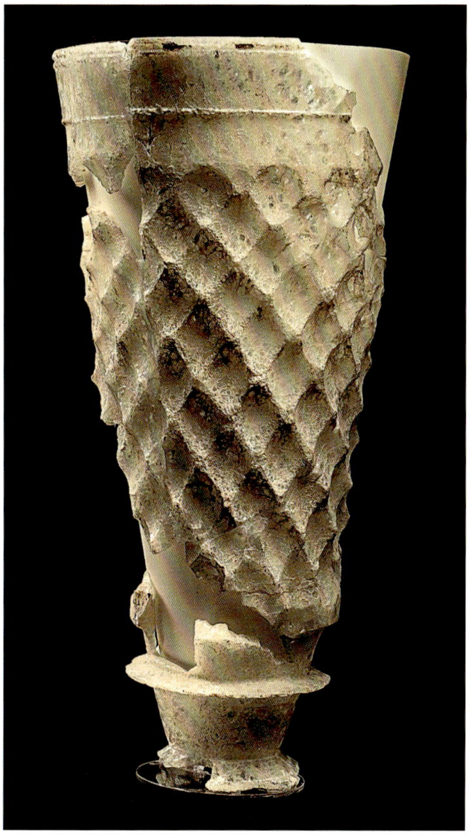

Fig. 9. Facet-cut beaker. Begram, Room 10, 1st century A.D. Glass, H. 22 cm, D. 10 cm. National Museum of Afghanistan, Kabul (04.1.112)

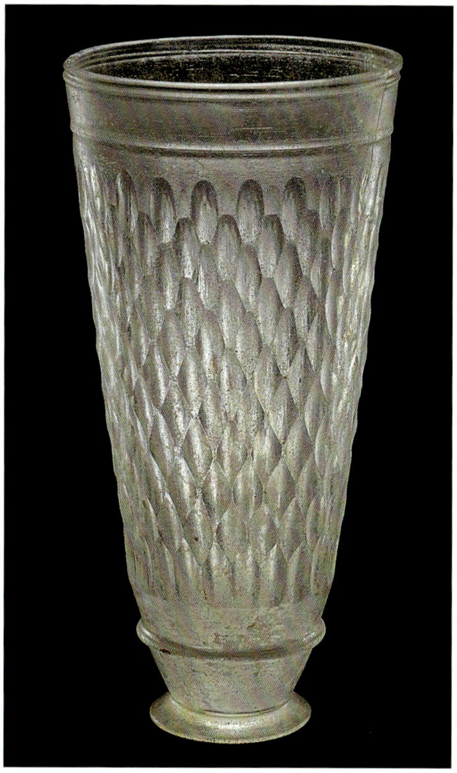

Fig. 10. Facet-cut beaker. Roman Empire, eastern Mediterranean, late 1st–early 2nd century A.D. Greenish colorless glass, blown, turned, and wheel-cut, H. 14.8 cm. The Corning Museum of Glass, Corning, New York (59.1.129)

open the door to regarding the Begram beakers as being of the first or the early second century.

Which brings us to the Roman cut glass: this large and varied group contains some twenty facet-cut objects,[29] objects decorated in intaglio or "negative relief,"[30] relief-cut vessels,[31] and, of course, the famous Lighthouse Beaker.[32]

The facet-cut vessels, most of which have an overall "honeycomb" pattern, include globular cups, pear-shaped jugs, a rhyton, barrel-shaped beakers, and conical beakers (fig. 9), which would have looked spectacular when new. Such objects have been found all over the Roman Empire (fig. 10). The earliest facet-cut glasses with honeycomb decoration date from the 60s of the first century A.D., and vessels with similar decoration seem to have continued in use until the mid-second century. Most examples from datable contexts, however, were deposited between about A.D. 75 and 125.[33]

A fragmentary bowl with intaglio decoration from Begram,[34] which must have been exceptional when new, is decorated with a Dionysiac scene. In terms of technique, it resembles a large plate, also with

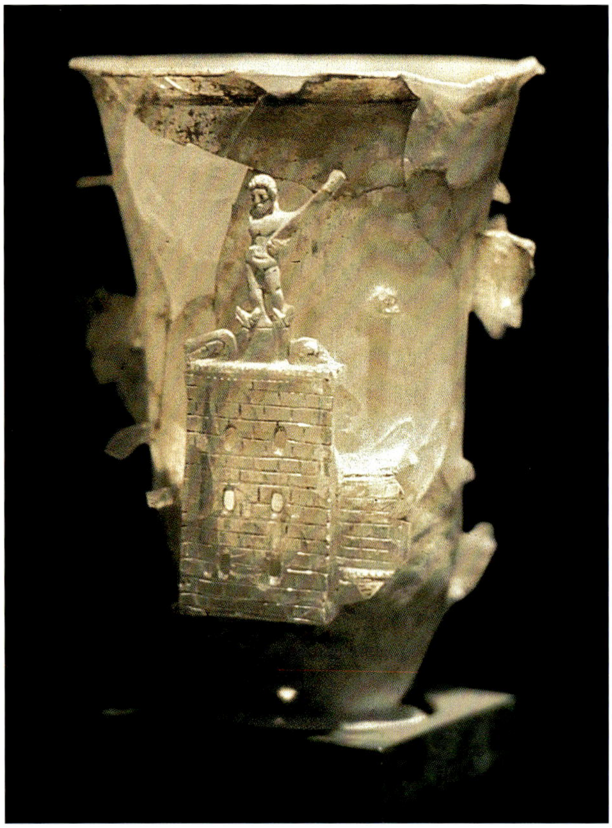

Fig. 11. Beaker depicting Lighthouse of Alexandria. Begram, Room 10, 1st century A.D. Glass, H. (as restored), 16.8 cm. National Museum of Afghanistan, Kabul (57.2.91)

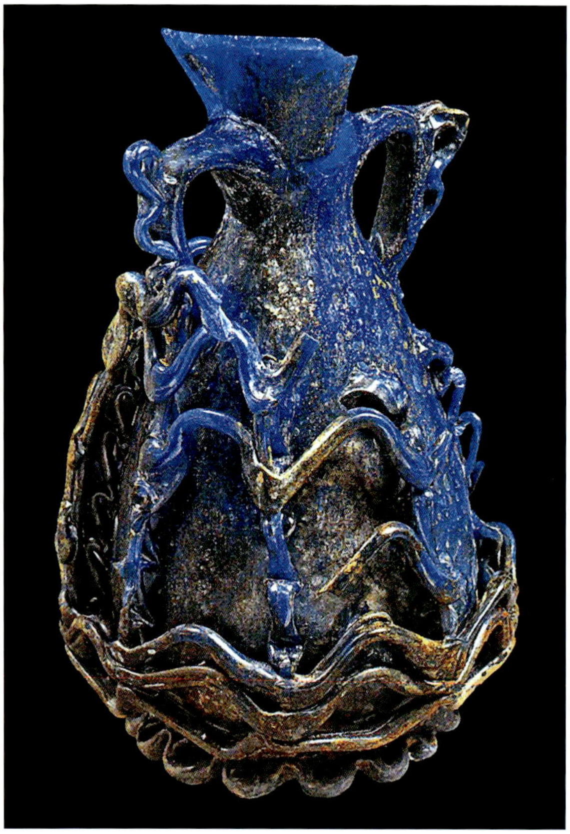

Fig. 12. Jar with applied decoration. Begram, Room 10, 1st century A.D. Glass, H. 22.7 cm. National Museum of Afghanistan, Kabul (04.1.41)

Fig. 13. Fish-shaped flask with applied decoration. Begram, Room 10, 1st century A.D. Glass, 8.7 × 10.7 × 20 cm. National Museum of Afghanistan, Kabul (04.1.45)

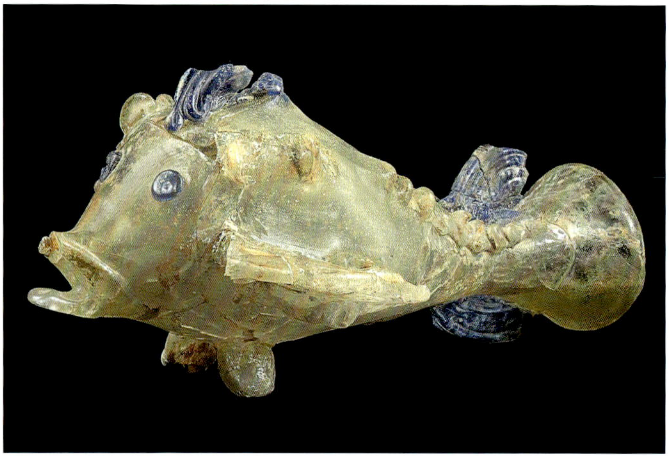

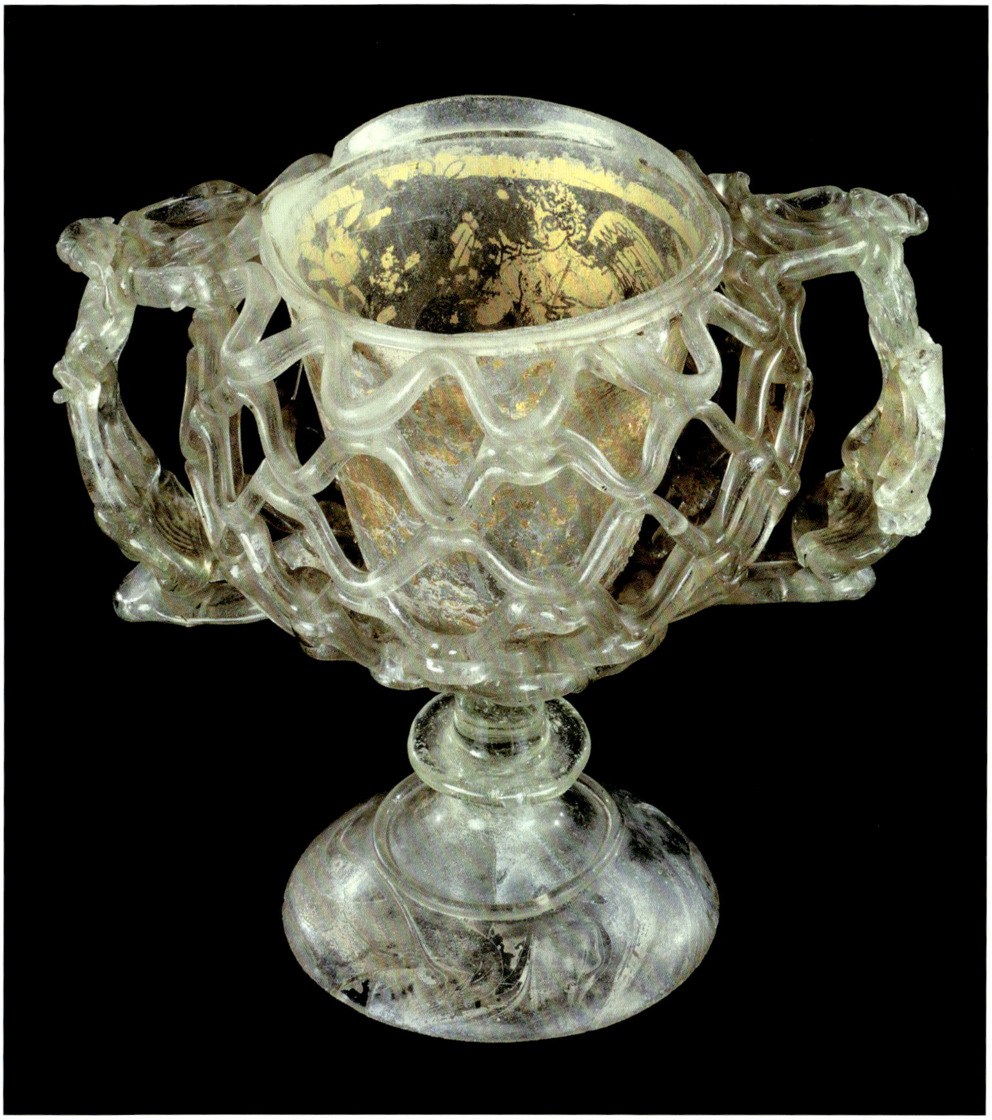

Fig. 14. Disch *kantharos*. Mediterranean or Germany, 3rd–4th century A.D. Transparent greenish colorless glass, blown, applied, gilded, H. 13.8 cm. The Corning Museum of Glass, Corning, New York (66.1.267)

Dionysiac figures, from an early second-century grave at Albenga in northern Italy.[35] The only relief-cut objects, of which substantial parts survive, are two beakers with vegetal ornament. A fragment of a similar beaker was found at Fishbourne in southern England, in a deposit of about A.D. 75–100.[36]

The Lighthouse Beaker (fig. 11) is usually compared with third- to fourth-century cage cups, which also have openwork decoration. However, the relief decoration on the Lighthouse Beaker seems to have been made by cutting blobs of glass that had been applied to the blank in a semi-molten state, whereas cage cups seem to have been cut from an exceptionally thick blank. In any case, at least a few glasses with openwork were made in the late first century A.D.[37]

Objects That Are Probably Not Roman

The objects that I believe are not from the Roman world consist of twenty-six beakers and jars with two handles (e.g., fig. 12),[38] twenty-two vessels in the form of fish and other creatures (e.g., fig. 13),[39] and five vaguely boat-shaped objects.[40] All of these vessels were formed by blowing. Despite the variety of forms, they have one common denominator: abundant applied ornament. The sides of the beakers and jars are surrounded by a network of horizontal wavy lines, which in some cases are supported on vertical trails attached to the wall of the vessel. The fish have trails on the body and very distinctive fins. Each fin is composed of several contiguous loops of a single trail, and many were crimped to produce a pattern of parallel ridges and furrows. The boat-shaped objects also have trails on the body and elaborate openwork handles.

The networks on the beakers and jars have been likened to the applied "cage" of the Disch *kantharos*, a third- or early fourth-century vessel found in Cologne (fig. 14).[41] The fish have been compared with fish of various shapes and sizes from different parts of the Roman Empire,[42] and the boats to a boat-shaped object from a site in Switzerland.[43] However, the only similarity between the beakers and jars from Begram and the Disch *kantharos* is the presence of a cage. Roman glass fish never have fins like the Begram fish, and the relationship between the boat from Switzerland and the boats from Begram is—at best—one of distant cousins. As far as I am aware, the only close parallel for these objects among the tens of thousands of Roman glass vessels in museums around the world is a colorless bottle from Padua, which was found in a well-dated late first- or early second-century grave.[44] Even here the difference in quality between the bottle from Padua and the vessels from Begram is striking. In fact, the most remarkable feature of the beakers, fish, and boats with extravagant trailed ornament is the almost total absence of parallels outside of Begram itself.

If chemical analyses demonstrate that the glass from which some of these objects were formed is typical of glass made in the Roman Empire, how can we reconcile their "Roman" composition with their "non-Roman" appearance? One possible answer is contained in the *Periplus of the Erythraean Sea*, a merchants' guide to maritime trade in the Arabian Sea, written in Egypt in the first century A.D.[45] According to the *Periplus* (49.23 and 56.19), raw glass (that is, glass intended for remelting and making into objects) was exported from Egypt to Barygaza, Muziris, and Nelkynda. All three were ports on the west coast of India. Barygaza was in the north, near the Gulf of Cambay, while Muziris and Nelkynda were farther south, in Kerala. This information does not tell us, of course, that the "non-Roman" glass objects from Begram were made in India, but it does show that, from time to time, raw glass made in the Roman Empire was used to form objects far from its place of origin, thereby explaining how "non-Roman" objects could be made from Roman glass.

A Note on Chronology

In conclusion, I wish to return to the date of the glass in the Begram treasure and its contribution to the question of when the treasure was deposited. The date of the majority of the Roman glass vessels is no longer in dispute: the earliest objects (the mosaic glass) were made between the late first century B.C. and the early first century A.D., while the latest were made between the middle of the first century and the early second century. With the possible (but, I think, doubtful) exception of the painted objects, most of the Roman glass was made between about A.D. 50 and 125: that is, some objects are as early as 50, while others could be as late as 125. In fact, like the ivories and the Chinese lacquer from Begram, I believe that they were made in the first century. If this is correct, the glass objects are consistent with the view that the treasure was concealed within a generation of the year A.D. 100.

1. This essay is a revised version of my lecture at the New York symposium. More information may be found in Whitehouse 2001a.
2. Afghanistan 2008.
3. Ibid., p. 147.
4. Ibid., p. 153.
5. Although I disagree with some of its conclusions, I recommend the monograph by Menninger (1996) on the glass and stucco objects from Begram, which includes (as far as can be assembled) the only published corpus of the glass and is a very accessible survey of material that is otherwise divided among earlier publications that are no longer easy to find.
6. This includes Afghanistan 2008, pp. 173–74, nos. 168 and 171.
7. See ibid., p. 173, no. 167.
8. Menninger 1996, p. 16, pl. 1.
9. Oliver 1967, pp. 17–18.
10. Ibid., p. 17.
11. Arveiller-Dulong and Nenna 2000, pp. 142–43, nos. 174–75.
12. Afghanistan 2008, p. 173, no. 167.
13. Grose 1989, pp. 241–62.
14. Afghanistan 2008, p. 173, no. 167.
15. Grose 1989, pp. 244–49.
16. Afghanistan 2008, p. 174, no. 171.
17. Grose 1989, pp. 244–49.
18. Afghanistan 2008, p. 173, no. 165.
19. Van Lith 1991.
20. Afghanistan 2008, p. 174, no. 170.
21. Whitehouse 1997, pp. 118–20, nos. 184–86. The painting is illustrated in Sampaolo 1986, p. 170, no. 340.
22. Afghanistan 2008, p. 197, no. 210.
23. Ibid., p. 200, no. 213.
24. Whitehouse 2001b, pp. 273–74, no. 866.
25. Whitehouse 1997, pp. 19–20, no. 483.
26. Hilgers 1969, pl. 5.
27. Afghanistan 2008, p. 170, no. 163, and p. 198, nos. 211–212.
28. Menninger 1996, pp. 52–71.
29. They include Afghanistan 2008, p. 169, no. 162, and p. 175, no. 172.
30. Menninger 1996, pp. 38–43.
31. Ibid., pp. 43–46.
32. Ibid., pp. 77–83.
33. Whitehouse 1997, pp. 233–36, nos. 395–399.
34. Menninger 1996, pp. 39–43.
35. Massabò 1999, pp. 145–55, no. 136.
36. Harden and Price 1971, pp. 333–36, no. 30.
37. Koster and Whitehouse 1989.
38. Afghanistan 2008, pp. 168–69, nos. 158–160.
39. Ibid., p. 172, nos. 164, 166, and 169.
40. Menninger 1996, pp. 75–76.
41. Whitehouse 2001b, pp. 275–77, no. 867.
42. E.g., ibid., pp. 199–201, nos. 754–755.
43. Berger and Fünfschilling 1986.
44. Bonomi and Tagliaferro 2006.
45. Casson 1989.

Sanjyot Mehendale

The Begram Carvings: Itinerancy and the Problem of "Indian" Art

Located approximately 60 kilometers northeast of Kabul, the ancient site of Begram (Bagram), near the modern town of the same name, was an important commercial center when the Kushan dynasty dominated the region in the first centuries A.D. In 1937 and 1939, two excavation campaigns, under the direction of Joseph Hackin of the French Archaeological Delegation in Afghanistan, revealed a first- or early second-century sealed-off cache of exquisite objects traded along the ancient Silk Road, among them glassware, alabaster, and bronzes of Roman manufacture and Chinese lacquer.[1] This essay focuses on the third large corpus of material from this site, the Indianesque ivory and bone furniture panels, and the theoretical dilemmas these objects present in terms of classification. Technique, style, and iconography suggest a complex system of Indic traditions informing the inspiration and production of the panels. Their discovery in what is now modern Afghanistan highlights issues of luxury production and exchange in the socio-politically fluid environment of early Central and South Asia. But it also emphasizes, I would argue, the importance of developing more complex frameworks for the classification of "Indian" art. This paper addresses the issue of itinerancy.

Although not directly the topic at hand, the nature and function of the ancient site at Begram remains a matter of controversy. Some scholars believe the city to have been established in the fourth century B.C. by Alexander the Great as the garrison town "Alexandria ad Caucasum." This temporary settlement would subsequently expand into a city under Graeco-Bactrian hegemony and Indo-Greek rule, prior to its annexation in the first century A.D. by the Kushan dynasty, under whose auspices it was reconfigured into a summer capital. Following this hypothesis, the Begram objects have been seen as a royal Kushan treasure amassed over the course of the first to third century A.D., with the rooms ultimately sealed up to protect the objects from the approaching armies (ca. A.D. 241) of the Sasanian Persian dynasty, whose eastward expansion would put an end to direct Kushan rule in the region.

It is important to note that, in the opinion of some scholars, including myself, the archaeological evidence in support of this "royal treasure" argument is weak. Rather,

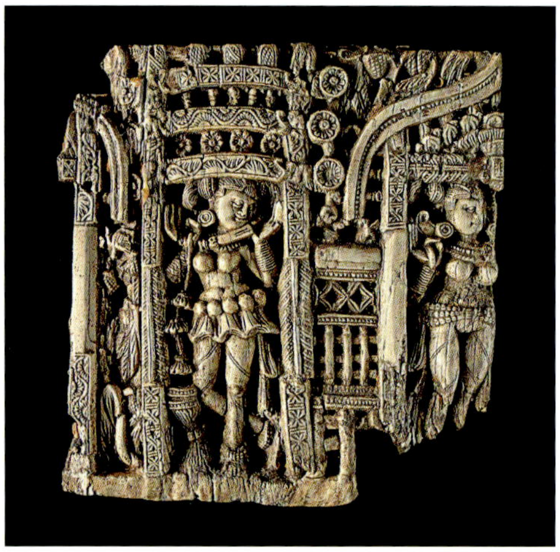

Fig. 1. Decorative plaque with women under gateways. Begram, Room 13, 1st century A.D. Ivory, 16 × 15.3 cm. National Museum of Afghanistan, Kabul (04.1.49)

there is sufficient evidence to hypothesize that the so-called treasure hoard was actually a collection of commodities exchanged along the ancient trading networks popularly known as the Silk Road.[2] Supporting this notion are comparative studies on the Roman and Chinese objects in the cache,[3] as well as the discovery of analogous ivory finds in Uzbekistan and Afghanistan. This evidence suggests that the overwhelming majority of the objects in the "treasure" can be dated contemporaneously to the first or early second century A.D. and that, via a combination of sea and land routes, they probably reached the site of Begram, where they may have been awaiting further distribution.

Turning to the ivory and bone objects themselves, the beautifully carved pieces consist of small plaques and bands, engraved or carved in high and low relief (fig. 1), and sculptures in the round (fig. 2). Together, the individual carvings formed the outer decorative layer of furniture, the wooden skeletons of which had long since decayed due to burial in humid soil. It is very probable that, originally, some of the Begram furniture was painted with red and black dye.[4] Some of the pieces carried marks on the reverse, which may have indicated their position in the larger ensembles.[5] The ensembles uncovered in what was designated Room 13 seemed to have formed the backs of elaborate chairs (fig. 3); the objects from Room 10 perhaps the accompanying footstools (fig. 4). Sets of furniture not unlike these are depicted on some of the Begram ivory carvings themselves (fig. 5). It is not inconceivable that they were traded as luxury wares along the ancient Silk Road, as is indicated by an analogous leg of an ivory table uncovered at the site of Pompeii (fig. 6).[6]

In terms of representations, the great majority of images on the Begram carvings are of women, and most of the scenes in which they are depicted are set in semi-enclosed spaces suggested by gateways, doors, and fences. The most beautiful and elaborate example of women standing under a gateway

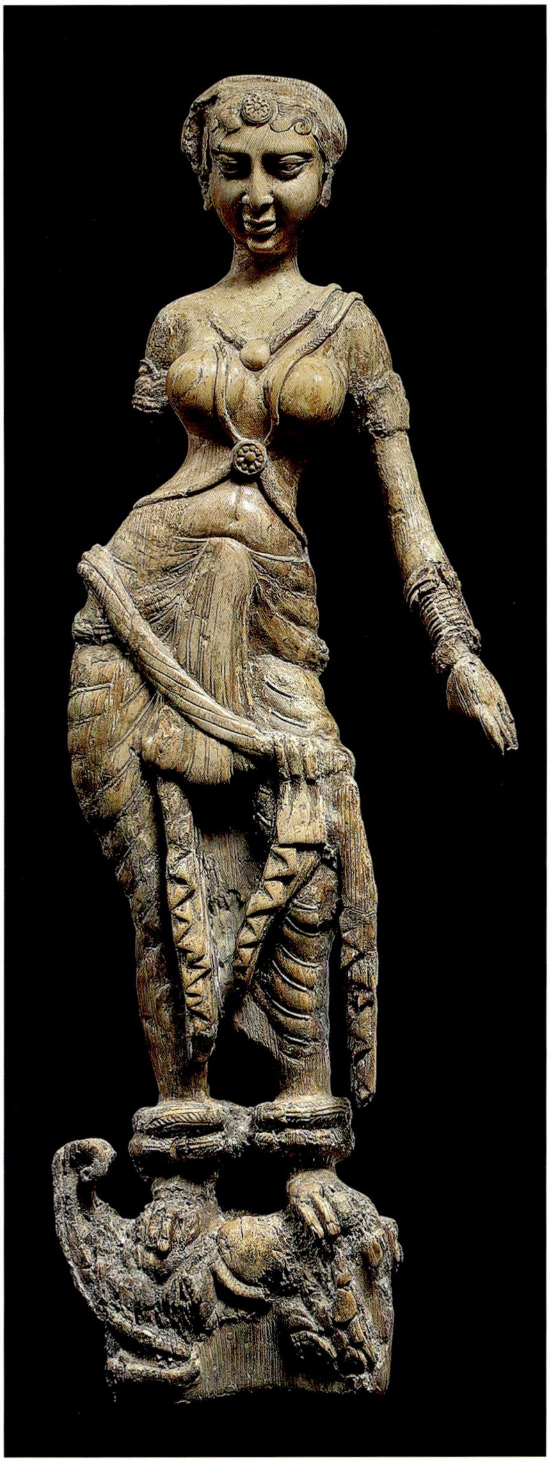

Fig. 2. Woman standing on a *makara*. Begram, Room 10, 1st century A.D. Ivory, H. 45.6 cm. National Museum of Afghanistan, Kabul (04.1.15)

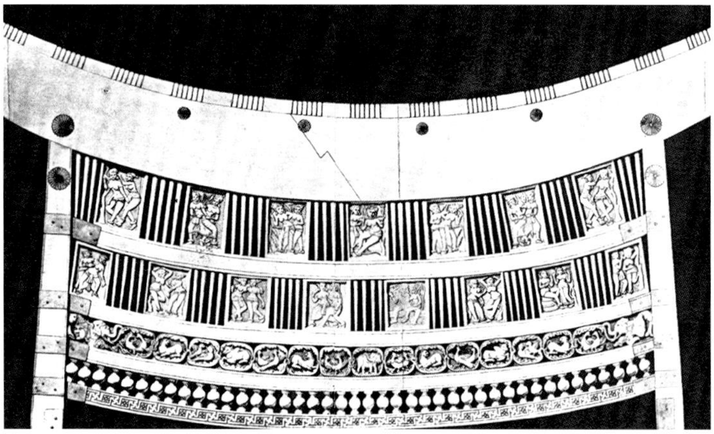

Fig. 3. Reconstruction drawing of a chair back from Begram, Room 13

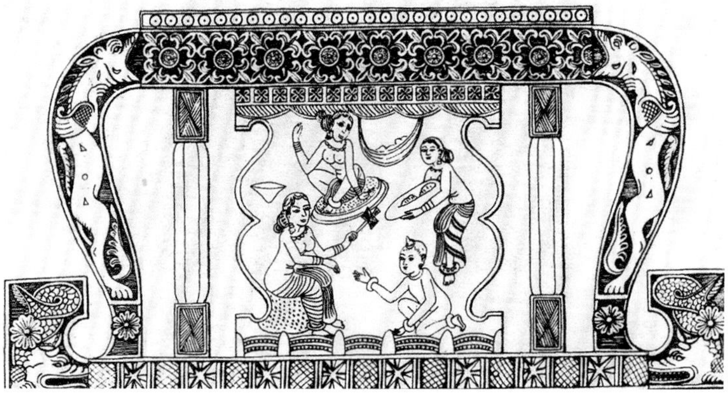

Fig. 4. Reconstruction drawing of a footstool from Begram, Room 10

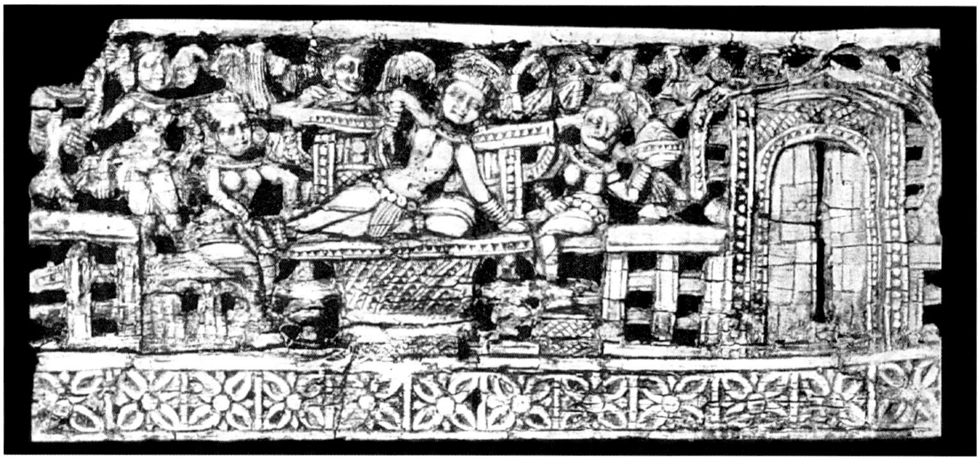

Fig. 5. Decorative plaque depicting a set of furniture. Begram, Room 13, 1st century A.D. Ivory, 8.3 × 18.9 cm. Musée des Arts Asiatiques–Guimet, Paris (MA 334)

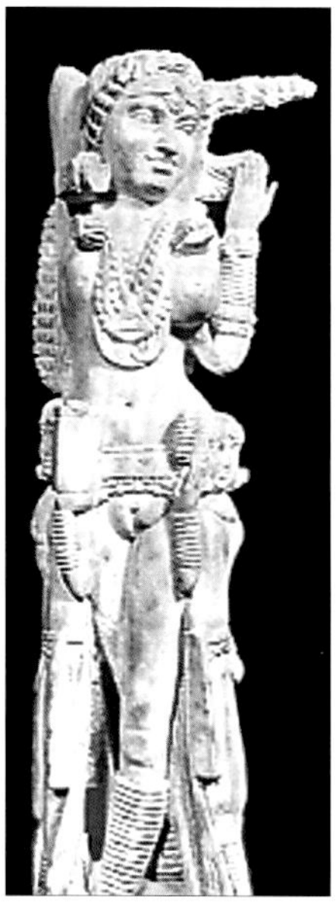

Fig. 6. Female figure. Pompeii, 1st century A.D. Ivory, H. 25 cm. Archaeological Museum, Naples (149425)

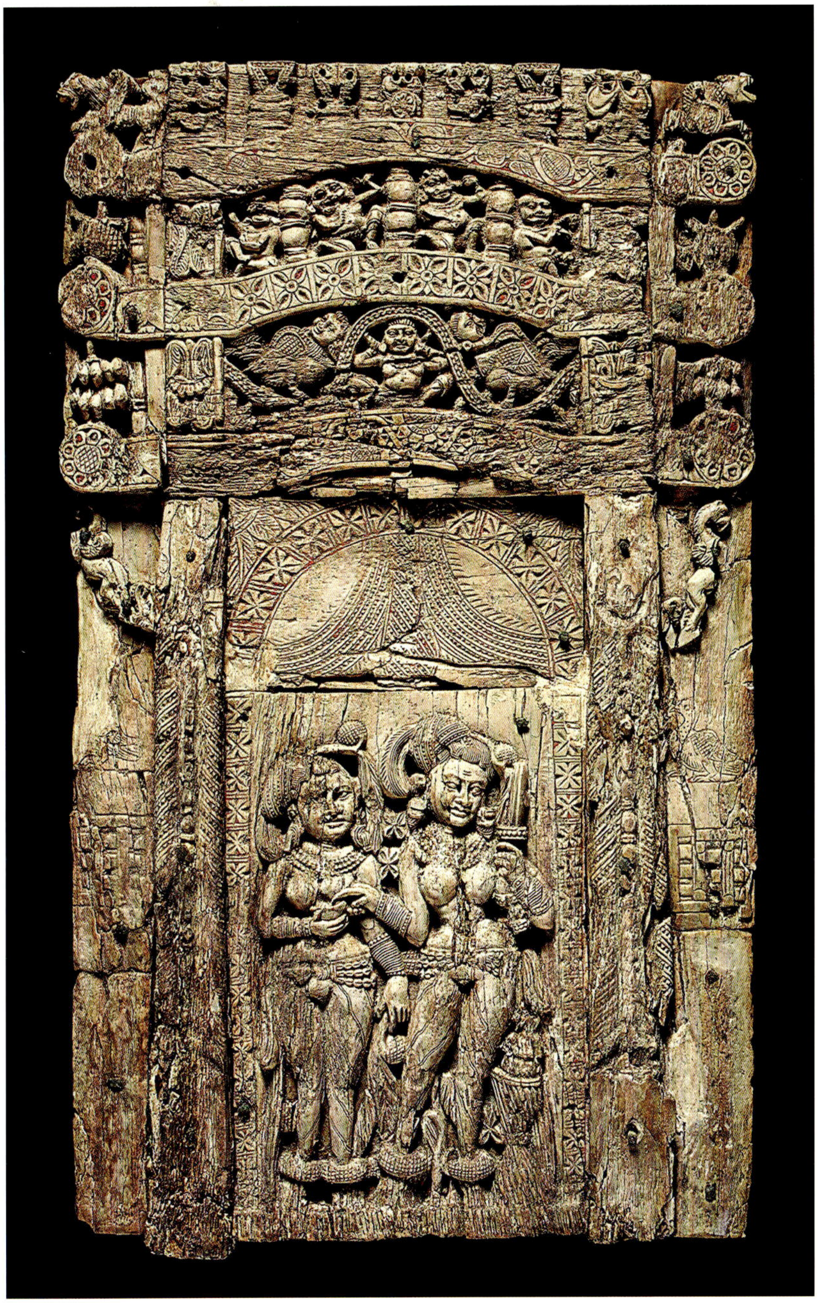

Fig. 7. Decorative plaque with women under a gateway. Begram, Room 13, 1st century A.D. Ivory, 42.7 × 24.6 cm. National Museum of Afghanistan, Kabul (04.1.113)

is presented by an ensemble of high-relief plaques in which the gateways consist of various types of carved pillars and architraves (fig. 7). A less intricately carved series of plaques shows similar scenes of pairs of women standing under an arched gateway (figs. 8, 9). On other plaques in which an entryway is not so clearly distinguishable, such as those which depict, within a square frame, pairs of women sitting on a bench or

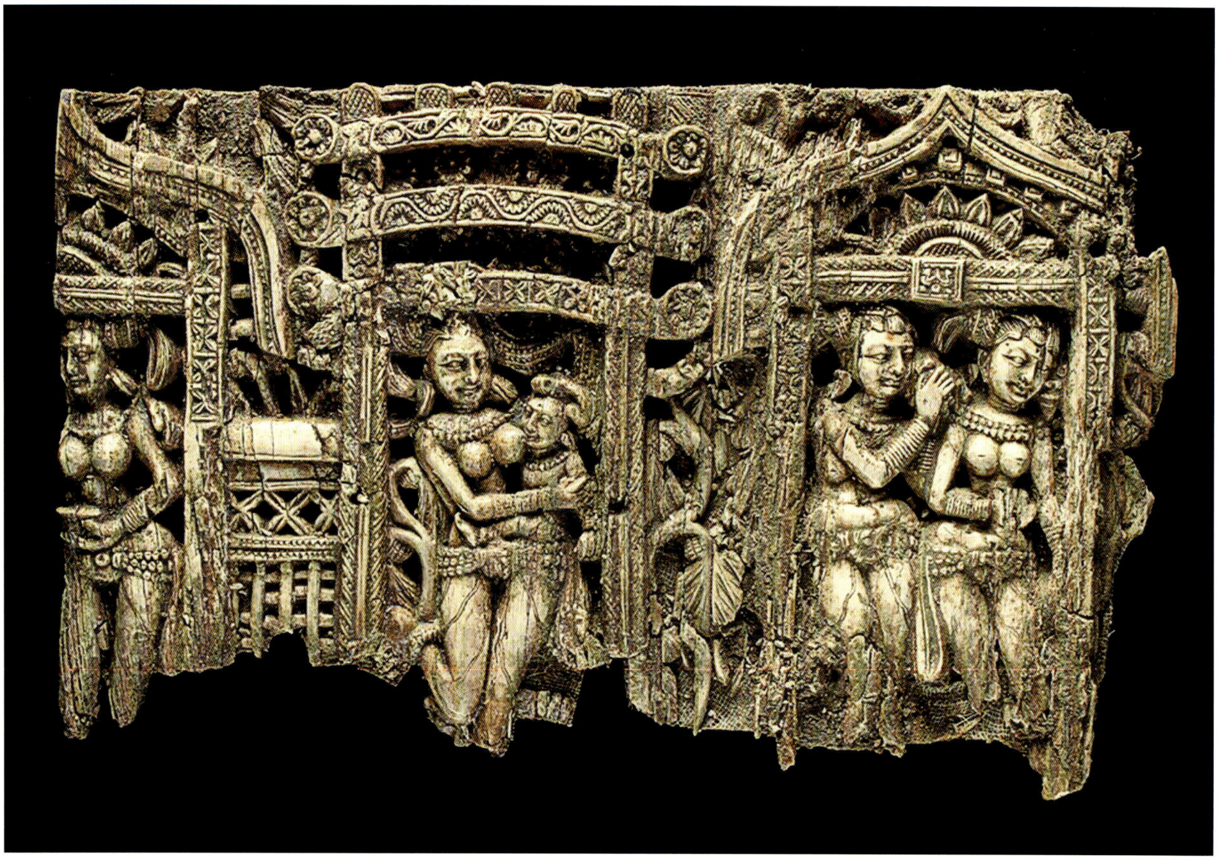

Fig. 8. Decorative plaque with women under gateways. Begram, Room 13, 1st century A.D. Ivory, 13.8 × 24.7 cm. National Museum of Afghanistan, Kabul (04.1.48)

bed, the frames give the viewer a sense of looking through a window or door (fig. 10).

Larger settings with groups of women are rendered in a series of plaques in relief. Small gateways are depicted at regular intervals, either topped by an arch or joined by slightly curving architraves (figs. 11, 12). Parts of balustrades are shown on either side of the gateways, which seems to indicate that the area was enclosed but not completely sealed off. Likewise, the doors of the gateways are left slightly ajar, as if to invite the viewer to experience the secrets behind them. Between the gateways are scenes of women relaxing and playing musical instruments. A few men are represented, but most other motifs are mythological creatures and auspicious signs symbolizing fertility and abundance.

What about the provenance of the carvings? As for the Chinese and Roman objects found at Begram, there has been no controversy regarding their place of manufacture, although David Whitehouse has suggested that some of the Begram glassware, those pieces without antecedents in the Roman world, could have been produced outside the Roman sphere with flint glass exported from the Roman Empire (see Whitehouse essay).[7] What can one then say about the provenance of the Begram ivory and bone carvings? Where were they produced and by whom? Those familiar with my work on

Begram may have been puzzled by my continued use of the terms "Indianesque" and "Indian-style" to describe the carvings. Why not just "Indian"—either they are or they are not. Even if one could agree upon an exact geographic and/or cultural definition of ancient India, a single identification of "Indian" is problematic for this Begram material.

A close examination of the individual carvings reveals that the styles and techniques presented by the ivory and bone objects are very heterogeneous. Some have simple engravings (fig. 13), others are in high relief (see fig. 7) or were made by gouging out undecorated parts to create a sunken relief with a flat surface (fig. 14). Some of the contours are stiffly executed, others very sinuously. The heterogeneity, coupled with the early assumption that the objects had been hoarded over time, offered most scholars the freedom to assign different sets of furniture to various regional schools in India. Indeed, almost all studies to date of the Begram ivory and bone objects have concentrated on the motifs and have been limited to a general stylistic placing of the carvings within the art styles of ancient India. In addition, nearly all stylistic comparisons have been made with stone sculptural art, individual "schools" of which are dated by their relationship with other styles, rather than by exact dates. The use of stone-relief comparisons was based on the scarcity of other ivory finds, at least before the discovery of analogous ivories from Afghanistan and Uzbekistan.

In the earliest studies of the ivory and bone objects, for example, Joseph Hackin compared some of the motifs to the mid-first century B.C. carvings of the gateways of Stupa I at Sanchi. Hackin compared the majority of other finds to the school of Mathura of the first–second century A.D. but stylistically placed one of the footstools (IX) at the end of the third or the beginning of the fourth century A.D.[8] J. LeRoy Davidson placed the objects in the first century

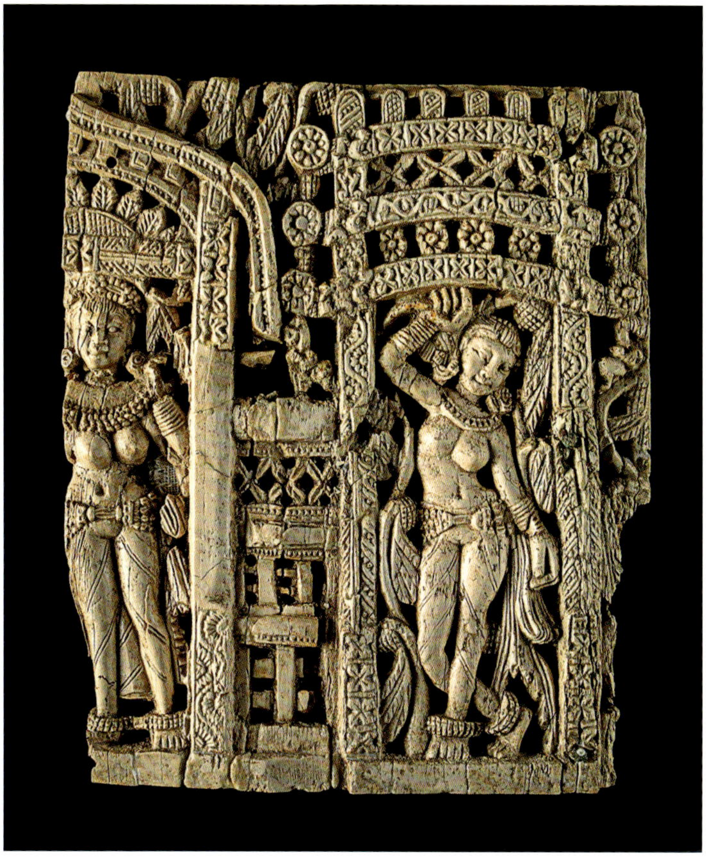

Fig. 9. Decorative plaque with women under gateways. Begram, Room 13, 1st century A.D. Ivory, 16 × 13.3 cm. National Museum of Afghanistan, Kabul (04.1.53)

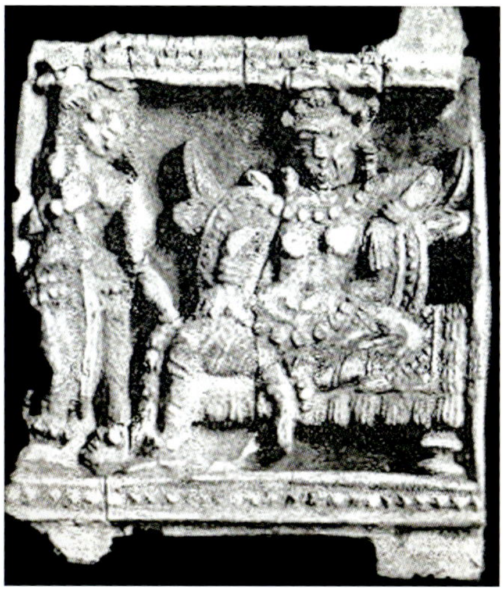

Fig. 10. Decorative plaque with a woman seated on a bed. Begram, Room 13, 1st century A.D. Ivory, 5.6 × 5.5 cm. National Museum of Afghanistan, Kabul (58.1.148)

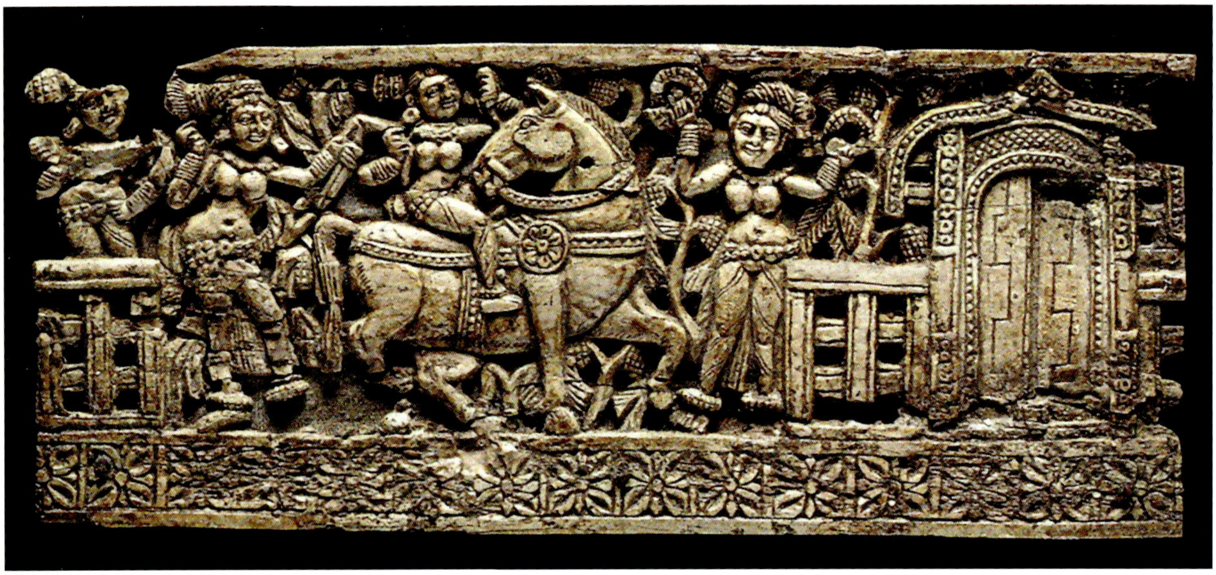

Fig. 11. Decorative plaque with a scene from the women's quarter. Begram, Room 13, 1st century A.D. Ivory, 8.2 × 19.7 cm. National Museum of Afghanistan, Kabul (04.1.74)

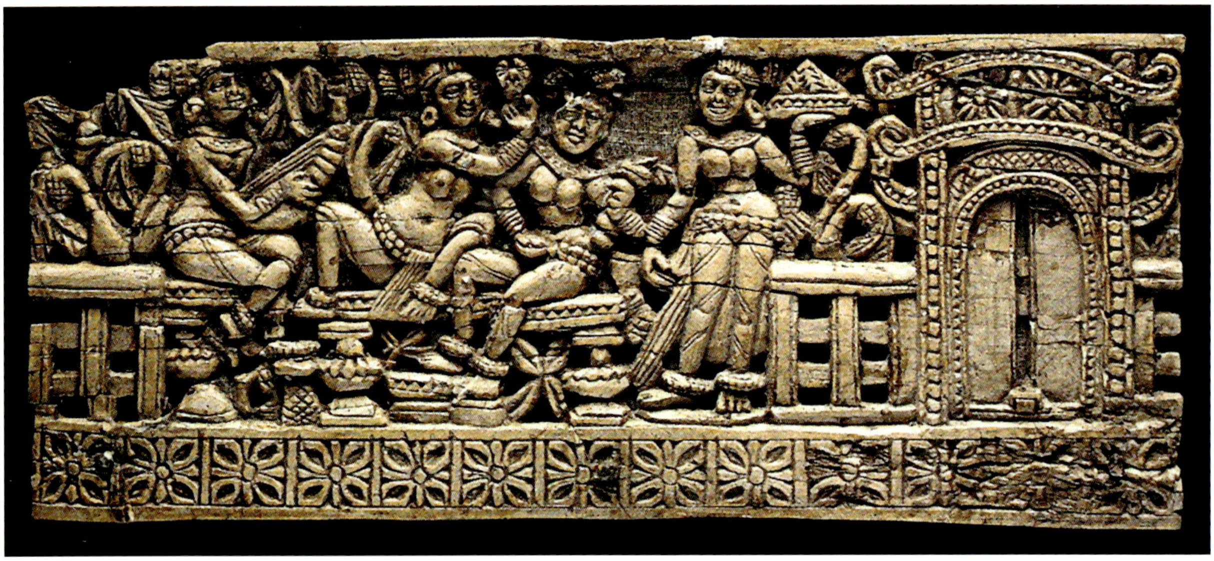

Fig. 12. Decorative plaque with a scene from the women's quarter. Begram, Room 13, 1st century A.D. Ivory, 8.3 × 20 cm. National Museum of Afghanistan, Kabul (04.1.75)

B.C., based on a stylistic comparison to the art of Sanchi I.[9] Philippe Stern viewed the Begram artifacts through the lens of texts and inscriptions, along with a stylistic examination of the development or transformation of motifs, and came to the conclusion that the carvings should be dated to the first and second centuries A.D., contemporaneous with the style of Mathura but later than the old style of Sanchi.[10] Elizabeth Rosen Stone, on the other hand, has assigned the latest dates for the Begram ivory and bone objects, asserting that they belong to the later phases of Andhra art, namely, at the end of the third or in the early fourth century A.D.[11]

The above and subsequent studies may suggest that the Begram ivory and bone objects were carved in different cultural centers of ancient India, at different times, and were transported to Begram over time to become part of a royal treasure. Careful examination of all of the ensembles, however, seriously challenges the assertion that the objects came from different regions. In the first instance, different styles and techniques appear in the same ensemble. It seems that the artisans quite purposefully used heterogeneous plaques to create a visual interplay among the pieces of the

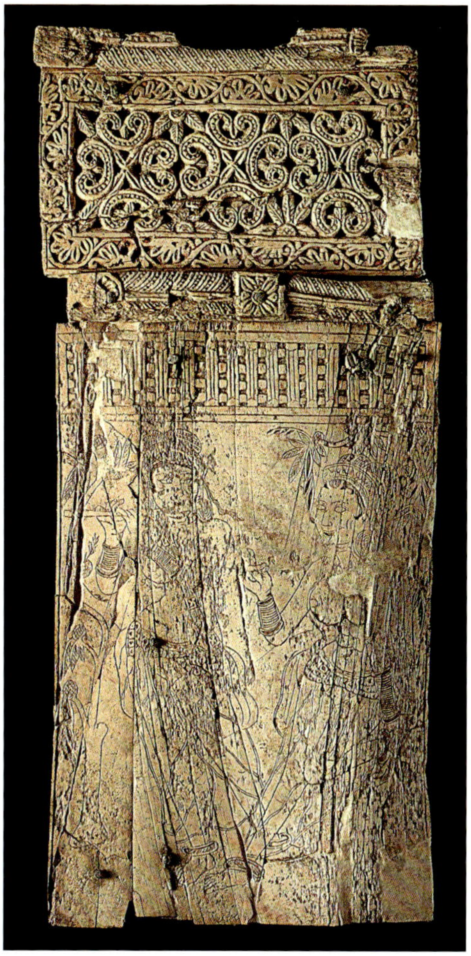

Fig. 13. Decorative plaque with a scene of a musician and a dancer. Begram, Room 13, 1st century A.D. Ivory, 34.6 × 15.4 cm. National Museum of Afghanistan, Kabul (04.1.21)

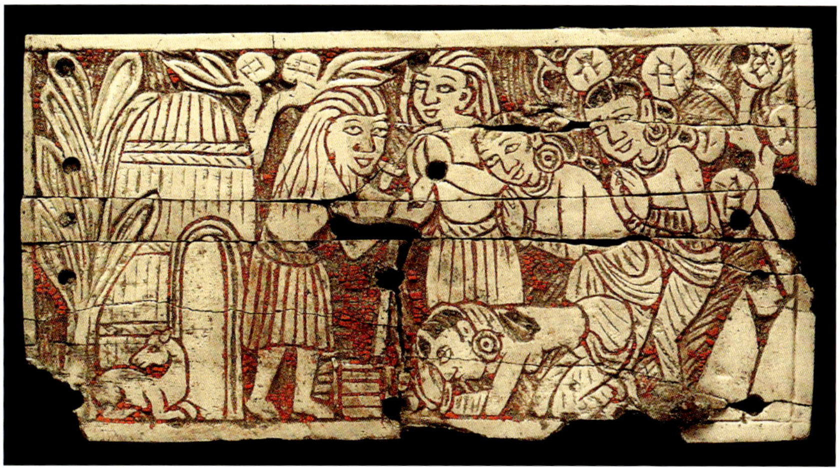

Fig. 14. Decorative plaque in sunken relief showing a group of men and women paying respect to a hermit in front of his hut, possibly a *jataka* story. Begram, Room 13, 1st century A.D. Ivory and paint, 5.9 × 11.3 cm. National Museum of Afghanistan, Kabul (04.1.23)

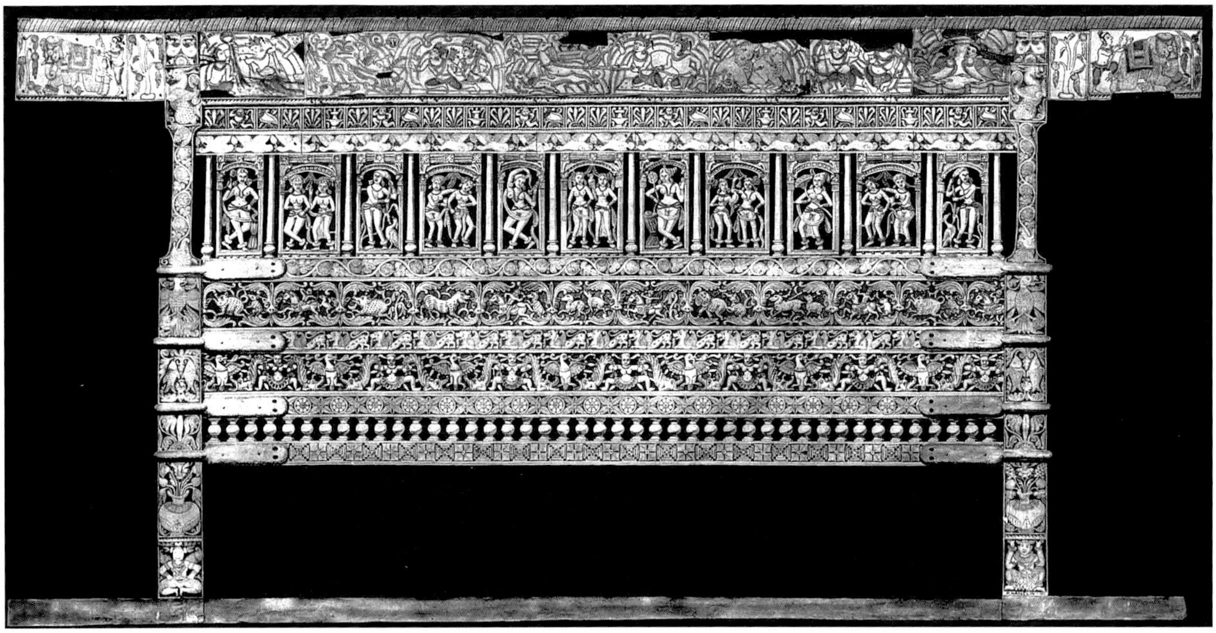

Fig. 15. Reconstruction drawing of a chair back from Begram, Room 13

same ensemble. In addition, despite the differences in style and technique, the majority of plaques are uniform in representation—women depicted centrally, framed by secondary bands of mythological, vegetal, and architectural designs (fig. 15). Because of these elements, I have little doubt that the furniture was carved in the same workshop or sets of workshops. This contention is further supported by analogous finds of ivory carvings uncovered in areas of modern Afghanistan and Uzbekistan that date to the first century A.D., providing additional evidence that the Begram carvings can be dated contemporaneously.

If the carvings originated from a single workshop, one must next consider its location. If India is posited as the place of origin, based on stylistic analyses of monumental stone sculpture, disputes immediately arise about which monumental sites provide the best comparative material. It is a somewhat arbitrary and ultimately not very satisfactory process that isolates a few motifs favoring one site, while another few motifs could favor a different site. Furthermore, a number of problems exist with the use of stone reliefs as comparative material. Differences in style between stone sculpture and the Begram carvings may be due to the smaller scale but also to the higher precision afforded by ivory and bone. Theoretically speaking, one might ask whether stone reliefs or monumental art always precede smaller arts and crafts; all previous comparisons seem to assume that stone reliefs are the seed that germinated the ivory and bone carvings. It should be kept in mind, however, that, despite similarities between a particular work of monumental art and later ivory pieces in different regions, monuments do not travel. Thus, the long-distance diffusion of motifs may have been the result of the exchange of small portable examples along trade routes.

Another problem concerning stone reliefs as comparative material is the issue of contemporaneity. Stone monuments tend to last for a long time and are seen by many people. Motifs of long standing on monumental stone reliefs might have triggered the imagination of an artisan at a much later period than that of the construction of the monument.

While stylistic analysis does not provide definitive evidence, Indian literary and epigraphic remains can be used in an effort to winnow information concerning the work environments of ivory-carving artisans and traders from the broader Indian subcontinent. Of the ancient textual evidence concerning the ivory carvers of India, the most famous is undoubtedly the stone *torana* inscription at Sanchi (ca. second century B.C.), which reads: "This carving has been done by the ivory carvers of Vidisa."[12] If the translation is precise and the inscription is to be taken literally, then it appears that these ivory carvers, at least, worked in more than one kind of material and in more than one location. Furthermore, the description of the carvers as a specific group suggests that they were organized in guilds and collectively contributed to the construction of these important monuments. The Ramayana, the ancient Indian epic, also mentions that both ivory carvers, *dantakarah*, and ivory traders, *dantapajivinah*, were organized into guilds.[13]

Furthermore, there is also ample evidence that ivory carvers were localized in urban districts. The *Silavanaga Jataka*, for example—the story of the Buddha's past in which he was born as an elephant and of his generosity betrayed by a greedy man—mentions the ivory carvers' bazaar, *dantakaravithi*, in Benares and the sight of artisans working on ivory in different shapes and forms.[14] The description of such a specific bazaar, with different types of ivory work going on in one place, seems to indicate that the ivory carvers gathered together in a particular part of the city and that the work was significantly organized.

Another issue that may be of importance concerns the buyers or patrons and the types of markets for which the artisans produced. In the same story of the *Silavanaga Jataka*, a forester inquires of the ivory carvers whether they would be interested in buying the tusk of a live elephant; the artisans reply that the tusk of a live elephant is worth much more than that of a dead one and that they would be willing to pay more. This indication that artisans were direct buyers of ivory may permit us to see them as working for themselves, as an active part of a commercial economy.

Other texts support this notion by indicating that buyers of ivory carvings were traders who dealt directly with the artisans. Such a reference, and perhaps a significant one in relation to Begram, occurs in the *Avasyaka Churani*, a Jain text of uncertain date, in which it is written that ivory trade was in the hands of the "Tanana Mlecchas." "Mlecchas" is translated as "not Indian," i.e., from the north. This suggests to J. C. Jain that, at least at the time of this particular text, some ivory trade may have been in the hands of people from the northwest.[15] The text goes on to mention that these traders in ivory traveled down from the northern region along the "Uttarapatha" (northern road) to the "Daksinapatha" (southern road) with their ivory, evidence for the existence of ivory-carving centers in the north and of trade in ivory objects between north and south. A similar suggestion concerning itinerant ivory traders, who may also have been carvers, can be found in the *Guttila Jataka*. This text is the story of the birth of the future Buddha into a musician's family. Mention is made of a group of traders, ready with their wares to set off on a trading journey from Benares to Ujjain. In some translations, instead of mere traders, the group is described as ivory workers setting off on a trading journey.[16]

From these various textual sources, we can deduce that ivory carving was a craft that was well established and well organized, localized in urban centers, and part of a commercial market. Additionally, the evidence indicates that some ivory carvers were itinerant.

It is this itinerancy that is important in our discussion of Begram. Three important

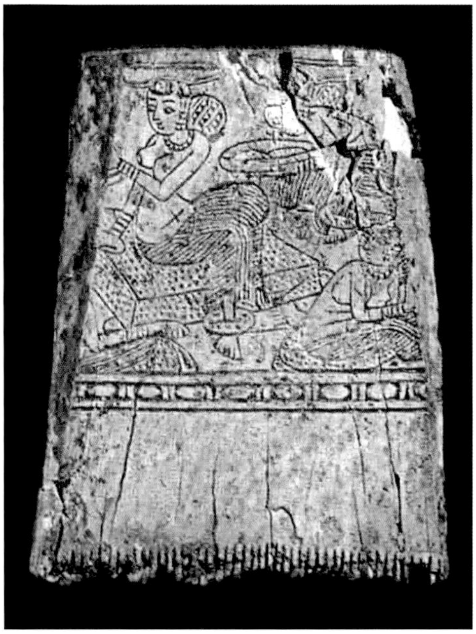

Fig. 16. Comb (obverse) with a scene depicting a group of women. Dal'verzin-Tepe, 1st–2nd century A.D. Ivory, 9.2 × 6.5–7.8 cm. Museum of Fine Arts, Tashkent, Uzbekistan

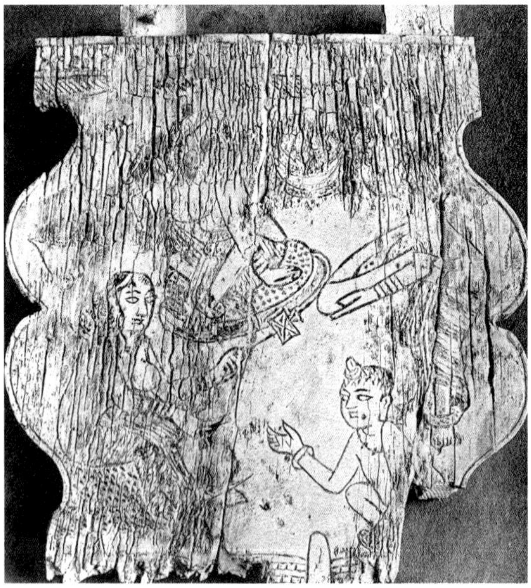

Fig. 17. Decorative plaque with a scene depicting a group of women and a young man. Begram, Room 10, 1st century A.D. Ivory, 11.5 × 11.7 cm. Musée des Arts Asiatiques–Guimet, Paris (MG 18977)

pieces of evidence from the site itself point to the intriguing possibility that the ivory carvings might have been made locally. First, three unfinished tusks uncovered by the excavators, although no longer extant, are suggestive, but certainly not conclusive, of a carving center at the site.[17] Second, an ivory comb found outside the two sealed-off rooms, in the residential area of Begram, indicates that ivory was used or perhaps traded at the site.[18] Third, a number of Begram carvings carry marks on the reverse in the Kharosthi script of the Kushan era.[19] Because of wear, it is impossible to say whether all of the Begram ivory and bone objects originally carried such marks. If most did, the marks may not have been signs of the artisans' authorship, but of the placement of the object in the ensemble to be attached to a wooden frame. The use of the Kharosthi script suggests that the persons who either carved or assembled the objects came from local workshops in what is now Pakistan or Afghanistan, rather than from the Indian heartland. If so, the Begram ivory and bone pieces may have been produced by carvers who actually lived and worked in the region, and not carved farther south and then transported to the northwest.

There is also ample archaeological evidence, based on finds, to suggest that ivory carving was as important a craft in the northern regions as it was in the south, with many scholars supporting the hypothesis that an ivory-carving center existed in Taxila.[20] The presence of Bactrian ivory workshops at or near Nisa in Turkmenistan[21] and at Aï Khanum in northern Afghanistan clearly shows that the raw material could be obtained in regions far north.[22]

The pre-Begram traditions of ivory carving in the north, mentioned above, are complemented by several contemporaneous ivory and bone finds, from the first to early second century A.D. The first secure date for analogous ivory and bone carvings is provided by an ivory statuette discovered at Pompeii that is very similar to the Begram ivory figurines.[23] The Pompeii figurine (see fig. 6) carries a *terminus ante quem* date of A.D. 79, when Vesuvius erupted and buried Pompeii under a layer of ash. It is unknown how long before this date the Pompeii ivory was carved. Some scholars date it to the mid-first century A.D., while others have placed it in the latter half of the first century B.C. on the basis of a comparison with the arts of Sanchi and Bharhut. Judging from the Kharosthi inscription on the base of the Pompeii ivory, however, and significantly for the argument here regarding local workshops in the region of Begram, it seems to have come from somewhere in the northwestern regions of India, Pakistan, or Afghanistan. If so, it would be problematic to date the Pompeii figure on the basis of the imagery from Sanchi and Bharhut in the heartland of India. Furthermore, since the building in which the Begram objects was discovered is dated to the first century A.D., the stylistic analogies between the ivory figurines from Begram and the known *ante quem* date of the Pompeii ivory would seem also to argue in favor of placing the Begram carvings in the first century A.D.

If the Pompeii ivory figurine represents the furthest extent of the trade in Indian-esque ivory and bone objects, intermediate stages in this commerce can be seen in finds from Dal'verzin-Tepe and Tillya Tepe. Dal'verzin-Tepe is situated on the east bank of the Surkhan Darya, five miles north of Surci in modern Uzbekistan. The excavations at Dal'verzin-Tepe reveal rich evidence of fortifications, religious and urban architecture, monumental sculpture in baked clay, frescoes, and ceramics. According to Galina Pugachenkova, the town, established in the last centuries B.C., reached its zenith during the Kushan period.[24] An ivory comb (fig. 16) discovered at a small sanctuary in Dal'verzin-Tepe is identical in style to some of the Begram ivory and bone carvings (fig. 17), so much so that it seems almost certain that both came from the same atelier and were even made by the same hand. The date assigned to the ivory comb from Dal'verzin-Tepe, first or second century A.D., correlates with the more recent dates attributed to the entire hoard discovered in the two rooms at Begram.

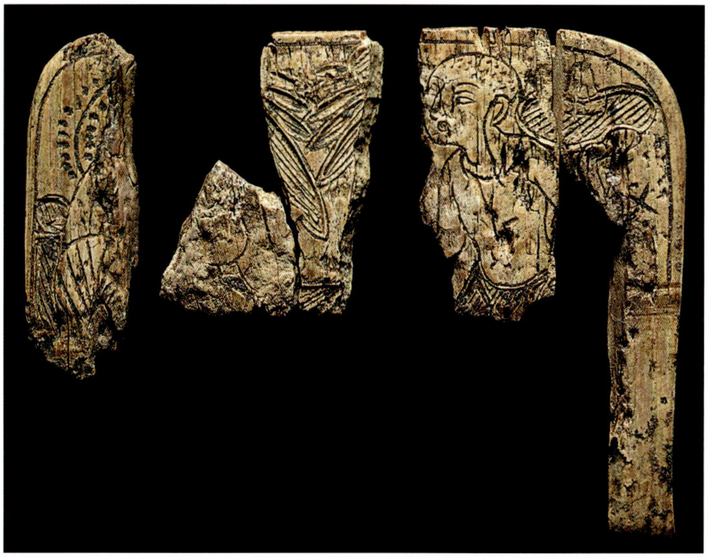

Fig. 18. Fragments of a comb with a scene depicting a young man. Tillya Tepe, Tomb III, 2nd quarter of 1st century A.D. Ivory, W. 5 cm. National Museum of Afghanistan, Kabul (04.40.227)

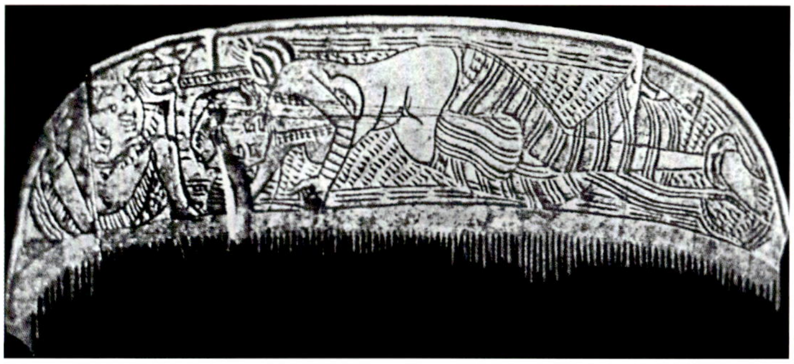

Fig. 19. Comb (obverse) with a representation of a reclining female. Taxila, 1st century A.D. Ivory

Other objects analogous to the carvings from Begram include a small ivory comb from the Tillya Tepe necropolis (fig. 18), dated to the early first century A.D., and an ivory comb from Taxila (fig. 19). On the basis of stylistic characteristics and the dating of the exact pits in which it was found, the Taxila comb has been assigned to the first century A.D.[25] All these analogous ivory and bone finds not only support a first century A.D. date for the Begram ivory and bone objects, but also suggest the strong possibility of one or more northern carving centers.

The hypothesis that there may have been an ivory-carving workshop at Begram itself remains, at this point, subject to further proof. In the future, there may be renewed excavation at the site, which could provide us with more data. The evidence for itinerancy among ivory carvers is strong, however, and may have interesting and important theoretical implications for our understanding of "Indian" art. Instead of always reaching for a place of geographic origin, which has been the basis of the main classifications of ancient South Asian art, one would also need to conceive of a *portable* artistry. In other words, what does it mean for our understanding of so-called Indian art when artisans and craftsmen move?

In the specific instance of Begram, itinerancy presents a challenge to scholars for whom style is rooted to place. For example, V. P. Dwivedi, although admitting "that the appearance of the Kharosthi alphabet on the [Begram] ivory would suggest that it was carved in the region where Kharosthi was used, Gandhara,"[26] nonetheless rejects a northwestern atelier on the grounds that, stylistically, it would be impossible to place the object in that region. The concept of itinerancy may help to bridge the divide.

Much classification of Indian art is based on stylistic analyses, the attribution of works to schools and historical periods, and regionalism. But when it comes to crafts and artisanship, as applied to monumental works, for example, the commonly used dynastic categories, such as Satavahana and Kushan, may not be very useful. First, determining the impact of a ruling clan on the production of all forms of artisanship across an empire is highly problematic. One can certainly argue that royal sponsorship of monumental constructions would have a determinative impact on the architecture of a structure and on the subject matter of reliefs. However, the styles of reliefs might instead be determined by the training of the artisans and the long development of styles in a workshop and in a region's artistic tradition. Second, dynastic classification is not very useful when comparing the art styles of "schools" that, while technically belonging to different states or empires, show more in common with each other than with some sites within the same dynastic political sphere. For example, the art of Sanchi, belonging to the Andhra–Satavahana dynastic tradition, can be viewed as closer in style to Kushan-period Mathuran art than to, say, Amaravati, which is also included in the so-called Satavahana school. Even the use of geographic, e.g., Gandharan or Mathuran, rather than dynastic, classifications as a basis for comparative studies of art styles provides only partial, unstable organizing tools, since rarely were regions either clearly defined or insular in antiquity.

And even if geographic classifications, i.e., regional schools, are adequate for understanding stationary stone monumental art, they lose much of their explanatory power when itinerant artisanship enters the picture, particularly if we consider artisans who are moving away from a center toward the periphery. For example, the locally made stone stelae uncovered in Sri Lanka that were based on Amaravati styles: are they Sri Lankan, or are they Indian?

Itinerancy, it is argued here, suggests that the current paradigms for the study of Indian art may not be fully adequate to understand the combined artistic, geographic, and socioeconomic complexities of the ancient past. Notions such as "Mathura school" or "Amaravati style" to delimit a regional art may be more complex than their common usage suggests. Regarding the current definitions in area studies of "South Asia" and "India," if one accepts that the Begram ivory and bone carvings could have been locally produced at or near the site, they would have to be reclassified as what we might call "ancient Afghan" art.

1. For the two excavation reports, see Hackin and Hackin 1939 and Hackin 1954.
2. Mehendale 2007.
3. See Elisséeff 1954 for a discussion of the date of the Chinese lacquers, and Whitehouse 1989 for a description of the Roman glass.
4. Hackin and Hackin 1939, p. 13.
5. Ibid., p. 24.
6. Levi d'Ancona (1950, p. 166) believed the ivory figurine to be a handle of a comb, but During Caspers (1981) proved that the object was a leg of a small table.
7. Whitehouse 1989.
8. Hackin and Hackin 1939, p. 22.
9. Davidson 1971.
10. Stern 1954.
11. Rosen Stone 1974–75, pp. 39–49.
12. Bühler 1894, p. 92.
13. Dwivedi 1976, p. 21.
14. Cowell 1973, pp. 174–77.
15. Jain 1984, p. 150.
16. Cowell 1973, p. 172.
17. Hackin 1954, pp. 188, 250 (cat. nos. 87, XXIII and XXIV). There are no known photographs or illustrations of these three pieces of ivory; because they had been stored at the National Museum of Afghanistan, Kabul, it is unclear if they have survived.
18. Hackin and Hackin 1939, fig. 237.
19. Ibid., pp. 74-75, figs. 113-115.
20. Dwivedi 1976, p. 76.
21. Masson and Pugachenkova 1982.
22. Rapin 1992.
23. During Caspers 1981.
24. Pugachenkova 1978, pp. 88–89.
25. See Sarianidi 1985 for a discussion of the Tillya Tepe comb, and Dwivedi 1976, pp. 75–77, for a description of the Taxila comb.
26. Dwivedi 1976.

Jane Hickman

Bactrian Gold: Jewelry Workshop Traditions at Tillya Tepe

Gold is often described as treasure. Jewelry from the Bactrian region of Central Asia surely fits that description. Two thousand years ago, gold jewelry and other ornaments were buried as grave goods in the tombs of wealthy nomads at Tillya Tepe in Afghanistan. In 1978, during investigation of a Bronze Age mound, six tombs were discovered and excavated by Viktor Sarianidi and an Afghan-Soviet archaeological expedition.[1] Gold jewelry and other ornaments—later known as the Bactrian hoard—were quickly taken to the National Museum of Afghanistan in Kabul. Political instability ensued, and this collection of over 20,000 artifacts was moved to a secure location.[2] Only a few people knew that the gold was moved again to a series of locked compartments within a vault. In 2001, Taliban ministers demanded access to the vault, but were not shown the Bactrian gold: Ameruddin Askarzai, a banker, had deliberately broken the key in the vault door.[3] If the Taliban had been able to enter the vault, the gold would have surely been confiscated.

Joan Aruz, in her introduction, has described the thrilling revelation when it was learned that the location of the gold had been kept secret by a few courageous individuals and that an irreplaceable part of Afghanistan's heritage had not been lost. The authenticity of the objects was assured when Viktor Sarianidi was able to confirm in 2004 that a temporary repair from 1978, made on the back of a hair pin, was his work (fig. 1; see also Massoudi essay, fig. 9).[4] This is a significant collection of jewelry, not only with a great story, but also with clear provenance and unambiguous evidence indicating how and by whom it was worn.

Tillya Tepe is located in northern Afghanistan in the Amu Darya Valley. In the local Uzbek language, Tillya Tepe means "hill of gold." The burial site may have been associated with a nearby settlement: Emshi Tepe.[5] Sarianidi and other scholars have suggested that those interred in the graves were ethnically Yuezhi or proto-Kushan. According to Karen Rubinson, the burials may have contained "ancestors of . . . kings [of the Kushan dynasty] who ruled in what is today northwestern India and adjacent areas of Pakistan and Afghanistan from the first to the third century A.D."[6] Basing his judgment on coins and Chinese mirrors found in the graves, Evgeny Zeymal dated the tombs to the middle of the first century A.D.[7] However, it remains unknown whether all individuals were buried at the same time.

Each of the graves contained a single burial interred in a wooden coffin. The coffins were wrapped in shrouds decorated with gold and silver disks.[8] A preliminary analysis of skeletal remains determined that the burials contained one male and five females. The tombs appeared to be undisturbed. Although parts of the headgear and multiple layers of clothing have perished, jewelry and other objects were recovered *in situ*.

Bactria was crossed by trade routes associated with the Silk Road, providing it access to raw materials as well as stylistic influences from a range of cultures. Sarianidi called some of the objects "cultural hybrid[s]," as they incorporated themes from eastern and western traditions.[9] A study of the Tillya Tepe jewelry reveals iconography from the Hellenic world, China, India, and the Eurasian steppes, in some cases rendered by local artisans.[10] We also see what may be native Bactrian inspiration, perhaps connected with the Graeco-Bactrian kingdom, which flourished in this region in the third and second centuries B.C.[11] For example, each of the two gold clasps from the female burial in Tomb III depicts a warrior wearing a helmet and Greek-inspired clothing (fig. 2; see also Boardman essay, fig. 10).[12] A pair of boot buckles from Tomb IV—the only male burial—portrays a man with Chinese features and clothing riding in what may be a Chinese-inspired cart or chariot (see Leidy essay, fig. 2).

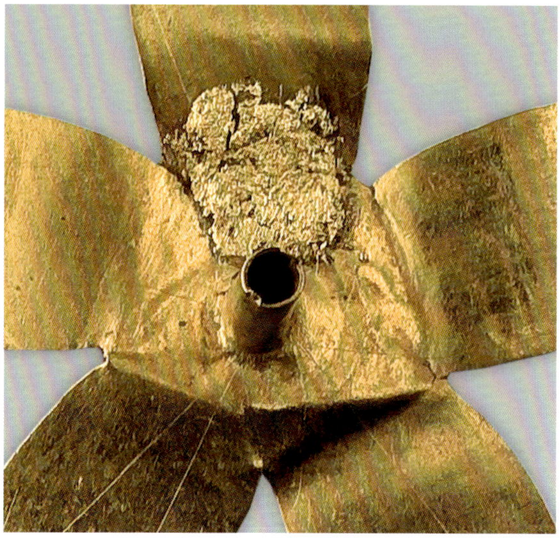

Fig. 1. Hair pin (see fig. 14) with "temporary" repair made by Viktor Sarianidi

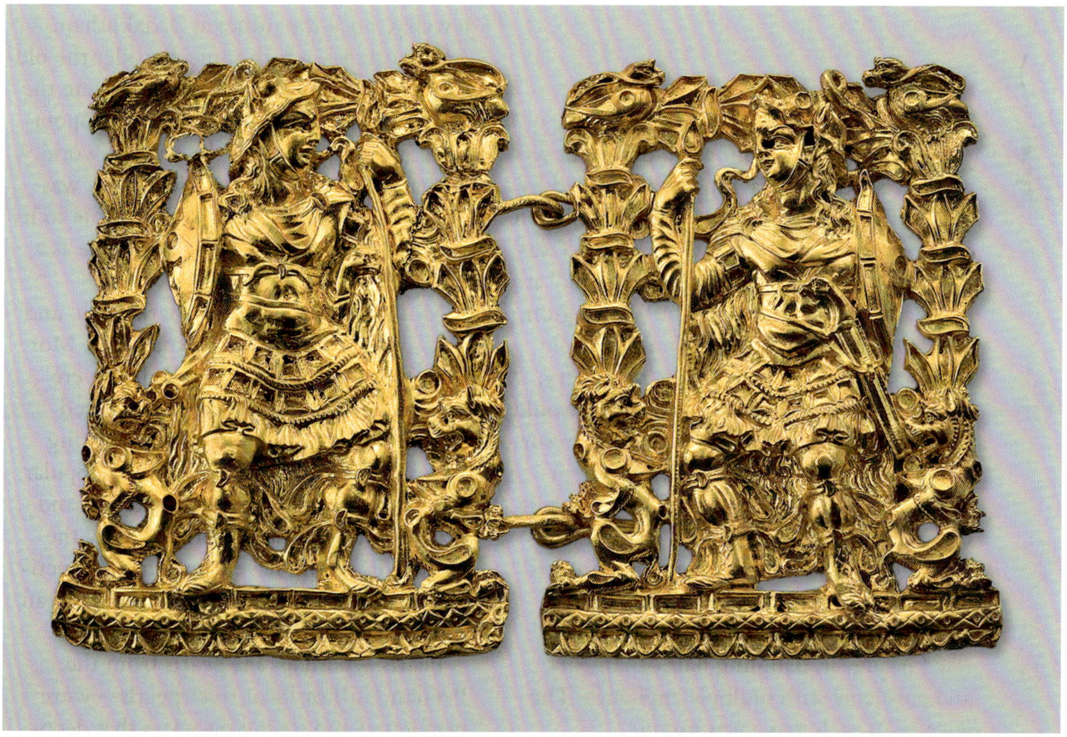

Fig. 2. Clasps showing warriors wearing Greek clothing. Tillya Tepe, Tomb III, second quarter of 1st century A.D. Gold, 9 × 6.3 cm. National Museum of Afghanistan, Kabul (04.40.245)

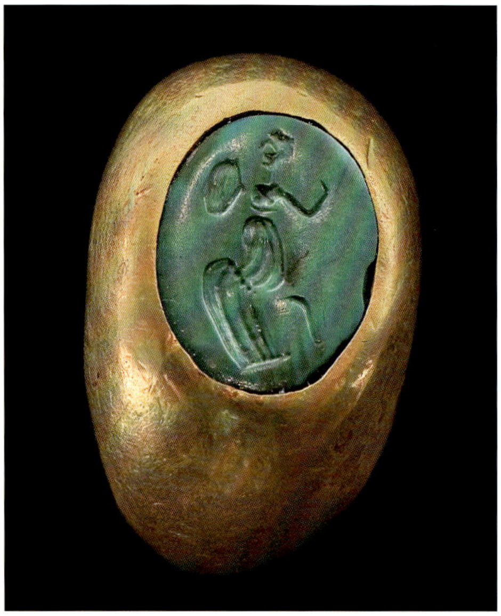

Fig. 3. Ring with inset intaglio depicting Athena. Tillya Tepe, Tomb II, second quarter of 1st century A.D. Gold and turquoise, 3 × 2.7 cm. National Museum of Afghanistan, Kabul (04.40.117)

In September 2008, nineteen objects or sets of objects from Tillya Tepe were studied by the writer, at the time of the de-installation of the exhibition "Afghanistan: Hidden Treasures from the National Museum, Kabul," at the National Gallery of Art in Washington, D.C. Objects were selected from different tombs and from various classes of jewelry, with an eye toward those pieces which would reveal the most information on manufacturing techniques. At least twelve different classes of jewelry were identified, from hair ornaments to anklets. All six individuals wore gold necklaces, bracelets, and anklets (or, in the case of the male burial, boot buckles). Four of the women wore decorated headgear, dangling hair ornaments, and garments with multiple appliqués. The jewelry in each grave was unique.

Virtually all of the jewelry was made of gold. X-ray fluorescence analysis (XRF) conducted in Paris by Thomas Calligaro on four ornaments indicated that, except for one ring, the objects had a very high gold content (95–97%) and a low silver and copper content.[13] XRF measures the proportion of gold on the surface of an object, and it is possible that some copper or silver leached out during burial. However, the results *do* suggest the use of native gold, at least in the manufacture of some objects, a finding consistent with a region that may have had supplies of gold. Sarianidi proposed that "local gold from Bactrian rivers" was used to make the jewelry.[14]

Color was important to the jewelry-makers and their patrons. Semi-precious stone inlays decorated many ornaments, including tiny appliqués sewn onto garments. Turquoise decorated every class of jewelry and exhibited a real richness when paired with gold. Semi-precious stones also included carnelian, garnet, lapis lazuli, amber, pyrite, amethyst, and nephrite jade.[15] It is surprising that more lapis lazuli was not used in the jewelry, since the mines at Badakhshan, Afghanistan—which some consider the oldest working mines in the world—were the source of lapis lazuli for Egypt, Mesopotamia, and other parts of the ancient world.[16] Perhaps lapis lazuli, available locally, was not considered exotic enough so close to its source and was instead more valuable as a traded commodity.

Mother-of-pearl, ivory, shark teeth, and glass paste also decorated ornaments. More than ten different shapes of inlays were used in the creation of mass-produced appliqués. Hearts (perhaps representing leaves) and droplets were especially popular, and may have symbolized vegetation and water. These appliqués, produced by the hundreds, would have been simple, repetitive work for apprentices learning the craft of jewelry-making.

Pearls—perhaps sea pearls from the Persian Gulf or local river pearls—were perforated and strung on wires that decorated many pins and pendants. Although most pearls have deteriorated or disappeared entirely, evidence indicates they were common decorative elements. For example, only two pearls survive on the Dragon Master pendant from Tomb II at Tillya Tepe (fig. 16, and Francfort essay, fig. 13).

Heirlooms or recycled pieces were used in the construction of jewelry from Tillya Tepe. Seams on a ring from Tomb II indicate that it was not cast, but constructed from hammered sheet gold. The inset turquoise intaglio depicting Athena is worn on its face and broken at its edges. It may have decorated another piece of jewelry before it was mounted in the ring (fig. 3).

An adjustable bracelet with sliding ends is from Tomb V, the burial with the least amount of jewelry (fig. 4). It is an unusual piece, as none of the attached ornaments is secured to the wire. All move freely, sometimes clustering together. The back of each element was covered with sheet gold before hoops were affixed. The sides of the ornaments—the granulation and filigree—are quite worn. The quality of craftsmanship is poor compared to other examples of granulation from the tombs. The stones are also worn, and the hoops on the back of the elements are of three different types. Perhaps this piece was created using the bezels of old rings. The extra set of hoops, which retain lumps of solder, indicates that one element is missing.

Several objects show evidence of wear, especially necklaces and bracelets that, during life, were worn directly on the neck or the wrist. Other objects show no obvious signs of wear, perhaps because they were attached to garments or headgear. A necklace from Tomb VI includes ten large, hollow, round beads (each with a diameter of over 2.5 cm) and two conical terminals, crafted from sheet metal (fig. 5). Golden granules, some now flattened from wear, were attached along crimped edges on each bead and on the terminals. The granules are quite smooth at the points of contact between beads.

A similar necklace from Tomb III is also decorated with granulation. Eight round beads

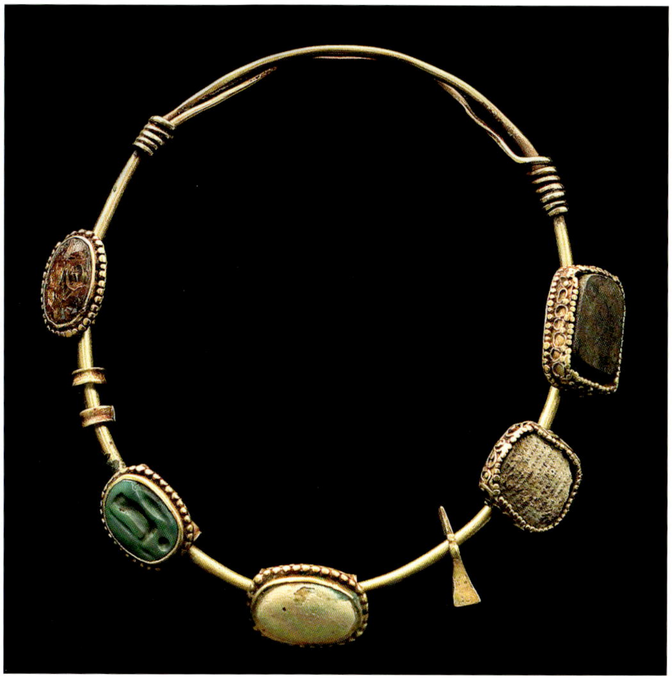

Fig. 4. Bracelet with sliding ornaments. Tillya Tepe, Tomb V, second quarter of 1st century A.D. Gold, turquoise, amber, lead glass, deteriorated stones, D. 6.7 cm. National Museum of Afghanistan, Kabul (04.40.134)

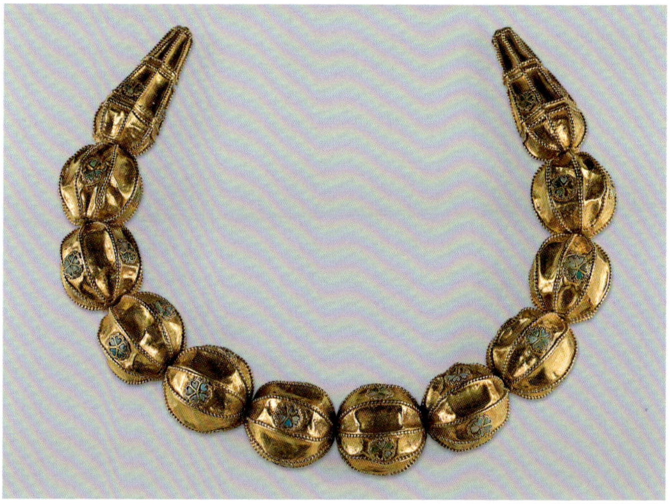

Fig. 5. Necklace decorated with granulation. Tillya Tepe, Tomb VI, second quarter of 1st century A.D. Gold and turquoise, D. of beads 2.5–2.8 cm. National Museum of Afghanistan, Kabul (04.40.51)

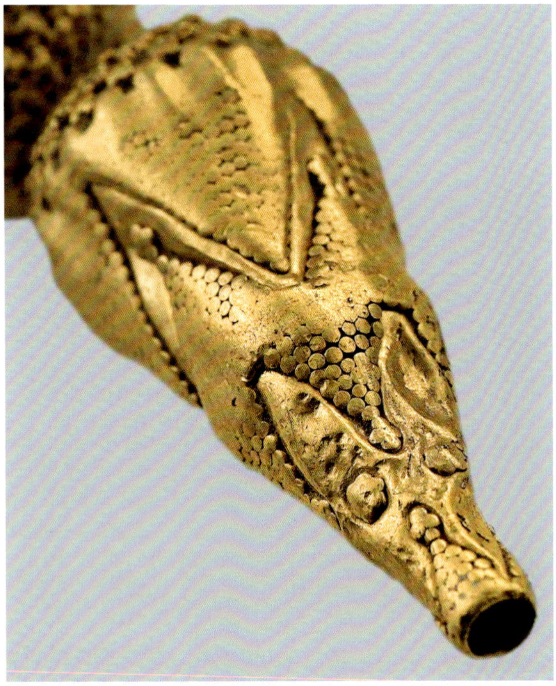

Fig. 6. Terminal of a necklace showing clear evidence of wear. Tillya Tepe, Tomb III, second quarter of first century A.D. Gold, L. 3.9 cm. National Museum of Afghanistan, Kabul (04.40.162)

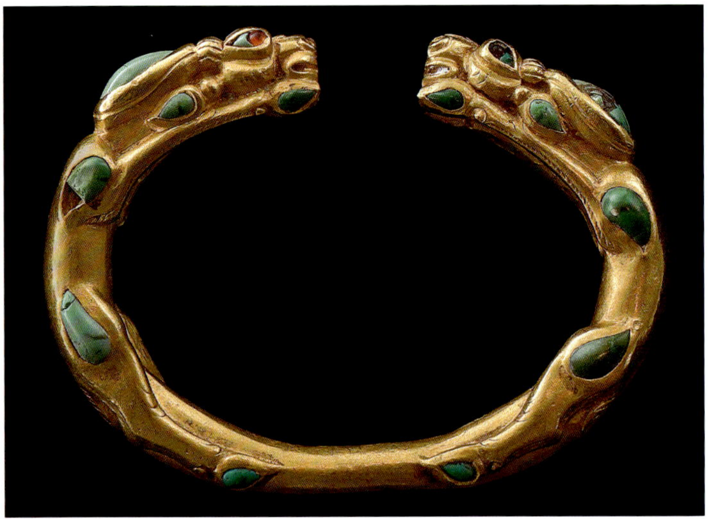

Fig. 7. One of a pair of antelope bracelets. Tillya Tepe, Tomb II, second quarter of 1st century A.D. Gold, turquoise, carnelian, 8.5 × 6.3 cm. National Museum of Afghanistan, Kabul (04.40.141)

include a dense pattern of closely placed gold balls. The granulation is smooth in places, and the cone-shaped terminals, originally decorated with very even granulation, are substantially worn. However, animals with pointed ears—perhaps antelopes, foxes, wolves, or bats—are still evident (fig. 6).

The antelope bracelets from Tomb II exhibit evidence of wear under the front legs of the animals, where the bracelets rested on the arms (fig. 7). These bracelets are heavy, as each weighs over 250 grams, a clear indication of the status of the woman who wore them. The bracelets may have begun as cast rods, with substantial hand work required to create the legs and the heads of the animals. Although the attitude is the same, each head is slightly different, illustrating the individual work that went into each piece. Elements such as the ears and eyes may have been soldered on. Fur is indicated by chased lines. After the turquoise and carnelian inlays were added, the gold was pressed up and over the stones, to better secure them, which also gave the antelopes' bodies a smoother, more graceful look.

Similar jewelry workshop traditions, related to the use of raw materials, decorative motifs, manufacturing techniques, and methods of joining and assembly can be observed in the gold ornaments from Tillya Tepe. This similarity indicates that some jewelry from all tombs was manufactured in the same workshop, one that included experienced artisans and apprentices with different abilities and skill levels. The workshop may have been independent, or, more likely, it was sponsored by elites who commissioned and wore the jewelry.

Ornaments made from gold and turquoise were common finds in all tombs and were, by far, the preferred combination for jewelry. Gold and turquoise may have been available locally, although Iran is also a possible source for both of these raw materials.

Although the form and decoration of objects vary, several motifs stand out. Flowers, fish, animals, and human figures (the last two groups both real and mythical) are

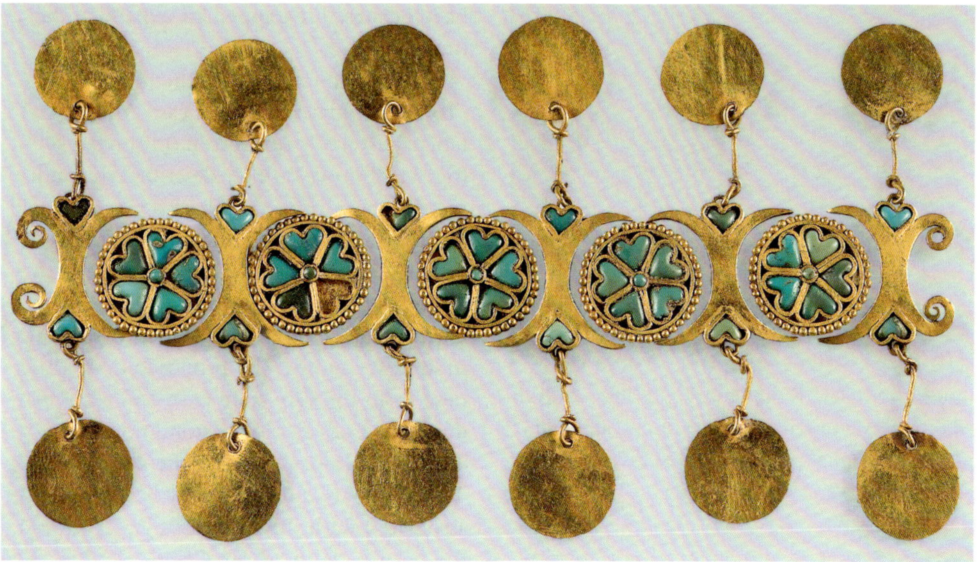

Fig. 8. Components of shoulder ornaments. Tillya Tepe, Tomb II, second quarter of 1st century A.D. Gold, turquoise, L. 18.3 cm. National Museum of Afghanistan, Kabul (04.40.95)

commonly depicted. What ties the Tillya Tepe jewelry together *stylistically*, however, are the shapes. Moons—full, crescent, or double crescent—and hearts are found in all tombs. Droplets and rosettes are found in all but one burial, Tomb V, which had only a few pieces of jewelry.

Ornaments from Tomb II (fig. 8) may have decorated the shoulders or upper portion of a garment.[17] They illustrate the use of the most popular motifs: the moon (full, crescent, and double crescent), heart, and rosette. The alternating disk and double crescent motif seen here is also found on other objects. On the reverse side, the elements are finished with sheet gold (fig. 9). Thread passed through soldered tubes, allowing for attachment to clothing.

Figures on ornaments were crafted in low, medium, and high relief, indicating the use of repoussé—working sheet gold from the back and front—and pressing metal into molds or over forms. Some pieces appear to have been cast. Detail was added by chasing and punching. Seven appliqués from Tomb I, each representing a man with a dolphin or large fish around his neck, may have been manufactured over a form. Although each appliqué is about the same size, differences are noticeable in the finishing (fig. 10). Punched dots on top of the head, indicating hair, extend further back on some pieces. Although the chin is in roughly the same place, details of the faces are different, as are the scales on the fish.

The warrior clasps (see fig. 2) were created by repoussé or perhaps cast in molds.

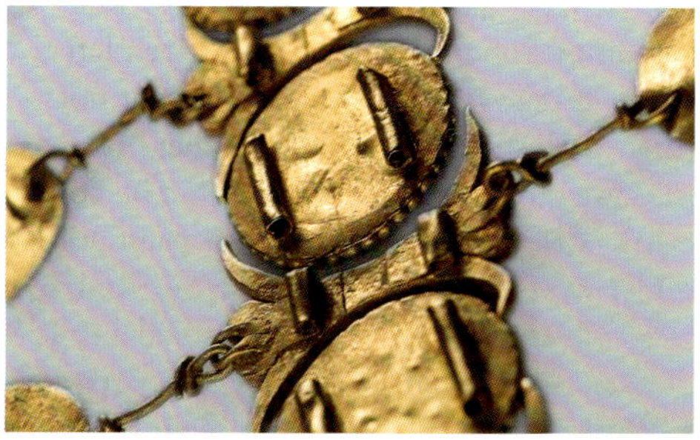

Fig. 9. Reverse of fig. 8

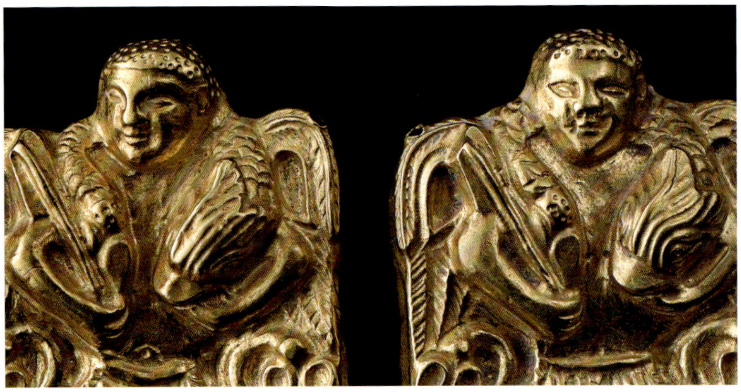

Fig. 10. Two of seven appliqués, with details showing slight differences in finishing. Tillya Tepe, Tomb I, second quarter of 1st century A.D. Gold, 4.1 × 2.9 cm. National Museum of Afghanistan, Kabul (04.40.303)

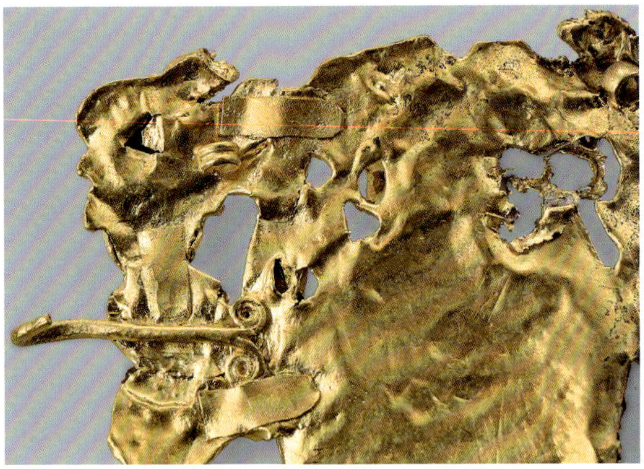

Fig. 11. Reverse of fig. 2, showing triangular "trap door" (at upper left) allowing expansion of air during soldering

Substantial effort was required to add detail to the front of each piece. Although similar, they are not mirror images. The option of stone inlays may have been left open, as depressions were created but not filled with stone. The backs of these objects are quite interesting (fig. 11). The covering of thin sheet metal and strips of gold solder were trimmed to expose the voids. Jack Ogden has previously described a type of triangular opening seen on the clasps as a "chisel-cut trap door."[18] The openings were added to avoid explosions that may have occurred if trapped air expanded during soldering.

The boot buckles from the male burial (Tomb IV) may have been cast. An unusual fabric pattern is impressed on the back (fig. 12). Emma Bunker described this indirect lost-wax process, where a mother mold is made, as the "lost-wax and lost-textile" process.[19] Katheryn Linduff has traced this process to late fourth to third century B.C. China; with evidence provided by ceramic models for molds, she proposed that Chinese from the Qin state (221–206 B.C.) produced cast objects for pastoral nomads.[20] The fabric impression is quite clear on the Tillya Tepe buckles and may have been associated with the first casting.[21] Although the figures clearly show Chinese influence (see Leidy essay, p. 113), it is curious that the use of inlays, especially the border of turquoise droplets, appears to be in the style of other locally produced objects. It is possible that the buckles were produced in China and traded westward,[22] but they may have been made in Tillya Tepe by Chinese craftsmen or by local craftsmen who learned the "lost wax–lost textile" technique in China or from Chinese metalsmiths.

Another popular manufacturing technique at Tillya Tepe was the cutting of ornaments from sheet gold. Perhaps the most unusual object made by this method is the collapsible crown from Tomb VI, which could be taken apart and packed away for safekeeping (see Leidy essay, fig. 7). The crown, weighing 213 grams, is comprised of six separate elements: a diadem or strip, which could be worn by itself, and five vertical attachments. Four of the attachments were cut in the form of trees, with dragon-like tails flanking the trunk and birds perched at the top, while the center attachment was taller and cut differently. Thin rods, slipped into tubes of gold on the back of the elements, were used to assemble the various elements (fig. 13). Decoration included disks of gold, secured by means of wire, and flowers with bent petals. Each flower had an eyelet soldered to the back that was stuck through the diadem or the vertical attachment and spread slightly to keep the element secured.

Crescent moon hair ornaments with three dangling elements were recovered from four tombs: I, II, III, and VI (fig. 14). Each object was constructed and assembled in a similar fashion, suggesting all were made in the same workshop. The elements were connected using short lengths of twisted wire. Although many have disappeared, pearls still remain on some of the ornaments.

Granulation was a common decorative technique at Tillya Tepe, and it was generally well executed. Necklaces from Tombs II, III, and VI, all consisting of large, hollow beads and conical terminals, were surely created in the same workshop, and perhaps designed by the same artisan. (See figs. 5 and 6 for two examples.) In the process of granulation, tiny gold granules of various sizes were attached to a gold surface by a bonding process. Granulation is found on many objects from Tillya Tepe, including on tiny appliqués that decorated garments.

Jewelry with multiple components utilized the same joining and assembly techniques, providing further evidence that at least some objects from all tombs were manufactured in the same workshop. Wire twists connected perforated elements, or wire was bent, flattened, and soldered to components. Small hoops and jump rings were used, and loop-in-loop chains connected elements on larger pieces.

Master craftsmen who made the Tillya Tepe jewelry were specialists in at least three kinds of jewelry-making: relief work, the cutting of carefully measured shapes from thin sheet gold, and detail work that included finer, more complicated granulation. These artisans may have also designed individual pieces and ensembles of jewelry and completed or supervised the final assembly of objects with multiple components.

Another class of jewelry-makers, perhaps not as skilled as the master craftsmen, may have manufactured components to be used in larger pieces or as appliqués for garments. It would have been easier and faster to simply stamp ornaments, such as the hundreds of tiny appliqués that were sewn onto garments

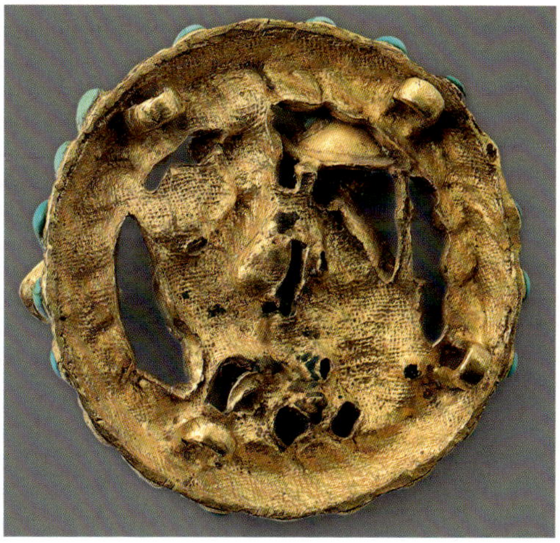

Fig. 12. Back view of boot buckle. Tillya Tepe, Tomb IV, second quarter of 1st century A.D. Gold, turquoise, and carnelian, H. 1.1 cm, D. 5.5 cm. National Museum of Afghanistan, Kabul (04.40.383)

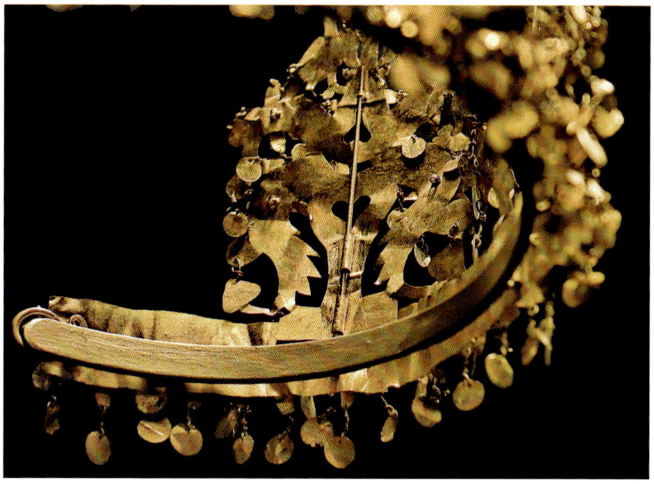

Fig. 13. Reverse side of element from crown. Tillya Tepe, Tomb VI, second quarter of 1st century A.D. Gold, imitation turquoise. National Museum of Afghanistan, Kabul (04.40.50)

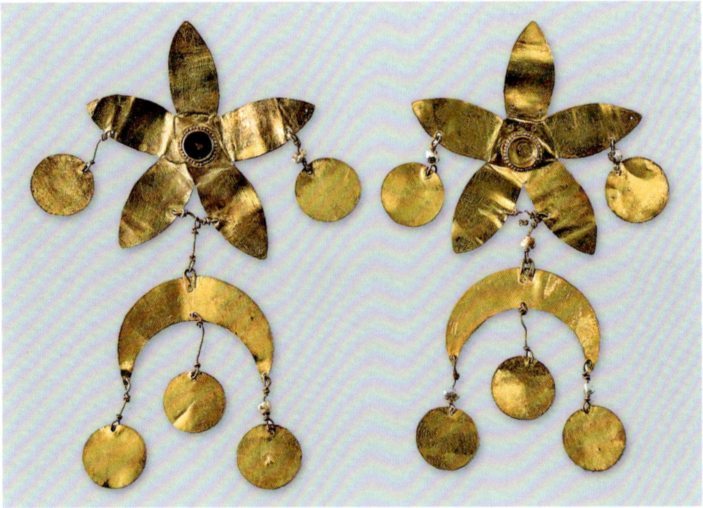

Fig. 14. Crescent moon and flower hair ornaments. Tillya Tepe, Tomb VI, second quarter of 1st century A.D. Gold and silver, D. (rosette) 7 cm. National Museum of Afghanistan, Kabul (04.40.1)

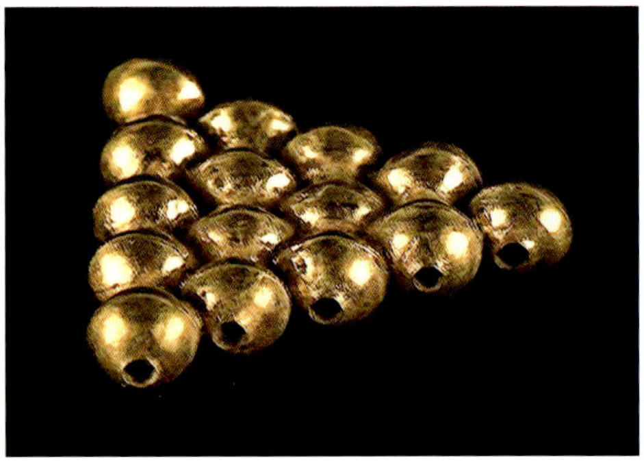

Fig. 15. Triangular appliqué. Tillya Tepe, Tomb I, second quarter of 1st century A.D. Gold, 1.3 × 1 cm. National Museum of Afghanistan, Kabul (04.40.323)

or decorated coffin shrouds. However, it appears that most of the appliqués, such as the gold ball and spiral forms, were handcrafted individually. The tiny balls on the triangular appliqués from Tomb I are hollow, and seams indicate that each ball was made from two soldered halves. Fifteen balls were then soldered together and drilled as a group, with each finished appliqué measuring about 1.3 × 1 cm (fig. 15). Almost one hundred of the spiral appliqués were cut freehand, without the use of a template. Four hoops were soldered to the back of each piece. The lack of time-saving measures would suggest the availability of labor—a workshop with assistants and apprentices to do simple or repetitive work—and the desire for high-quality finished pieces.

There was also work for less skilled apprentices. Hammering gold to create sheets of uniform thickness is a time-consuming job. Apprentices probably made wire, which was manufactured in several forms: round-section wire (including strip-twisted wire, evidenced by a diagonal or spiral seam), square-section wire, and beaded wire. Other tasks included making links and assembling loop-in-loop chains, creating gold thread, making and sorting different sizes of gold balls for granulation, cutting blanks for the backs of appliqués, and cutting and polishing semi-precious stones for inlays.

The Dragon Master pendants from Tomb II (see Francfort essay, fig. 13) incorporate many of the techniques and motifs seen in jewelry from all of the burials. The pendants were attached to a hat decorated with appliqués; they may have hung over the ears. Stone inlays included turquoise, garnet, lapis lazuli, and carnelian. The evidence for pearls is quite clear, although only two survive. One reveals the concentric pattern of its interior, resembling the layers of an onion (fig. 16). Many short lengths of wire that remain on this pendant must also have originally held pearls.

The pendants were built up from many separate elements. Their plaques—illustrating a male figure dressed in a robe holding two mythical creatures—were two-sided, soldered together. They may have been made over the same form, with details of the figures later chased. Cells containing stone inlays were created within the figures or by the use of square-section wire. Moving from the top down, separate elements on each side included a wire ring, the large central element with the Dragon Master, two separate creatures, beaded wire horns on the animals and a ring of beaded wire at the base of the horns, separate wings, a small piece of wire near the hooves (perhaps a tail), and twenty-four individual wire cells holding turquoise droplets or rounds. Numerous elements were attached with loop-in-loop chains made from strip-twisted wire. The smaller elements included plain gold disks and appliqué-like ornaments: round cabochon garnets, small hearts set in circles, and droplets and rounds surrounded by granulation.

Creating these pendants was surely a collaborative effort. A skilled artisan must have designed and assembled the pieces, with the mundane work of preparing materials and smaller components carried out by assistants and apprentices. An analysis of manufacturing techniques indicates that some of the objects from all of the tombs were manufactured in the same workshop. The Bactrian gold from Tillya Tepe reveals a culture that drew inspiration from the east and the west, yet also relied on local traditions. This is demonstrated not only by those who wore the jewelry but also by those artisans who created such memorable works in gold.[23]

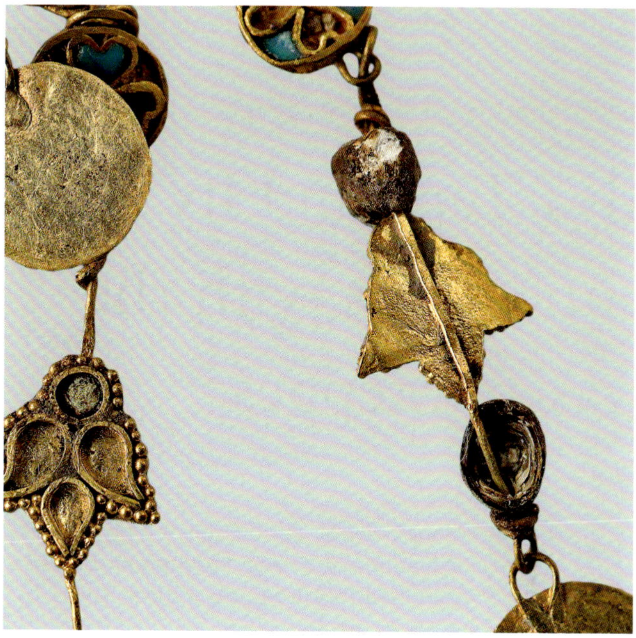

Fig. 16. Reverse (detail) of Dragon Master pendant. Tillya Tepe, Tomb II, second quarter of 1st century A.D. Gold, turquoise, garnet, lapis lazuli, carnelian, pearls, 12.5 × 6.5 cm. National Museum of Afghanistan, Kabul (04.40.109)

1. Sarianidi 1985; Sarianidi 1989; Sarianidi 1990; Sarianidi 2008; Afghanistan 2008.
2. Kabul Museum 1995.
3. Wonacott 2009.
4. Fredrik Hiebert, personal communication.
5. Sarianidi 1985, p. 7; Boardman 2003b, p. 348.
6. Rubinson 2008, p. 51.
7. Zeymal 1999, p. 243.
8. Sarianidi 1985, p. 18.
9. Sarianidi 1990, p. 52.
10. Boardman 2003b, p. 348.
11. Sarianidi 1985, p. 17.
12. Boardman 2003b, p. 355.
13. Calligaro 2006, p. 293.
14. Sarianidi 1990, p. 55.
15. Afghanistan 2008, pp. 232–93.
16. Bowersox and Chamberlin 1995, pp. xi–xii.
17. Afghanistan 2008, p. 251.
18. Ogden 1982, pp. 40–41.
19. Bunker 1988, p. 222. See also Bunker and Ternbach 1970; Linduff 2009, pp. 93–94. My thanks to Sir John Boardman and Karen Rubinson for directing me to these sources.
20. Linduff 2009, pp. 90, 93–94, fig. 5.
21. Sir John Boardman, personal communication.
22. Karen Rubinson, personal communication.
23. My thanks are due to the National Museum, Kabul, Afghanistan, and particularly to the museum's director, Omara Khan Massoudi, for permission to examine and photograph jewelry from Tillya Tepe. This study was suggested and facilitated by Dr. Fredrik Hiebert of the National Geographic Society, and was conducted at the National Gallery of Art, Washington, D.C., under the direction of Michelle Fondas, registrar of exhibitions. Photographs are by Michael Furlong and Leslie Furlong.

Henri-Paul Francfort

Tillya Tepe and Its Connections with the Eurasian Steppes

Along the 40th parallel runs a long steppe and mountainous zone throughout Eurasia, from the Black Sea to the Yellow River. To the south are deserts and irrigated oases where cities and empires developed and extensive networks of communication, notably the "Silk Road," flourished from the first century B.C. onward. In the steppe zone, nomads developed their cultures, based on mounted herding, and from there they penetrated into the southern "sown" oasis zone at various periods. The most important remains left by the steppe cultures are the burials, the kurgans, with their grave deposits. The steppe and the sown, however, were never truly separate. The history of their relationship is very long, extending from at least the Bronze Age, when steppe peoples moved to the south with their oxen carts and their horse chariots.[1] This occurred before the advent of riding and of mounted nomadic herding, which took place in about 1000 B.C. The new way of life proved to be most effective and has lasted until the present day, with large caravans passing yearly through the oasis, going from their winter to their summer pastures. The use of the land by agricultural and pastoral communities was interpenetrating, and it was not uncommon to see, at the same time, tents or yurts in villages. Many kinds of settlements and seasonal mobility were the rule, and the Tillya Tepe "nomadic cemetery" in the oasis of the Bactrian Shirin Tagao Valley is no exception, belonging as it did to this sort of mixed culture. We must ask what the historical and cultural context was in which these individuals lived and were buried.[2] Who was ruling in Bactria, about A.D. 50, and who were their neighbors?

The Parthian empire (247 B.C.–A.D. 224) was the great power in the Near East, in contact with Rome, then under the rule of the Julio-Claudian dynasty (27 B.C.–A.D. 68).[3] The Parthians, originally nomads from the steppes, were settled by the third century B.C., although, under the reign of Gotarzes II (ca. A.D. 40–51), they continued to maintain contacts, as allies or enemies, with the eastern Scythians, the Saka.[4] To the northeast and east, the Kushan empire was still in formation, and perhaps not yet firmly established in Bactria. Kujula Kadphises (ca. A.D. 30–80), the empire builder and great Kushan sovereign at the time, may have ruled Bactria under the names of Heraios Sanab and, perhaps, Soter Megas.[5] In the south, the "Indo-Parthian" Gondophares (ca. A.D. 20–46) was ruling from Herat to the Indus. As has been observed by Paul Bernard, his distinctive collar, as depicted on coinage (fig. 1a), is very similar to the necklace of the man buried in Tomb IV at Tillya Tepe (fig. 2). This similarity may suggest that he was a vassal or an ally of Gondophares.[6] The helmeted head struck as a countermark on an older Parthian coin found at Tillya Tepe may signify some kind of allegiance to the Parthians.[7] Tillya Tepe, indeed, was located precisely in the border area between the Parthian and the expanding Kushan empire.[8] Many scholars agree that a Saka ruler was buried at Tillya Tepe (a view supported by the number of steppe-type artifacts in the tomb), rather than a Yuezhi, as initially thought. Based on coins with a

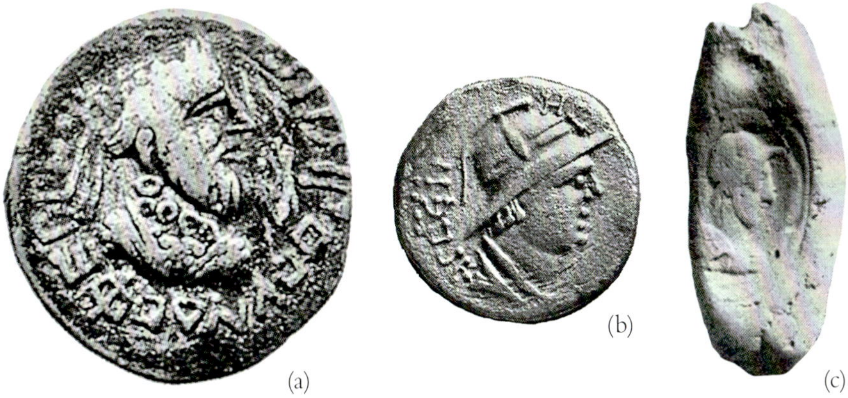

Fig. 1. (a) Silver drachm showing the Indo-Parthian ruler Gondophares wearing a collar; (b) Bactrian coin of Arseiles with helmeted head (Senior Collection, Ashmolean Museum, Oxford); (c) bulla from Djiga Tepe (Bactria) showing helmeted head

helmeted king in the Graeco-Bactrian tradition of Eucratides, however, it is possible that some "Scytho-Bactrian" rulers were in power in the region: Arseiles (20–1 B.C.?; see fig. 1b), Spalirizes, and Pulages.[9] The reverses of their coins are the earliest evidence for the introduction of Nanaia into Bactria from Mesopotamia via the Parthians, a deity who became very important as a Kushan dynastic goddess.[10] The helmeted figure also appears on the cameo of the Tillya Tepe prince's necklace (fig. 2, detail)[11] and on a bulla from Djiga Tepe (see fig. 1c) in the Bactra oasis, 100 kilometers to the east of Tillya Tepe.[12] Whether they were descendants of the nomadic Saka invaders of Bactria who overcame the Greeks about 150 B.C., or newcomers from the steppes, the Tillya Tepe rulers in their small oasis were clearly not in a position to compete with either the Parthians or the rising Kushan empire. Thus, they soon disappeared, while the art of Tillya Tepe is the singular and unique flash of brilliance of their complex hybrid culture.

Miraculously, the Tillya Tepe "cemetery," located about 500 meters north of a circular site named Emshi Tepe, was preserved practically intact. Trenches there revealed Graeco-Bactrian and Kushan material, but nothing diagnostic of the period from the second

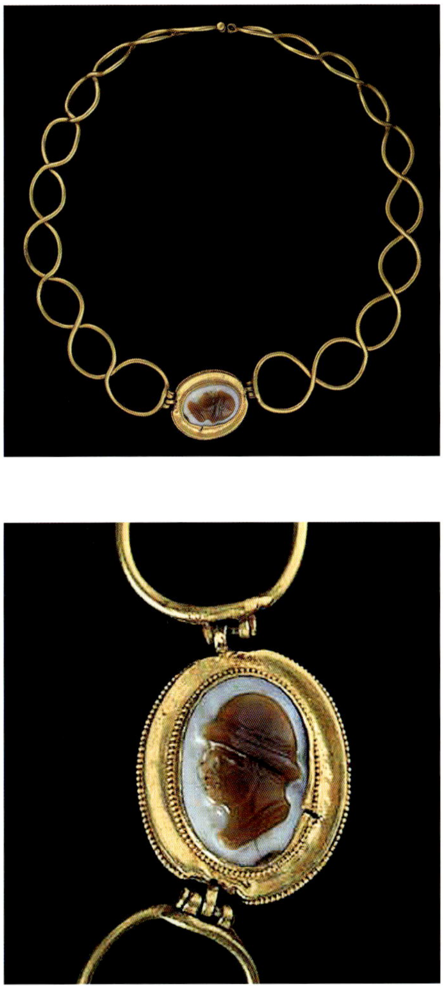

Fig. 2. Necklace, with cameo (detail) showing helmeted head. Tillya Tepe, Tomb IV, second quarter of 1st century A.D. Gold, sardonyx, L. 65 cm, D. 21 cm (necklace). National Museum of Afghanistan, Kabul (04.40.378)

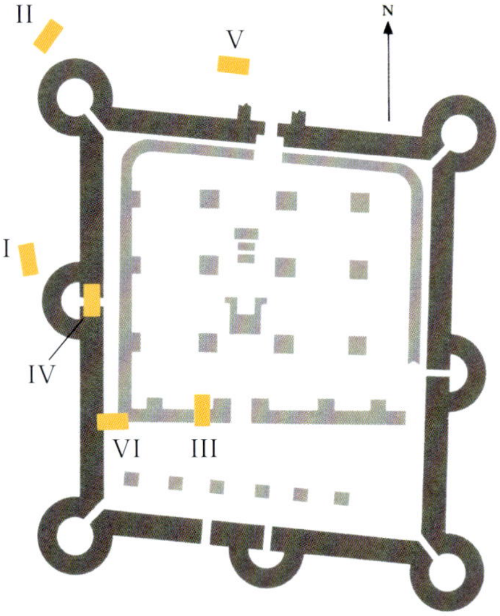

Fig. 3. Drawing of the disposition of tombs at Tillya Tepe

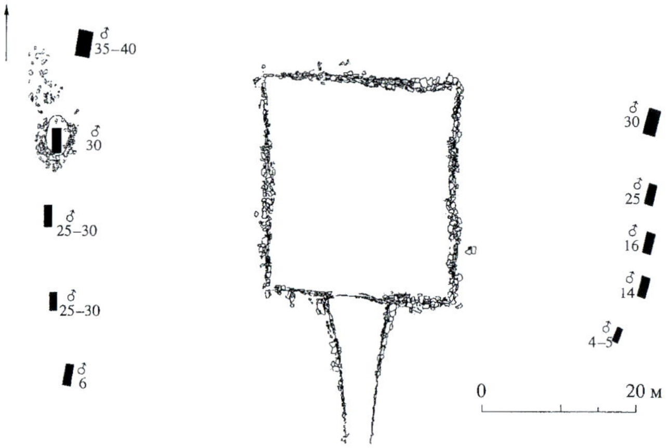

Fig. 4. Drawing of the disposition of Xiongnu elite burials at Tsaram (Buriatia)

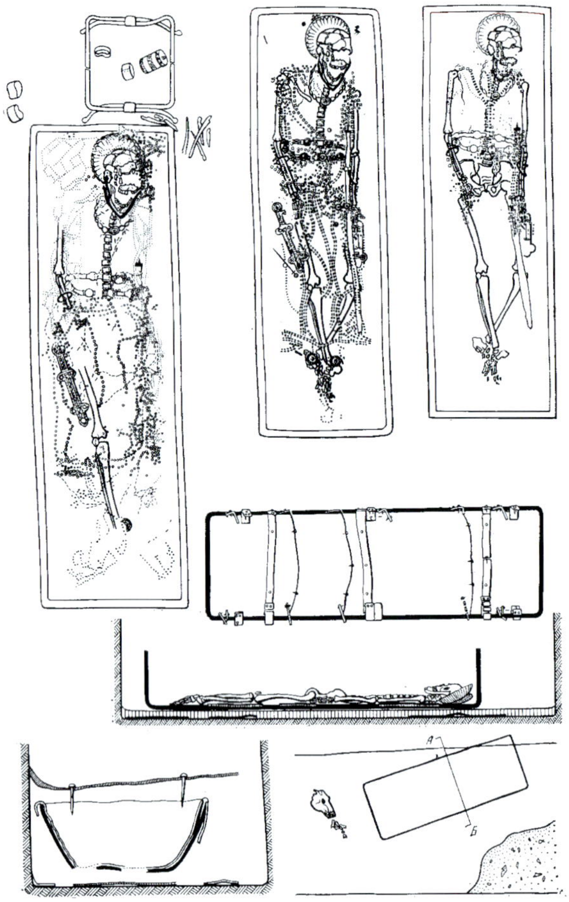

century B.C. to the second century A.D.[13] The big capital cities of Merv in Margiana (continuously under Parthian rule) and Bactra also had circular citadels. About 100 kilometers east of Tillya Tepe and Emshi Tepe is another site with a circular citadel, Delberjin-Tepe, which was excavated by the Afghan-Soviet mission in the 1970s. There also, as at other Bactrian sites, the Tillya Tepe period (first century A.D.) is represented by very little material or by destruction layers. Only one site, Khalchayan in the Surkhan Darya Valley, yielded significant remains from the mid-first century, notably a building decorated with clay sculptures.[14] With a number of nomadic cemeteries dated second century B.C.–A.D. second century, the evidence is scanty and the amount of antiquities contemporaneous with Tillya Tepe is very small.[15] Nothing matches the quantity of recovered remains from Graeco-Bactrian or Kushan times,

Fig. 5. Plans and sections of Tomb IV, Tillya Tepe, showing a horse's head and legs (lower right) and a folding stool (upper left)

revealed by excavations and surveys to be the largest agricultural occupations and populations in the history of the region. Whether this paucity is a consequence of a lack of archaeological research, the result of depopulation, or a shift to nomadic herding, we cannot answer, but examination of the steppe material from the cemetery does provide some surprises.

The Tillya Tepe cemetery is actually a single collective elite burial, a group of seven graves, six fully excavated and one partially. From the gender composition, one male and five female burials, and the wealth of the deposit, it is generally considered that the individuals were interred at the same time and that the man was a ruler. The tombs were dug on the top of a huge Early Iron Age mound,[16] resembling a gigantic kurgan. Its layout suggests that the male burial (IV) is central and the others peripheral (fig. 3), reminiscent of the general disposition of elite burials with adjacent tombs among the Xiongnu (Hun) in Mongolia and in Buriatia (Noin Ula, Gol Mod, and Tsaram, fig. 4),[17] in the Altai foothills and Ob Valley, as well as in the middle Sargat culture. From the trans-Ural region to southern Siberia, a main burial surrounded by adjacent ones is the rule.[18] The use of wooden coffins at Tillya Tepe is also common among the Xiongnu, but more typical of these tribes is the disposal of a horse skull and leg bones outside the coffin, in the burial pit (in Mongolia and Xinjiang). To my knowledge, Tillya Tepe Tomb IV (fig. 5) is the only example of this practice in Bactria.[19] The Tillya Tepe ruler had no chariot; nevertheless, the chariot represented on his boot buckles, with two wheels and an umbrella (see Leidy essay, fig. 2), is reminiscent of the actual Chinese-inspired chariots in the burials of Xiongnu princes (at Noin Ula, Gol Mod, and Tsaram, fig. 6).[20] The tombs of Mongolia and the trans-Baikal region are remote from Bactria, but, according to Chinese sources, we know that the Xiongnu were in Xinjiang at this time, that is, just beyond the Yuezhi, east of Bactria.

Insignia of kingship were shared over long distances, as is shown by the folding stool found outside the prince's coffin (see fig. 5).[21] It is a typical *curule* chair, the official "throne" of a Roman ruler. We see an

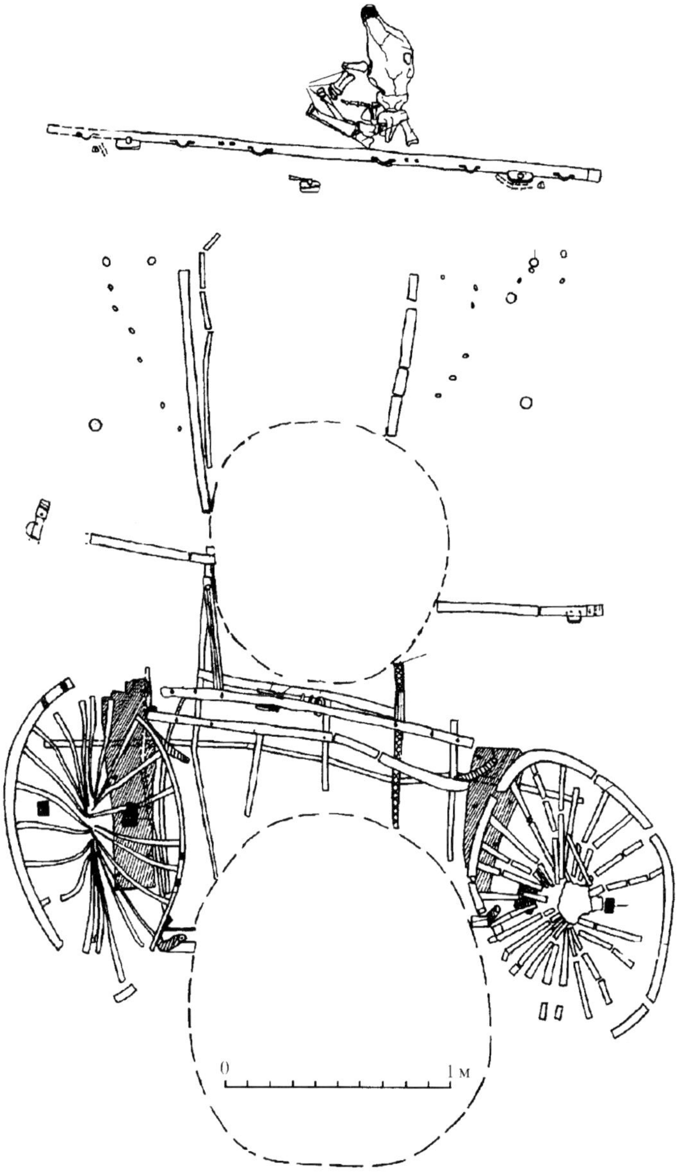

Fig. 6. Drawing of a chariot from a Xiongnu prince's burial at Tsaram (Buriatia), with (above) a horse's head and legs. The two broken outlines show the later entry of tomb robbers.

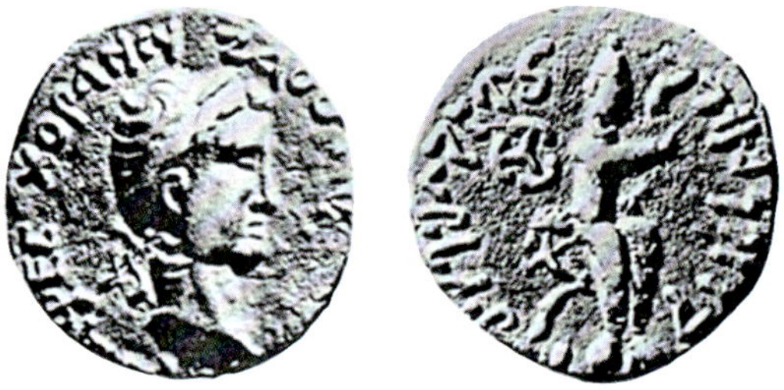

Fig. 7. Copper coin of Kujula Kadphises in imitation of Augustus, showing *curule* chair on reverse. American Numismatic Society, New York

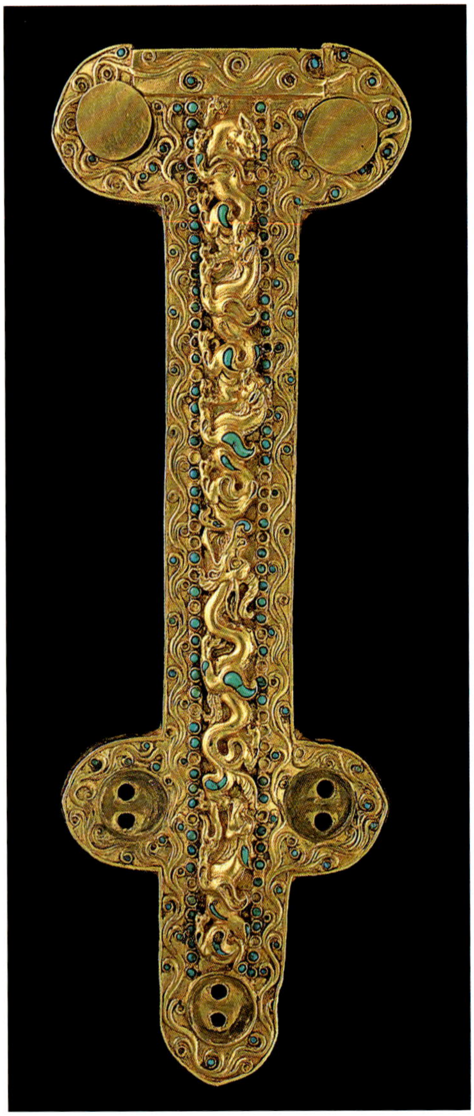

Fig. 8. Dagger sheath. Tillya Tepe, Tomb IV, second quarter of 1st century A.D. Gold and turquoise, 23.5 × 9 cm. National Museum of Afghanistan, Kabul (04.40.382)

example on a contemporaneous coin of Kujula Kadphises imitating Augustus (fig. 7).[22] Was the Tillya Tepe prince, in using such a folding chair, inspired directly by the Romans or by some type of allegiance to the Yuezhi? The question is open.

Long distances are also involved in the widespread distribution of a well-known, typical Scythian artifact among the weaponry of the Tillya Tepe ruler: the four-lobed dagger sheath (fig. 8).[23] The most ancient examples, in wood, are found in Altai burials dating to the third century B.C. A very close parallel for the Tillya Tepe weapon appears at Datchi, near Azov, in a Sarmatian context. The four-lobed dagger sheath, convenient for tying the weapon to the leg of a horseman, was in use among the Parthians, as is shown by coins and belt plaques[24] and, for instance, on the bronze statue from Shami in western Iran,[25] on which two daggers, like those found at Tillya Tepe, are represented, inserted in the rider's leggings; a variant appears on the Nemrud Dağ reliefs in southeastern Anatolia.[26] Furthermore, the same type of sheath is depicted on sculptures exhibiting Iranian features at the Syrian caravan city of Palmyra.[27] North of Bactria, in the Zeravshan Valley, some contemporary coins of a king named Hyrcodes (mid-first century B.C.) represent the same four-lobed sheath (fig. 9).[28] At Niya, in Xinjiang, one was found with the belt, the second knife, and the straps (though without the dagger).[29] Another one in bone, carved with steppe motifs, comes from the Ili Valley (Jilingtai) north of the Tianshan Mountains (fig. 10).[30] A very important depiction of this form of sheath appears on a fragment of a tapestry from Noin Ula tomb 6, again representing the lower part of a man with the dagger tied around his trousers with a strap (fig. 11).[31] Noin Ula tomb 6 is definitely the tomb of a Xiongnu prince, a *shanyu*, but these tapestries, with their classical motifs and human representations, belong to another culture, probably related to Bactria. In fact, the four-lobed sheath never appears in Xiongnu,

Yuezhi, or Kushan archaeological contexts. It is a typical Saka and Parthian accessory.

Saka artistic creativity can be seen in a very specific stylistic element: non-natural reverted hindquarters for animal representations. This convention is typical of steppe art and very widespread. The most ancient instance appears on small gold belt ornaments discovered in the recently excavated Arjan-2 kurgan in Tuva (more distant from Tillya Tepe than the Altai), from the late

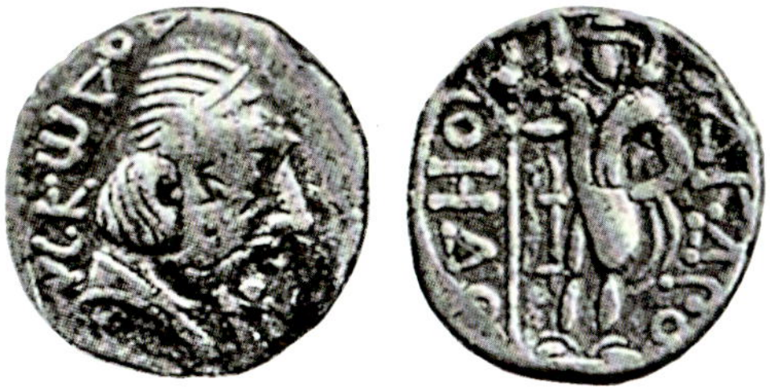

Fig. 9. Copper coin of the Sogdian ruler Hyrcodes, showing four-lobed dagger sheath on the reverse

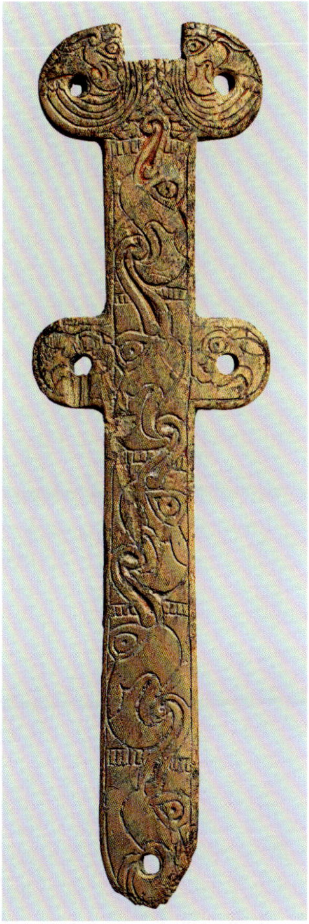

Fig. 10. Four-lobed dagger sheath from the Ili Valley, Xinjiang. 10th–6th century B.C. Bone, L. 15.2 cm, W. 4 cm. Xinjiang Institute of Archaeology

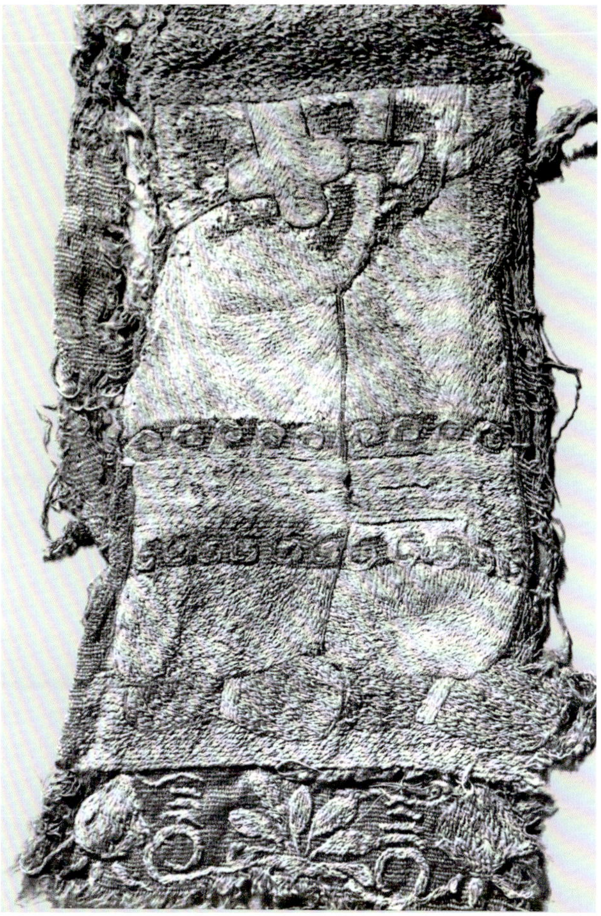

Fig. 11. Tapestry depicting four-lobed dagger sheath. Noin Ula, Tomb 6. National Museum of Mongolian History, Ulanbaatar

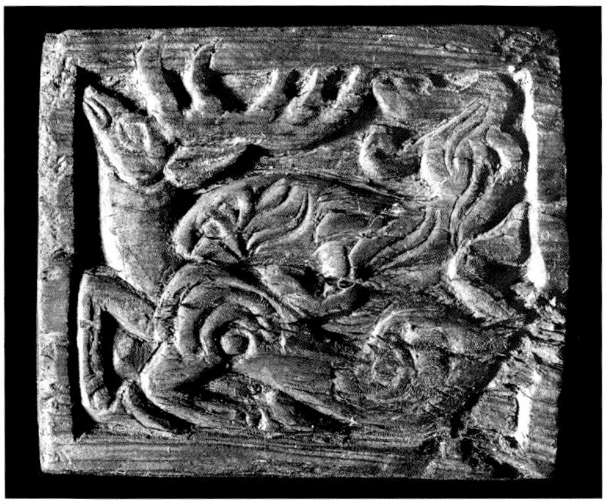

Fig. 12. Belt plaque with animal attack scene. Berel' (Altai, Kazakhstan). Wood. Institute of Archaeology, Almaty

seventh century B.C.[32] The motif becomes widespread in the art of the Altai during the fifth to third century B.C.: on a tattoo from Pazyryk,[33] a wooden belt plaque from Berel' (fig. 12),[34] and on gold ornaments found at Alagou in the Xinjiang Tianshan.[35] The Chinese adopted this convention—a fine example can be found on the Mawangdui coffin—but they abandoned it by the second century B.C.[36] The same seems true of the rest of Central Asia. Therefore, the Tillya Tepe dragons with reverted hindquarters on the ear pendants from Tomb II (fig. 13) and on the strap decorations from Tomb IV (fig. 14) are not only among the latest representations of this old Saka convention, but also its westernmost and southernmost occurrences.[37] Does its presence here signal the long use and reuse of artifacts, or is it an artistic archaism or a "quotation" (in the postmodernist sense)?

A scene of predation, with a carnivore attacking an herbivore (or another carnivore), is one of the most dynamic compositions in the art of the steppes. This subject is beautifully crafted on the appliqués found in the prince's burial (Tomb IV). On one a winged feline (leopard) attacks a saiga, a steppe antelope not found in Afghanistan,[38] while on another two felines fall upon a crouching horse,[39] their heads seen "en face" and their bodies in profile, just as on a Pazyryk tattoo (among others)[40] and on several northern Chinese belt plaques.[41] Another detail is worth noting. The Tillya Tepe horse is depicted in relief with a long mane, indicating Greek influence, and is comparable to those on the pectoral from the Tolstaya Mogila burial in the Black Sea area.[42] The horse with reverted hindquarters depicted on a plaque in the Siberian collection of Peter the Great, however, is a wild horse with a short mane.[43]

The style of the Tillya Tepe feline wings is typical of Central Asian steppe art, while some other stylistic elements are also highly significant indicators of Tillya Tepe's steppe connection:

(1) The two mountain sheep heads with split face and horns, on the sheath from Tomb IV,[44] are comparable to heads rendered on horse trappings from Pazyryk kurgan 1.[45]

(2) The twisting of the body parts, with the head seen from above or "en face" with the body in profile, appears to be very similar on the Tillya Tepe Tomb IV sheath[46] and on two carved wooden saddle decorations in Pazyryk kurgan 5.[47]

(3) The segmented tail of the felines or monsters is also identical at Tillya Tepe and in the art of its Altai predecessors, although the segmented tail derives ultimately from ancient Achaemenid Persian models of scorpion tails attached to the bodies of horned lions on Persepolis reliefs. This stylistic trait (among others) traveled from the Achaemenid empire to the Altai region, was adopted by the Saka during the fourth to third century B.C., and possibly returned to Bactria with the subsequent Saka migrations in the second century.

Three other stylistic elements at Tillya Tepe are worth mentioning:

(1) The coiled felines or monsters on belt and strap separators, such as those from Tomb IV,[48] are ubiquitous in the art of the steppes, as well as in Bactria (Takht-i Sangin).[49]

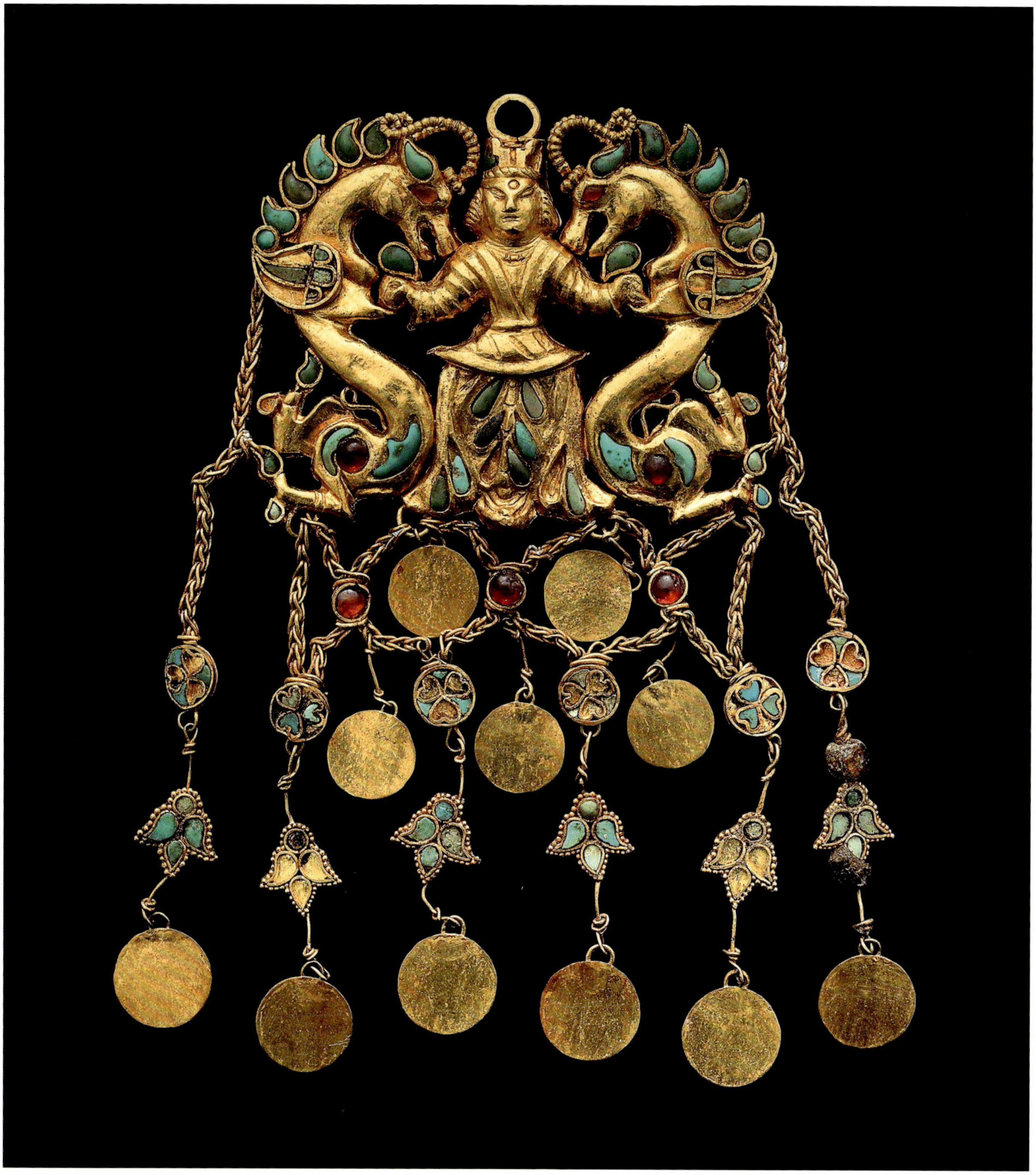

Fig. 13. Dragon Master pendant. Tillya Tepe, Tomb II, second quarter of 1st century A.D. Gold, turquoise, garnet, lapis lazuli, carnelian, pearls, 12.5 × 6.5 cm. National Museum of Afghanistan, Kabul (04.40.109)

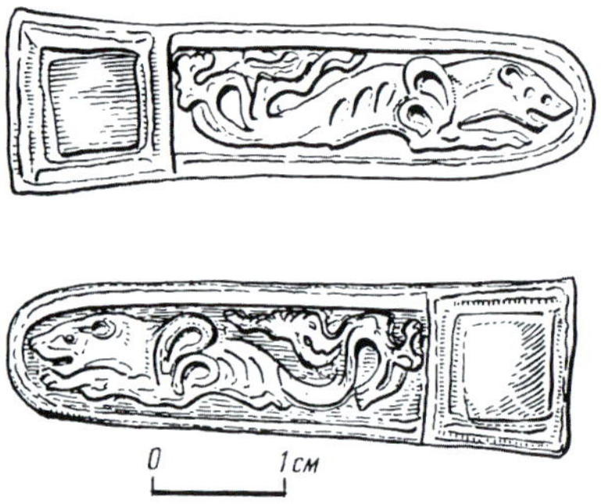

Fig. 14. Two strap decorations showing animals with reverted hindquarters. Tillya Tepe, Tomb IV, second quarter of 1st century A.D. Gold, 4 × 1.2 cm. National Museum of Afghanistan, Kabul (04.40.393)

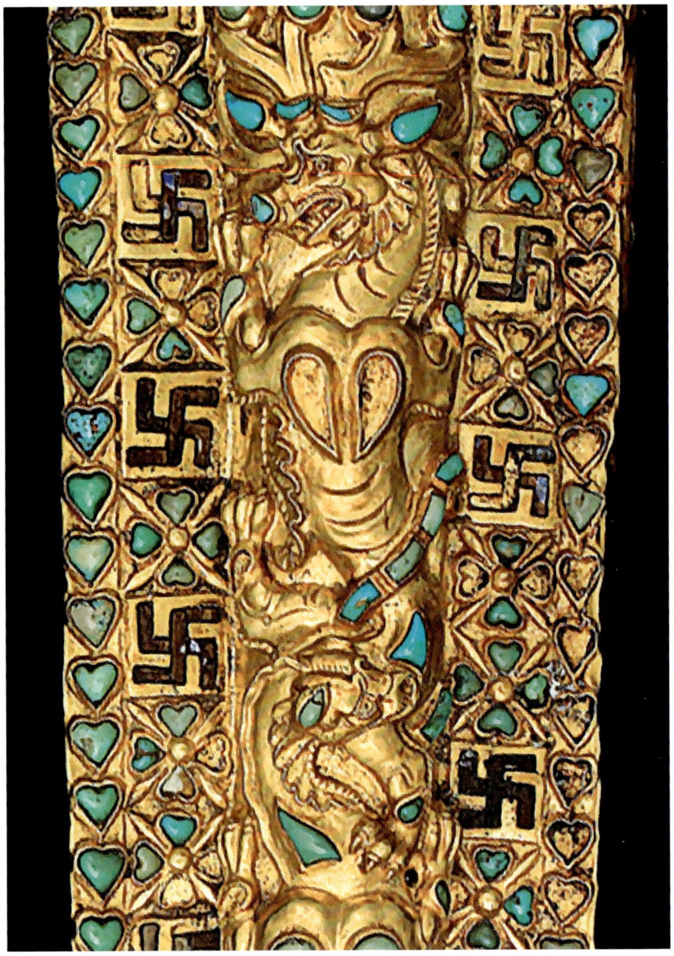

Fig. 15. Dagger sheath (detail) with antlered feline. Tillya Tepe, Tomb IV, second quarter of 1st century A.D. Bronze, gold, turquoise, H. 26 cm. National Museum of Afghanistan, Kabul (04.40.388)

(2) Depictions of isolated mountain sheep heads in profile appear to be very similar at Tillya Tepe[50] and at Bashadar in the Altai region.[51]

(3) The feline with stag antlers on the Tillya Tepe Tomb IV sheath (fig. 15)[52] also derives from the Altai, a motif known in Tuekta (fig. 16),[53] and is especially widespread in the eastern part of the steppes, in northern China, as at Aluchaideng (fig. 17).[54] At Shanpula (Hetian, Xinjiang), beautiful textiles contemporary with Tillya Tepe display friezes of antlered beasts of prey of the same iconographic tradition (fig. 18).[55]

More significant objects from Tillya Tepe point toward the steppe world. One of the most striking features of the head gear in the Scythian world is a very high assemblage with animal, vegetal, and other material ornaments: mountains, trees, feathers and birds, and mountain goats or sheep. All allude to high places or to a world rising in tiers. Similar crowns are well known not only in the Altai (Ukok)[56] and in Kazakhstan (Issyk)[57] but also from the Black Sea to China (Liaoning) and Korea (Silla; see discussion by Leidy, p. 119).[58] Two such crowns come from Tillya Tepe, one from the male Tomb IV[59] and the other from female Tomb VI (see Leidy, fig. 7).[60] They resemble trees, and, in the first case, a mountain sheep was probably attached at the top.[61] Two unusual pieces were discovered in Tomb III. The first, an ear or head pendant, represents a pair of addorsed horse protomes and again finds parallels at Pazyryk[62] and Issyk,[63] on two plaques from a Scythian Aral Sea tomb (Tagisken),[64] and on one comb from the Koktepa nomadic princess burial near Samarkand.[65] The second, two gold shoe soles of the lady buried in the tomb, are reminiscent of those from Pazyryk kurgan 2,[66] Noin Ula,[67] Shihuigou,[68] and Korea,[69] pointing again toward northeastern Asia, home of the Xiongnu.

Achaemenid connections must also be explored. The Master of Animals is a very ancient Near Eastern composition adopted into the art of the Achaemenid empire.

The pendants from Tomb II at Tillya Tepe beautifully exemplify this composition (see fig. 13).[70] Leaving aside the problem of the lower part of the body of the central figure (a rider's costume or a vegetal chalice), we may notice the typical Saka jacket, the very Asian eyes, and the distinctive crenellated crown. This crown, similar to one represented on a hood from Pazyryk kurgan 3,[71] clearly derives from Achaemenid art. (The type was rarer during the Hellenistic period and hardly appeared in Parthian times.) The dragon with horns, mane, wings, inlaid paws, segmented tail, and reverted hindquarters is, as was noted above, a fine example of steppe art. But now let us compare it with the lion-dragon framing the representations of Greek warrior-kings on two clasps from Tillya Tepe Tomb III (see Hickman essay, fig. 2).[72] Here the same elements are present, but the treatment is different: looking carefully at the lion's head with the horn, ear, mane, and a collared feature, we recognize the tradition of Achaemenid horned lions, as evident in the Oxus treasure[73] and in the art of the Persian royal court.[74] As for the composition of the Master of Animals, controlling two dragons (interpreted differently by John Boardman, pp. 110–11), we may make two observations:

(1) The perfectly frontal position of the Master of Animals, with strict symmetry of the monsters, is typical of steppe vegetation deities, while the Persian royal hero is in profile. Do we see here a manifestation of the nowadays neglected Parthian artistic rule of frontality?

(2) A prominent thematic characteristic of steppe "deities" or "heroes" is that they are never represented fighting or killing the felines or dragons. Instead the animals are held or shown tamed. The intention here is one of presentation, not of narration. Tillya Tepe craftsmanship follows this tradition, reintegrating into steppe scheme and style, after a considerable time lag,[75] some

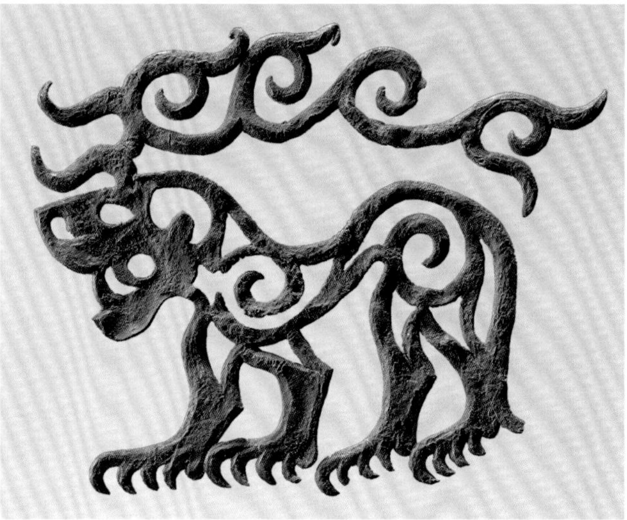

Fig. 16. Appliqué of an antlered tiger. Tuekta (Altai culture), 6th century B.C. Leather, 13 × 14 cm. The State Hermitage Museum, St. Petersburg (GE 2179/912)

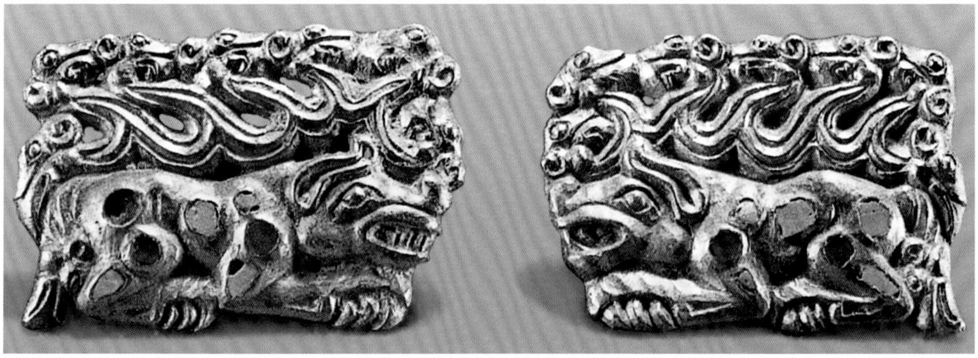

Fig. 17. Plaques with antlered tigers. Aluchaideng. Gold inlaid with turquoise

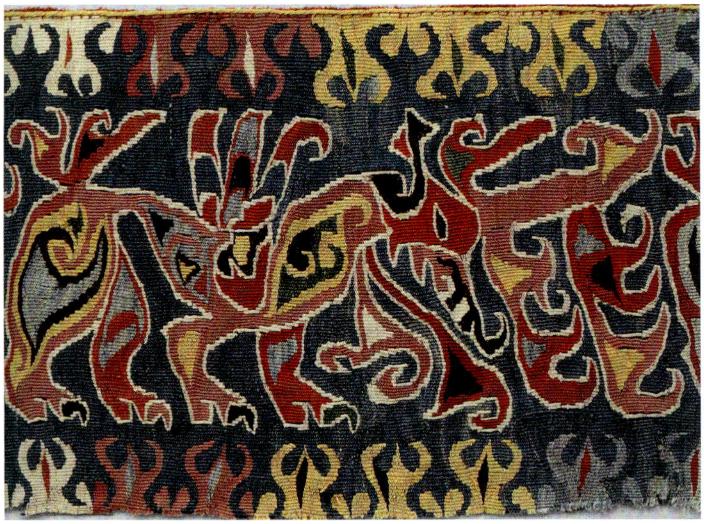

Fig. 18. Textile with detail showing antlered and winged felines. Shanpula (Xinjiang). Wool tapestry band, H. 20.5 cm, W. 225.5 cm. Abegg-Stiftung, Riggisberg

Achaemenid elements that were either brought back from the Altai or were already rooted in Bactria.

At Tillya Tepe, Hellenized forms were also inserted within a specific and intentional steppe artistic scheme. The Greek-Macedonian warrior-king on the clasps from Tomb III (see Hickman essay, fig. 2, and Boardman essay, fig. 10)[76]—which resembles one appearing on a coin of Kujula Kadphises (fig. 19, reverse) of about the same time[77]—is inserted in a frame. The side pillars are quite unusual: the lion-dragon, already discussed, is at the bottom; in the middle runs a vertical row of palmettes reminiscent of the stucco decor of a Parthian Iranian architectural niche; and at the top sits a bird (not a griffin). Such an odd composition is perhaps simply a goldsmith's (or his patron's) view of the three-tiered vertical steppe imaginary vision: the dragon (snake, fish) for water and the underworld, the vegetal (and animal and human) for the terrestrial world, and the bird (sky, etc.) for the celestial world. Thus, the king is possibly here included within the larger universe of steppe structure.

We turn now to the divine Mistress of Animals, depicted on a pendant from Tomb VI (fig. 20).[78] The image derives from a Greek tradition that passed into Graeco-Parthian and Indo-Parthian iconography (see the Taxila Sirkap jewelry).[79] But here, again, the vertical structure of the frame is the same three-tiered one: a dragon or fish head below, a bird above, and, in the middle, a harnessed fish-dragon (apparent from the belly strap) with a vegetal tail. Thus, the Hellenized human form appears here also inserted into what is probably a steppe (or Bactrian) structure. But at Tillya Tepe the lady of Tomb VI is even more informative. Her crown, typical of the steppe world,[80] repeats once more the same vertical three-tiered structure: a fish-dragon, a tree, and, above, a large bird (see Leidy essay, fig. 7). Such large birds are found, for instance, on the so-called "priestess" headgear of Ak-Alakha 1.[81] While each Tillya Tepe deceased had gold chin straps tying the maxillaries,[82] she was the only one to keep Charon's obole in her mouth, originally a Greek custom.[83] At the same time she was the only one to exhibit an artificial skull deformation,[84]

Fig. 19. Copper coin of Kujula Kadphises, with image of a Greek-Macedonian soldier on the reverse. American Numismatic Society, New York

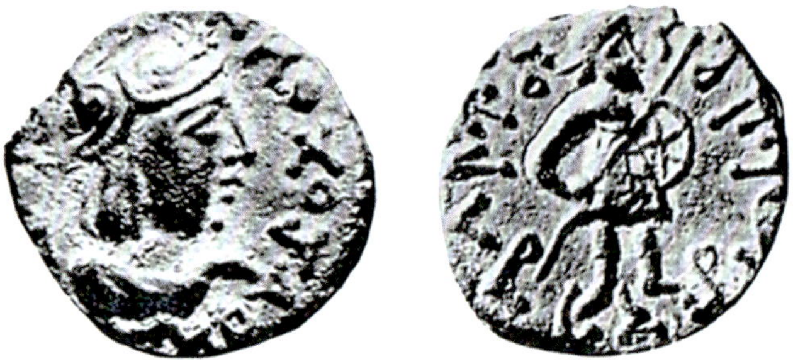

reminiscent of contemporary Yuezhi sculptures from Khalchayan and the similar portrait of a sovereign on coins of Heraios.[85] Does this necessarily indicate that she came from a Yuezhi family (an issue also addressed by Boardman, pp. 105–107, and Leidy, p. 120)? It is difficult to confirm since, according to studies by anthropologists, many similar artificial skull deformations appear in the second century B.C. and later in the nomadic Saka (?) cemeteries of Bactria. Was she, with her gold wand,[86] a magician or a priestess? This question is also difficult to assess.[87]

To summarize this brief and sketchy presentation of a large topic, we see that the connections of the Tillya Tepe peoples with the arts of the steppes are very complex, indeed. For instance, some steppe elements had long been integrated into Parthian art, and, conversely, Achaemenid forms had long before found their way deep into the heart of Eurasia. Parthians, Yuezhi, and Kushans were all originally steppe nomads, but the eastern Scythians, in particular the Saka, had developed a long-term relationship with the oasis agriculturalists and empires. The Tillya Tepe "Scytho-Bactrians," to our present knowledge, left no cultural descendants. Their artistic creations and the complex cultural and imaginary universes, which we find at the cemetery, were not transmitted. They faded, jammed as they were between the Parthians and the Kushans, the Romans and the Chinese. The missing element, as always, is the local Bactrian, but we must remember that a large part of this population was Zoroastrian and left no burials and no funerary goods.

In concluding, let us reiterate some important facts:

(1) The Tillya Tepe grave deposits not only exhibit links with the western steppes and the Sarmatians, but also show strong connections with the Altai Saka and, farther east, with the Xiongnu, who at that time were living in Xinjiang.

(2) The time lag between the earlier arts of the Altai and that of Tillya Tepe is comparable to or longer than the gap between the end of Graeco-Bactrian power and the burials at Tillya Tepe. We have many hypothetical scenarios to try to fill the historical gap, but some links are undoubtedly missing.

(3) It is relevant to note that some components similar to Tillya Tepe are found from the trans-Ural region to southern Siberia, not only in the Sarmatian and Hunno-Sarmatian culture, but also in the Sargat culture farther north. For instance, at Isakovka I there are comparisons in the disposal of burials under the kurgan, the inlaid gold steppe art, the four-lobed sheath, Chinese artifacts, and Achaemenid and Hellenistic metal phiales with Chorasmian and Parthian inscriptions.[88]

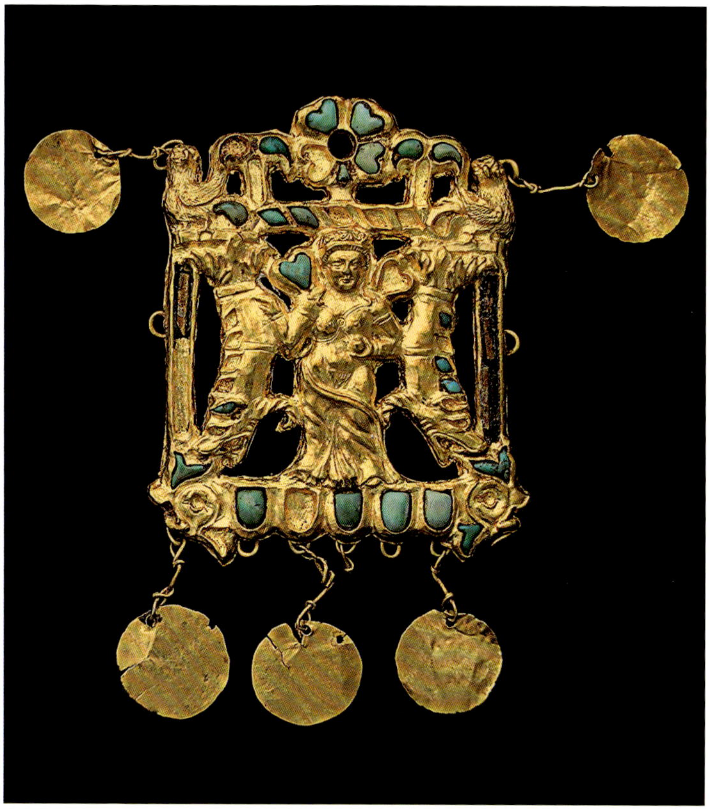

Fig. 20. Mistress of Animals pendant. Tillya Tepe, Tomb VI, second quarter of 1st century A.D. Gold, turquoise, 5.8 × 0.5 cm. National Museum of Afghanistan, Kabul (04.40.52)

(4) The connection with the art of the steppes is most apparent in the prestigious headgear and weapons in the man's tomb, while in the female burials the nomadic elements are less prominent and are mixed with local Bactrian ones.

Finally, we must consider the following: the deliberate display of kingship paraphernalia, including horse-riding and archery equipment, in the Tillya Tepe "Scytho-Bactrian" princely tomb; the presence of five or six elite female burials accompanying this "prince" to the other world; links with the Parthians, Yuezhi, Indo-Parthians, Greeks, and perhaps even Romans; and the wide range of parallels demonstrating connections with the so-called Sarmatians and above all the Xiongnu. In that light, would it not then be interesting to consider the possibility that this complex burial is the tomb of one of the so-called "small kings," the "Pulagids," of western Bactria (see fig. 1b)?[89]

1. Anthony 2007.
2. The *terminus post quem* is the Tiberius coin struck in Lyon in A.D. 21. The accepted date of A.D. 50 is a convenience, nothing more.
3. Schneider 2007.
4. Olbrycht 1998.
5. Cribb 2007; Widemann 2009.
6. On the Indo-Parthians, see Bivar 2007 and Bopearachchi 1993. On the Gondophares and Tillya Tepe collars, see Bernard 1987a. For the collar of Gondophares on coins, see Cribb 2007, nos. 42, 43.
7. For the Parthian coin of Phraates IV, see Sarianidi and Koshelenko 1982, no. 2. See also Sarianidi 1985, 6.3, p. 186, p. 258 (ill. 129).
8. Rtveladze 1995.
9. On this still discussed question, see, for instance, Rtveladze 1993–94; Rtveladze 1995; Callieri 2005; Rtveladze 2007; Cribb 2007; Widemann 2009.
10. Ghose 2005.
11. Sarianidi 1985, 4.10, pp. 122–23, p. 248 (ills. 68, 69).
12. Kruglikova 1984, fig. 3, no. 17. The bullae of Djiga Tepe are from the Kushan-Sasanian period; this one, certainly more ancient, is of Graeco-Bactrian type, probably Graeco-Bactrian period or a later imitation, possibly contemporary with the Tillya Tepe cameo.
13. Kruglikova and Moustamindy 1970.
14. Pugachenkova 1966; Bernard 1987b; Bernard and Abdullaev 1997.
15. Rapin, Isamiddinov, and Khasanov 2001; Abdullaev 2007; Rapin 2007.
16. This Yaz 1 to Yaz 3 Early Iron Age mound (ca. 1400–900 B.C.) is one of the few important sites in Central Asia for this period.
17. Sarianidi 1985, map p. 6. See Rudenko 1969 for Noin Ula; Desroches 2003 for Gol Mod; Minjaev and Sakharovskaja 2007a and Minjaev and Sakharovskaja 2007b for Tsaram; Brosseder 2009 for Xiongnu elite burials in general.
18. Troickaja 1997; Koryakova 2007; Koryakova and Epimakhov 2007.
19. Sarianidi 1989, pp. 84–86, fig. 30,5.
20. See note 17 above for references. For the chariot representation from Tillya Tepe, see Sarianidi 1985, 4.1, pp. 182–83, p. 246 (ill. 124), and commentary in Pfrommer 1996; Pugachenkova and Rempel' 1986; Schiltz 2006, with scholarly notes, pp. 270–83.
21. It is depicted and mentioned in Sarianidi 1989, pp. 84–86, fig. 30,1.
22. Rosenfield 1967, pp. 13–14, type II, pls. 4, 5, p. 14, fig. 1; Cribb 2007, p. 353, no. 80.
23. Commentary and parallels are found in Schiltz 2006.
24. Ghirshman 1979, pl. II,2; Winkelmann 2006.
25. Amiet 2001, with bibliography, ill. 28 for the Shami bronze, and ills. 25 and 26 for the stone sculptures from Susa.
26. For reliefs depicting Antiochus of Commagene, see Ghirshman 1962 p. 66, fig. 79.
27. Seyrig 1938.
28. Cribb 2007, p. 351, no. 67.
29. Wang 1999, p. 124, from Niya burial M3.
30. Tokyo 2005, p. 100, no. 51.
31. Rudenko 1969, pl. LXIV.
32. Cugunov et al. 2006, pl. 38,18.
33. For example, on the man in kurgan no. 5, ca. mid-third century B.C. See Rudenko 1970, figs. 53, 54.
34. From 286 B.C.; see Samashev et al. 2000, p. 12, fig. 15.
35. From the third century B.C.; see Wang 1987, p. 34, figs. 3 and 4.
36. Pirazzoli-t'Serstevens 2008, p. 7, fig. 6, with relevant steppe Chinese and Sino-steppe documents and parallels. The Marquise of Dai coffin is dated shortly after 168 B.C.
37. Sarianidi 1985, ear pendants with a human figure "mastering" mythic animals: 2.7, pp. 98–103, p. 231 (ills. 44–47); belt ornaments with felines: 4.4, p. 155, p. 257 (ill. 98). On the "dragons," see also Boardman 2003a and Boardman 2007.
38. Sarianidi 1985, 4.35, p. 180, p. 251 (ill. 123).
39. Ibid., 4.36, p. 178, p. 251 (ill. 122).
40. Barkova and Pankova 2005.
41. Notably on plaques from Aluchaideng. See Bunker et al. 1997, p. 51, fig. A57.
42. Schiltz 1994, pp. 58–59, fig. 34; pp. 196–97, figs. 145–48; pp. 368–69, fig. 276.

43. Ibid., fig. 40. The monster feline and the horse are both depicted with reverted hindquarters.
44. Sarianidi 1985, 4.9, pp. 220–23, p. 248 (ills. 162, 164–165).
45. Schiltz 1994, p. 42, fig. 25.
46. Sarianidi 1985, 4.9, p. 248 (ills. 162–163).
47. Rudenko 1970, pl. 116F.
48. Sarianidi 1985, 4.5–7, pp. 206–7, pp. 247–48 (ills. 148–152).
49. Pitschikjan 1992, p. 155, fig. 40.
50. Sarianidi 1985, 2.8, p. 208, p. 232 (ill. 153).
51. Bashadar kurgan 2: Rudenko 1960, pl. CXVI,2, a saddle ornament in felt appliqué, partially gilded.
52. Sarianidi 1985, 4.9, pp. 220–223, 248 (ills. 162–165). The animal is sometimes erroneously described as a "deer."
53. Rudenko 1970, p. 270, fig. 137B, from Tuekta barrow 1.
54. Bunker et al. 1997, p. 50, fig. A55. Felines and canids with antlers are widespread in northern China, in the Ordos; they also appear in the Siberian Collection of the State Hermitage Museum in St. Petersburg.
55. Museum Archaeology 2001, p. 204, no. 399, pp. 214–16, nos. 409–411. See also Keller and Schorta 2001, figs. 1, 13, 14, 15, and so on, where they are called "deer," which they are not, as indicated by the paws, the beak or wolf's head, the tail, the wings, etc. In spite of stylistic conventions and the specific textile schematization, they are recognizable as antlered carnivorous monsters.
56. Polos'mak 2001.
57. Akishev 1978.
58. Cambon 2006.
59. Sarianidi 1985, 4.28, p. 177, p. 250 (ill. 121).
60. Ibid., 6.1, pp. 70–75, p. 254 (ills. 12–15).
61. Ibid., 4.3, pp. 173–75, p. 247 (ills. 112–120). A sheep was not found attached to the "tree," but its position in the tomb makes it possible to see it as part of the headgear.
62. Rudenko 1970, pl. 164B, a saddle ornament from kurgan 5.
63. Akishev 1978, p. 16, fig. 7, pp. 18–19, fig. 9.
64. Moshkova 1992, p. 355, pl. 5, no. 6, and color pl.; Rapoport, Nerazik, and Levina 2000, p. 133, fig. 5, no. 2.
65. Rapin et al. 2001.
66. Rudenko 1970, pls. 64A and 152C.
67. Rudenko 1969, pl. LXX, 2, from kurgan 6.
68. Bunker et al. 1997, p. 55, fig. A68.
69. Cambon 2006, fig. p. 296.
70. Sarianidi 1985, 2.7, pp. 98–103, p. 231 (ills. 44–47).
71. Rudenko 1970, pl. 155B, a man's headdress.
72. Sarianidi 1985, 3.1, pp. 138–43, p. 236 (ills. 81–84).
73. Dalton 1964, pl. I, no. 23.
74. At Persepolis, a door jamb of the Harem of Xerxes depicting the "Royal Hero" fighting with the horned winged lion with raptor claws and scorpion tail; see Boardman 2000, p. 109, fig. 3.31. See also the same theme on the seal in fig. 5.26. For horned lions on horse trappings from Berel', see Francfort, Ligabue, and Samashev 2000, pp. 796–98; Francfort, Ligabue, and Samashev 2007, p. 123, fig. 15.
75. For such transfers by deconstruction and reintegration into another style scheme in our area, see Francfort 2007.
76. See also note 72 above.
77. Rosenfield 1967, p. 15, type V, pl. I, nos. 8–9.
78. Sarianidi 1985, 6.4, pp. 104–7, p. 254 (ills. 48–50).
79. Marshall 1951, pls. 190–196, esp. pl. 191, nos. 96–98.
80. See notes 55–59 above; also Kuz'mina and Sarianidi 1982.
81. Polos'mak 2001.
82. Rubinson 2008 for the chin straps.
83. Sarianidi 1985, 6.33, p. 258 (ill. 129): it is the countermarked silver coin mentioned earlier. Another coin, in gold, was deposited with her—in her hand—with a countermark representing a frontal bust (6.32, p. 258 [ill. 129]).
84. Sarianidi 1989 (p. 130, fig. 46) proposes a reconstruction of the profile of the lady.
85. Pugachenkova 1966; Pugachenkova 1971; Bernard 1987a. This is a well-known and illuminating parallel, but it is complicated by questions of the date, identity, and minting system of Heraios. See Widemann 2009; Zeymal 1983.
86. Sarianidi 1985, 6.19, p. 256. We must also note the number of symbolic "apotropaic" pendants she was wearing, although she was not alone in this in the Tillya Tepe burials. It is difficult, however, to be sure of a specialized sacerdotal function. The study of the religious and magical finds of Tillya Tepe has still to be carried out, but apparently these finds are linked to the female tombs. The ideological aspects of the male burial are of another category, one encompassing power and strength, but this is not the place for such an anthropological study.
87. See also the discussion in the essay by John Boardman.
88. Livshits 2003; Koryakova 2006; Treister 2009.
89. I would like to express my thanks to The Metropolitan Museum of Art and to all the organizers of the remarkable symposium. I would also like to take this opportunity to pay tribute to Viktor Sarianidi, the discoverer and excavator of Tillya Tepe, to whom we all owe a great debt, as well as to Afghan colleagues and authorities.

John Boardman

Tillya Tepe: Echoes of Greece and China

Afghanistan is much in the news these days, but it always has been. Its location explains much. It lies across the main routes, east-west and west-east, of the Old World: from the Mediterranean, Mesopotamia, and Persia to the Asian steppes, India, and China, the traditional silk routes. Crossroads are busy and informative places, especially for those who live there, as well as for those who pass by them on their business. It is not always easy for a crossroads to have a character of its own; rather, it reflects the changing fortunes and interests of those who visit. It is also often dangerous. People, objects, and ideas are absorbed, and there is a constant challenge to any historian or archaeologist who attempts to unravel connections, influences, and, not least, names and sources for those who passed by or who stayed.

Afghanistan is also a beautiful country, everywhere also revealing its history. It combines the ruggedness of the neighboring Pamir and Karakoram mountains with rich plains and river valleys, and it breeds and has always bred a folk whose independence of mind and action has more than once been the bane and often the downfall of attempts by many other and greater powers who have approached it.

A view of the Bamiyan Valley (fig. 1) shows in the foreground ruins of one of the many ancient but destroyed villages; at the back the massive range of the Hindu Kush rises majestically, while below it is the cliff with the tall niches that enveloped the massive Buddha figures destroyed in 2001 by the Taliban. The ruined town, of which there are many in the country, is commonly described as having been destroyed by Genghis Khan—which might be true for some of them. To the south is Kandahar, also much in the news these days. Two kilometers of cliffs (see fig. 2, where they are partially visible) surround the ancient town, which contains native, Persian, and Greek remains. Out of sight to the right, the cliffs terminate in a great Buddhist stupa, which is barely accessible now, and at the center of the old town stands one of the largest of the country's ruins, the remains of the great brick citadel built by the Persians in the fourth century B.C. Beyond it is the site of British excavations, which in the 1970s yielded, among other things, Greek inscriptions.

Moving north from the present capital, Kabul, through the steep passes of the Hindu Kush, one comes to the broader plains, bisected by the Oxus River, which ran from the Pamirs toward the Caspian Sea. To the south of the Oxus stand the massive ruins of the so-called Mother of Cities, Balkh, the ancient Bactra, home of Zoroaster. To the east along the Oxus lies the Greek city of Aï Khanum, excavated by French archaeologists, to whom we owe most of our recent knowledge of the country's history. (See the essay by Paul Bernard in this volume.) It was founded by Greeks who decided to remain in Bactria after Alexander the Great's eastern expedition. They were from Alexander's own army and, no doubt, from the Persian army, in which there were even more Greeks, since the Persians had embraced in their empire many Greek cities. The Greeks, we are told, were tired of fighting and of moving eastward, and Alexander himself could be a cruel and unsympathetic master. Though he may have chosen himself as the avenger of what the

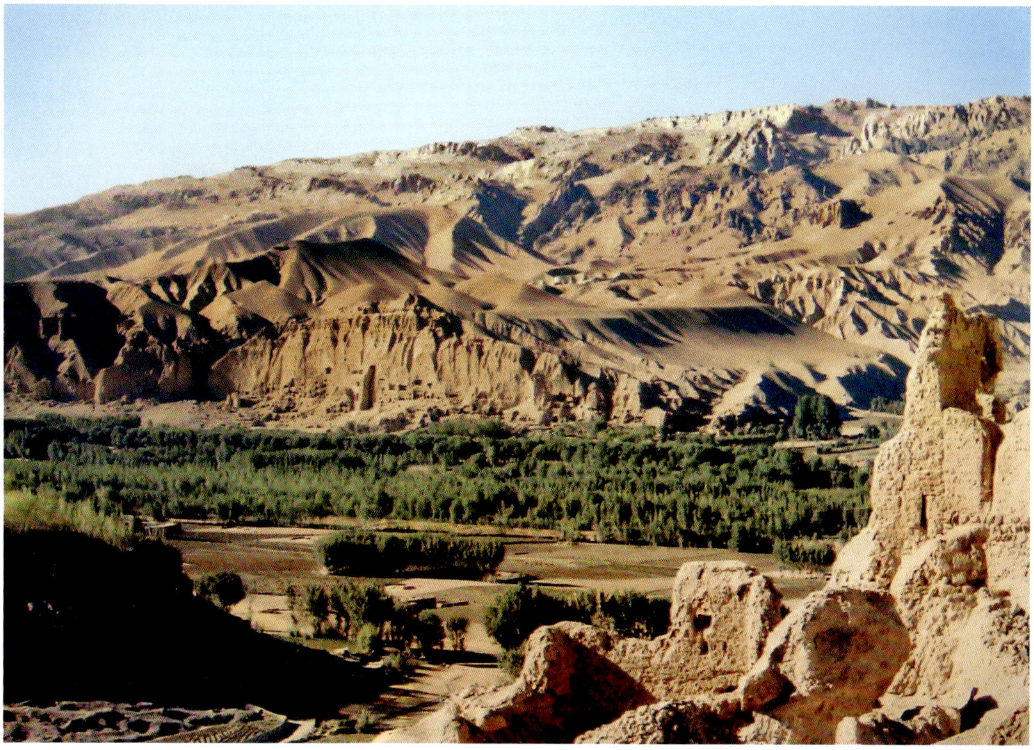
Fig. 1. Bamiyan Valley

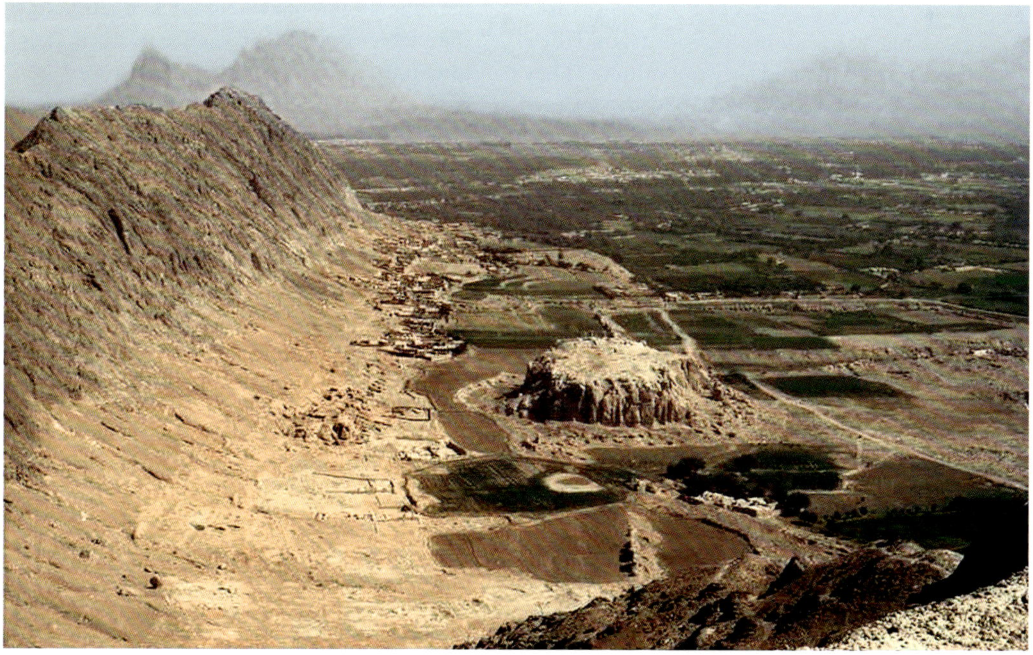
Fig. 2. Cliffs above the ruins of the ancient town of Kandahar

Persians did to Greece, he was otherwise generally indifferent to the Greeks. It was thus not long before the Greeks in Bactria organized themselves into a proper Graeco-Bactrian kingdom, and the usual dynastic differences arose, as well as the beginning of a move southward toward India, where they were to found the city of Taxila and soon to meddle in Indian affairs. One of these "Indo-Greek" kings, Menander (155–130 B.C.), even became a Buddhist scholar. Their coinage rivaled in its quality and variety that of the Greek homeland, with which links were, it seems, maintained. (See the essay in this volume by Frank Holt.) Foreign—Chinese—observers noted that in their walled cities south of the Oxus they had not seemed ostentatiously warlike, but that they were busy tradesmen—like Greeks anywhere, at any time.

Farther along the Oxus, beyond Balkh, lies Tillya Tepe.[1] It attracts our attention not only for the variety of sources of the finds there, from Roman coins to Chinese mirrors, but especially for the variety of influences that worked on the artists supplying the site: great variety, yet a degree of uniformity in the products of the local craftsmen. The majority of the finds from Tillya Tepe are of gold, and they are minute. They are the most evocative, yet they are not easy to judge because they are so small and require considerable enlargement to appreciate the nuances of detail that betray the mixture of their artistic origins, let alone the details of the figures on them. One can easily excuse scholars for mistaking male and female, details of dress and armor, let alone the puzzling and seemingly unique iconography. To understand these pieces properly, one has to enlarge them, then draw them.

The finds come from the wooden coffins of six tombs, which, it is presumed, had been moved for safekeeping from their original burial place.[2] It was clearly a makeshift operation because such important persons would have been interred in a far more impressive manner; indeed, the pressure of time seems to account for the fact that one of the workmen left his tool kit behind in one of the tombs.[3] But the bodies and their dress were not seriously disturbed in the move, which must have happened very soon after the first interment—or even, just possibly, before it had taken place. Their original burial or intended burial was probably at the nearby settlement site, Emshi Tepe, where there are also Greek finds. Tillya Tepe itself was mainly an earlier religious site. The tomb finds are a vivid demonstration of how much a single site can add to our knowledge—and leave us speculating about what remains to be found.

One of the burials is of a princely or royal warrior, the others are of what we may take to be his five female consorts or close family, killed, no doubt, to commemorate his funeral, after a fashion well known in many parts of the east. The burials are of about the middle of the first century A.D. The area had been settled a century or more earlier by a once-nomadic people, who had moved west from the borders of China. We know them as the Yuezhi, who had enjoyed a long and distinguished career in east Central Asia, harrying the Chinese kings as well as neighboring nomad kingdoms. Eventually they were moved on by more powerful fellow nomads, the Xiongnu, whom some have seen as the first Huns and who were also attacking China, but had been repulsed by the time of our graves. But the Oxus was merely a new starting point, and already before the first century A.D. the Yuezhi had begun to move south, behind the Greeks whom they had displaced, and eventually to found the great Kushan dynasty (1st–3rd centuries A.D.) of northern India and to adopt Buddhism.

It is no surprise, then, that among the finds at Tillya Tepe there are Chinese things, mainly works in bronze or gold, but also many in techniques suggesting that a great part of this collection of different objects and subjects was the work of local artisans, open to the traditions of widely different sources: their eastern homeland near China, the homeland of the Greeks who had previously inhabited the area, and, to a lesser degree, the steppes.

In the tomb of the prince, for example, we find a sheath for a Chinese short sword and another designed to hold three daggers; another dagger has on the roundel at its top a very typical figure of a Chinese dancing bear (see Leidy essay, fig. 4). A far odder Chinese subject, though not in a specifically Chinese style, is the scene on two boot buckles (fig. 3; see also Leidy essay, figs. 2 and 3), again not too easy to decipher.[4] We see a Chinese chariot-like cart with an umbrella top and with what looks like a Chinese man aboard, which is pulled not by horses, but by feline monsters. Similar travel scenes are found in Asian arts, particularly on belt plaques, but they suggest images from the real world. The monsters here evoke the divine realm, not that of mortals. The roundels, interestingly, were cast using a textile backing for the model, a technique new to this part of Asia, but one well attested to the northeast, in China itself.[5]

There are a number of purely Greek objects in the Tillya Tepe tombs, generally jewelry, not because the craftsmen necessarily specialized in jewelry, but because grave goods are bound to consist mostly of personal ornaments. The female burial in Tomb VI was no less rich in gold than the others, but there were differences. The decorative headdress she wore (see Leidy, fig. 7) was a feature of many burials found elsewhere in Central Asia, but the Greek character of the decoration of the objects in her grave was far more pronounced. She also had perfume bottles that had been brought from the Mediterranean.[6] She was, herself, no immigrant Greek or of pure Greek stock, as her skull had been deformed at birth in the local manner, evidence that she was brought up in Central Asia. Yet, it is tempting to think that, like many regal families to the south that still boasted Greek names, she entertained ideas about her Greek heritage and background and may even have been proud to display them by her way of life and, indeed, way of death.

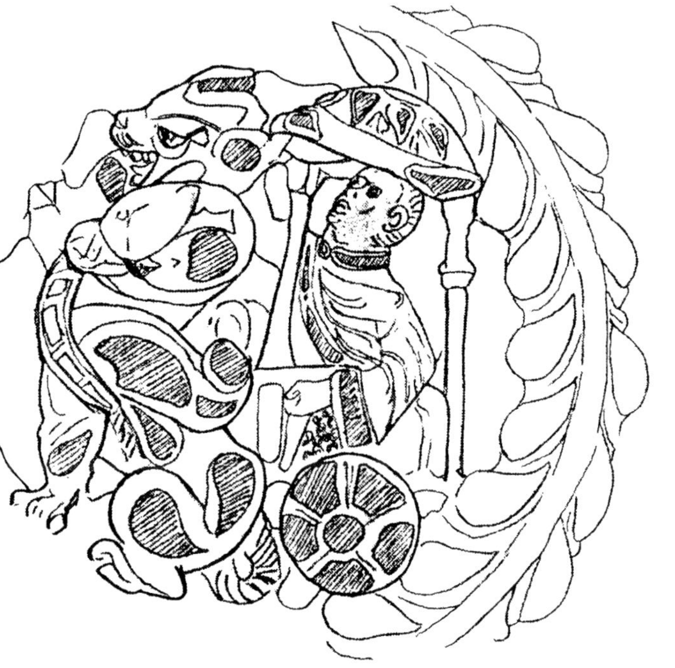

Fig. 3. Drawing of a gold and turquoise boot buckle with a man in a carriage drawn by monsters. Tillya Tepe, Tomb IV, second quarter of 1st century A.D. National Museum of Afghanistan, Kabul (04.40.383)

We cannot even conjecture her name, but intermarriage produced Greek names in non-Greek families farther south.

Looking at some of her jewelry we find a pair of clasps only two and a half inches high, which are easier to understand in a drawing (fig. 4).[7] Each shows the very Greek composition of the god Dionysos, wearing his animal skin, seated with his consort Ariadne in full Greek dress side by side on a lion. The god holds a wine cup. This area of Central Asia was no stranger to the vine, possibly earlier than Greece, and to Greek wine cups; indeed the Indians remarked on the bibulous behavior of the northerners. A shaggy Greek satyr squats beneath the lion's head, holding up his drinking horn to catch the drips from the god's cup. Behind the couple a figure of Victory flies up to crown them, so this is a celebration of the god, his wine, and his marriage. It could hardly be

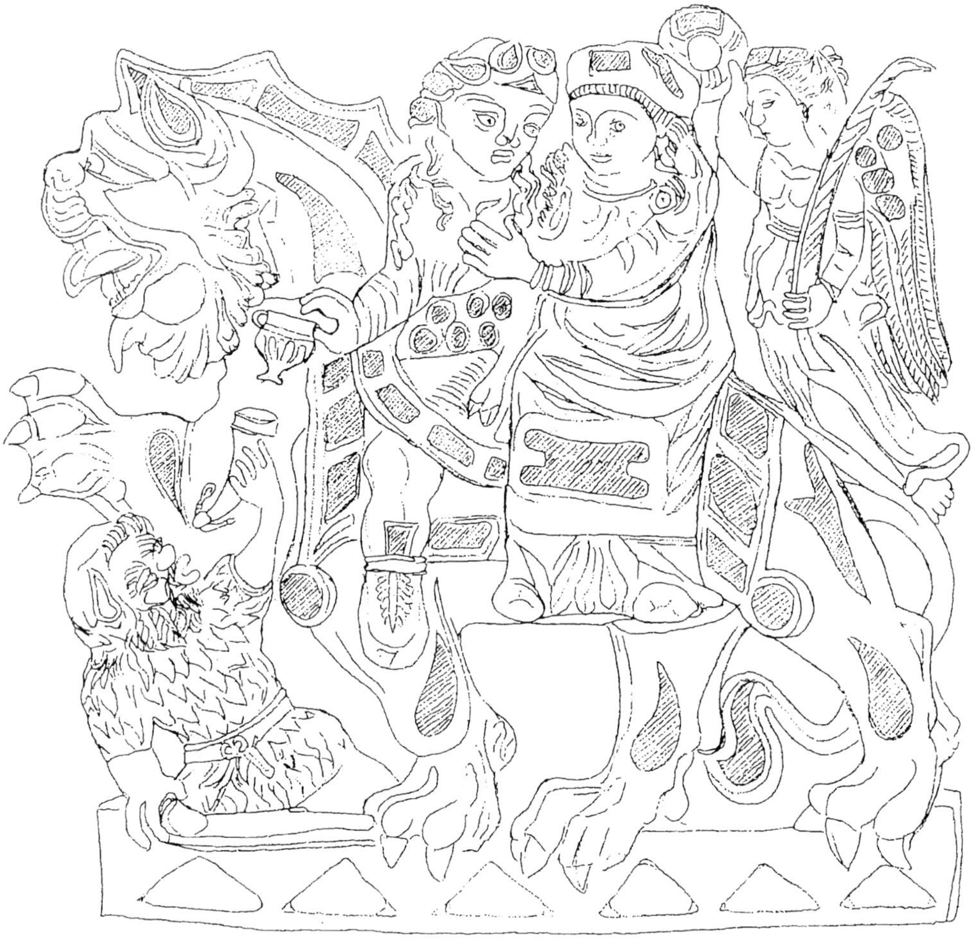

Fig. 4. Drawing of one of a pair of gold clasps showing Dionysos, Ariadne, and Nike. Tillya Tepe, Tomb VI, second quarter of 1st century A.D. National Museum of Afghanistan, Kabul (04.40.53)

more Greek in concept and detail, yet overall it is unique and not exactly matched in the Greek homeland. The lion itself, with "leafy" ridges on its neck and body, is not quite Greek, but exhibits characteristics we see more often on griffins, and it has a griffin's zigzag mane. These are features we see elsewhere on Hellenizing creatures in the east, and the lion in particular becomes important in Buddhist iconography. The Victory crowning the couple is perfectly canonical in every way, but odd in this context, though understandable if the wedding of Dionysos and Ariadne is being celebrated, while it also carries a hint of the Triumph of Dionysos, who had conquered the east. She is like many such flying figures of friendly females that were widely copied from Greek art, appearing in the east, from India (*apsaras*) to China, over many centuries. Thus, while every detail here can be matched in Greek art, the whole is a novel composition by an artist who, though fully conversant with Greek style and iconography, had his own ideas about composition and detail.

The lady in Tomb VI had Greek cupids for earrings and other jewelry showing Aphrodite/Venus herself, once with wings, emphasizing her divinity (fig. 5). Most significant of all, perhaps, the buried princess was found holding a coin in one hand and another in her mouth. This was a Greek custom, little copied elsewhere, of the dead carrying the fee for carriage over the river Styx to the underworld. Surely this find is a clear reference to lingering Greek beliefs, expressed in a very different environment, but one in which familial memory, of the west as well as the east, remained potent.

Turning to the prince's burial, we find a splendid belt of gold roundels, of a type met from China to Parthia to India.[8] On each roundel is a figure (fig. 6) wearing a short skirt and boots and holding a wine cup while seated on a lion. A woman riding a lion recalls an Indian goddess, Nana, and the dress and boots here are not quite Greek, although they are quite appropriate in a Dionysian context. But the cup is Greek, like several in silver that have been found in Afghanistan with relief decoration of Dionysian subjects.[9] In Greek terms, this would be a maenad, a wild woman follower of the god Dionysos, a very popular motif in the east, while the

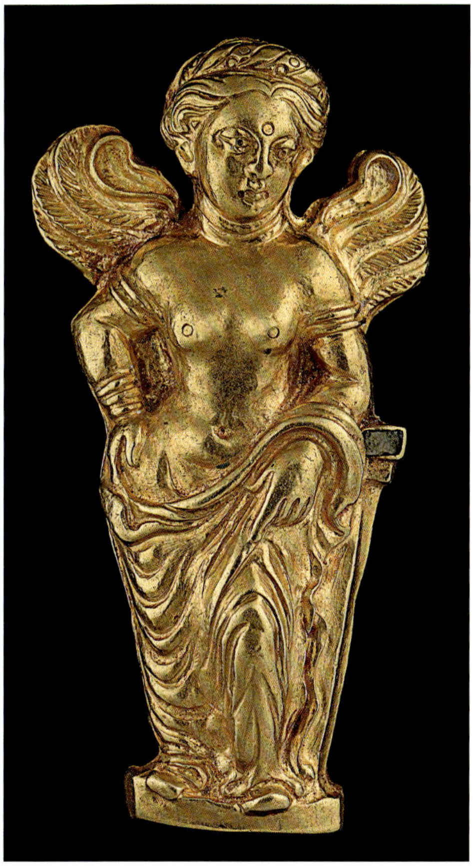

Fig. 5. Appliqué of a winged Aphrodite. Tillya Tepe, Tomb VI, second quarter of 1st century A.D. Gold, turquoise, 5 × 2.6 cm. National Museum of Afghanistan, Kabul (04.40.9)

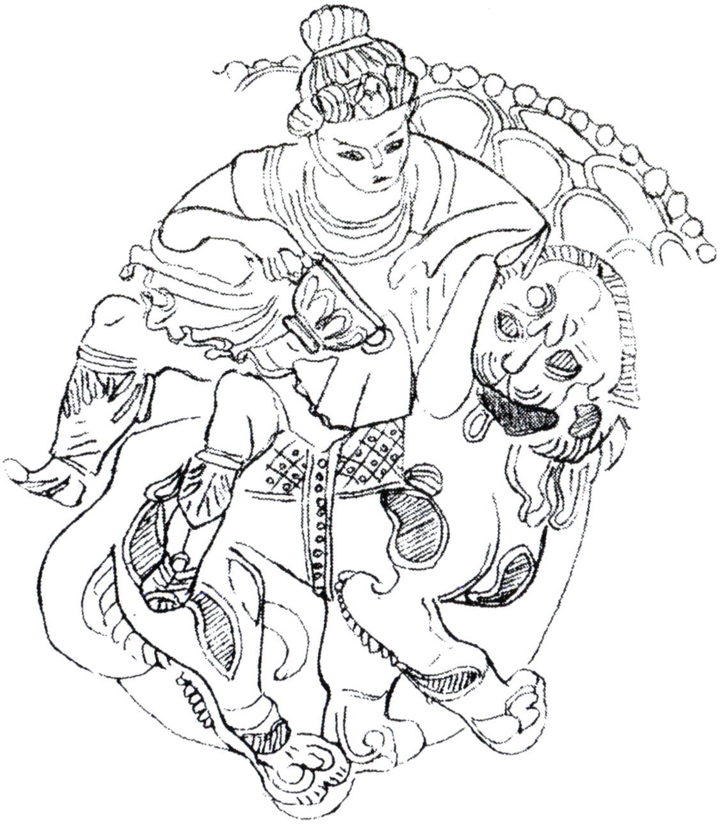

Fig. 6. Drawing of a gold belt roundel with a figure on a lion. Tillya Tepe, Tomb IV, second quarter of 1st century A.D. National Museum of Afghanistan, Kabul (04.40.384)

association of a wine cup and lion would be no less appropriate for any member of the Dionysian entourage. We have seen them already with Dionysos himself and his consort. There is one close parallel in Greek, or Greek-made art, that could be significant. It is on a gold appliqué plaque, where the maenad riding a lion holds a cup (fig. 7).[10] It is from the great Bliznitsa tumulus on the northern Black Sea, from the fourth to the early third century B.C., a site with much Greek goldwork and Scythian subjects. The Bliznitsa maenad's dress is at first sight Greek, but beneath it we can see on her outstretched arm a thick, patterned sleeve, such as was worn by Scythians and their women. So, she is a Scythian maenad and a significant predecessor of the Tillya Tepe figures.[11]

There is another suggestion of split identity in a figure repeated on seven plaques from Tomb I (fig. 8; see also Hickman essay, fig. 10). He is what the Greeks would call a Triton, because he has fishy legs.[12] Like Tritons in Greece he holds a dolphin, but he wears it around his neck, like a college scarf, and, like Tritons in Greece, he carries an oar over his shoulder, with the usual rather square blade. But no Greek Tritons carry both a dolphin and an oar, while in the east there are Indo-Greek coins and gems with such a figure (fig. 9).[13] They all seem to be personifications of rivers, and some have acanthus or seaweed-like appendages on their bodies. So this is, perhaps, a personification of the Oxus River—a very Greek concept—and one executed in Greek style and manner near the river itself for royalty buried at Tillya Tepe.

A fine pair of clasps from Tomb III shows warriors in Greek-Macedonian armor, who also wear an eastern straight

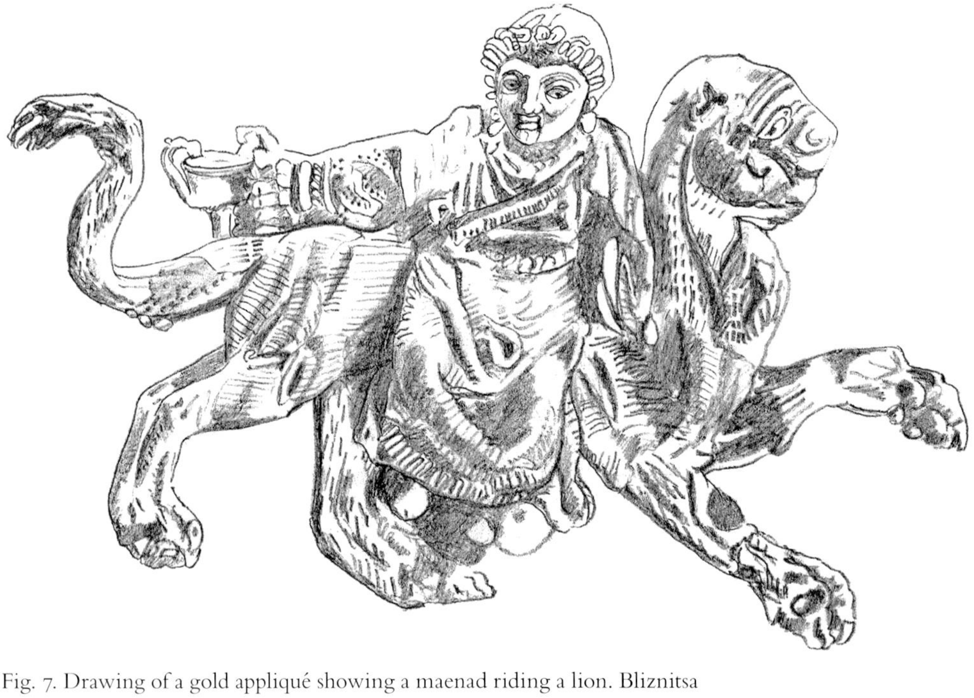

Fig. 7. Drawing of a gold appliqué showing a maenad riding a lion. Bliznitsa tumulus (Ukraine), 4th–early 3rd century B.C.

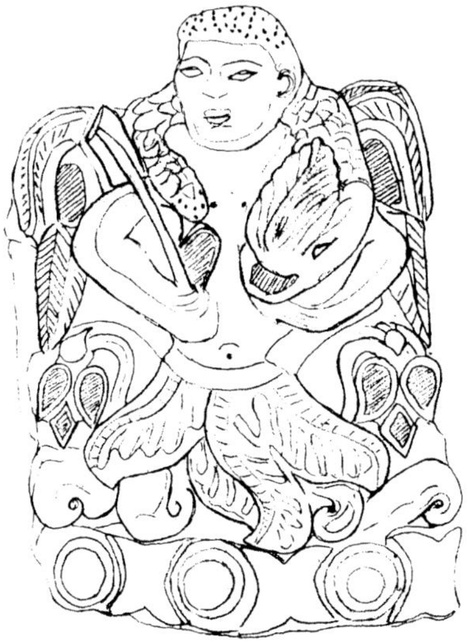

Fig. 8. Drawing of a gold appliqué showing a Triton carrying a dolphin and an oar. Tillya Tepe, Tomb I, second quarter of 1st century A.D. National Museum of Afghanistan, Kabul (04.40.303)

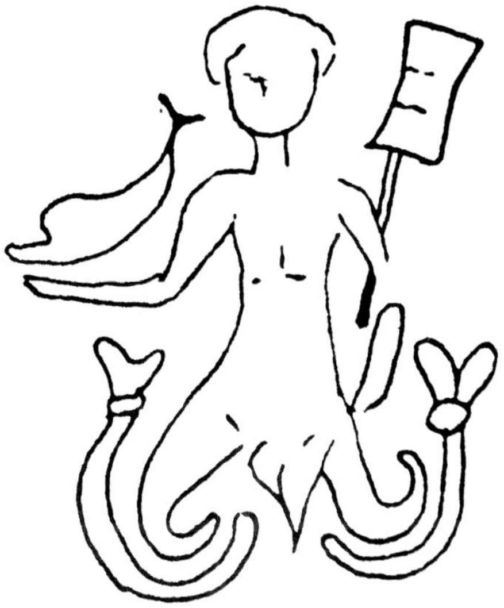

Fig. 9. Drawing of a coin of Hippostratos (65–55 B.C.) showing a Triton carrying a dolphin and an oar

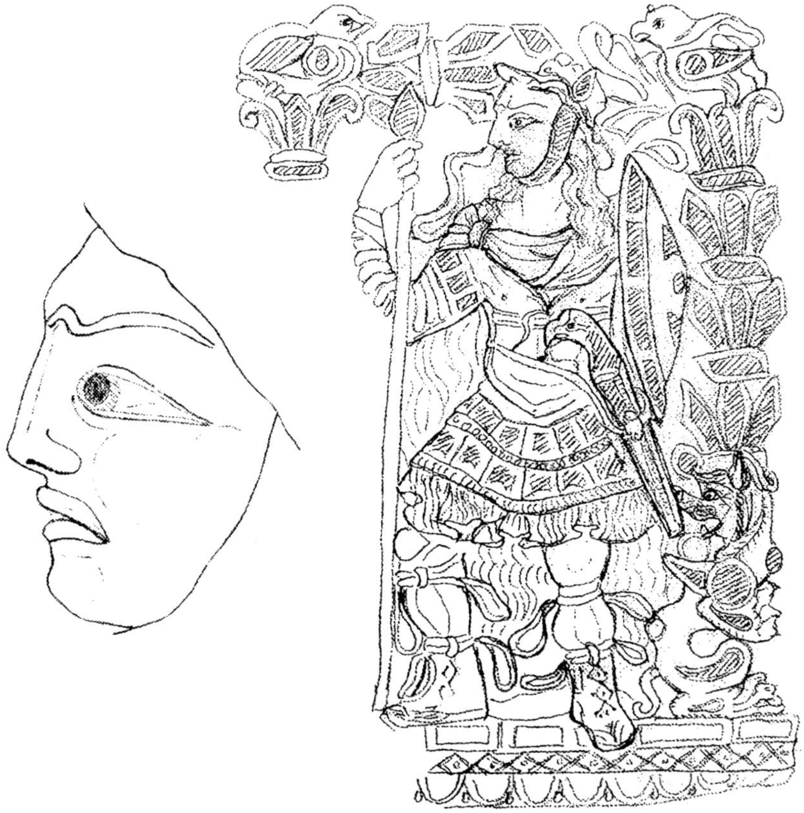

Fig. 10. Drawing (right) of a gold clasp with a warrior and (left) a detail of his profile. Tillya Tepe, Tomb III, second quarter of 1st century A.D. National Museum of Afghanistan, Kabul (04.40.245)

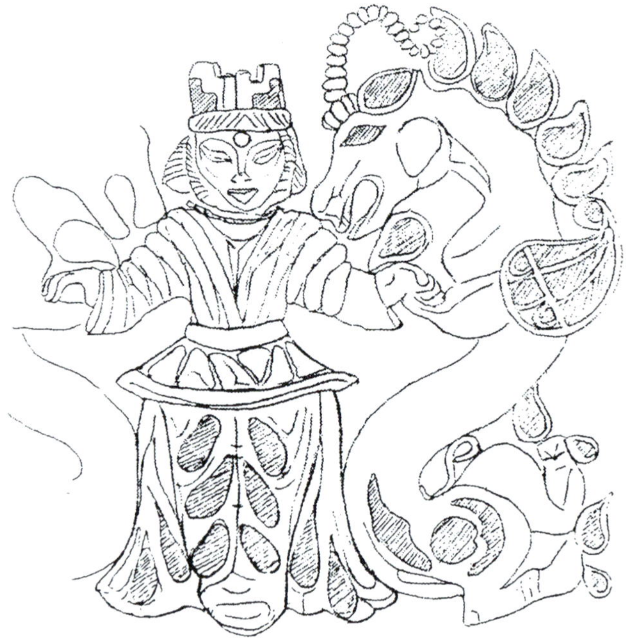

Fig. 11. Drawing of Master of Divine Horses pendant (detail). Tillya Tepe Tomb II, second quarter of 1st century A.D. National Museum of Afghanistan, Kabul (04.40.109)

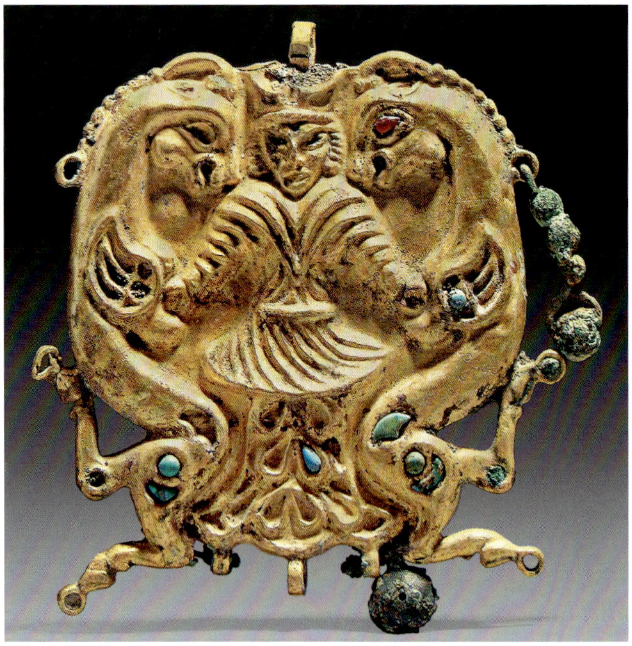

Fig. 12. Master of Divine Horses pendant, probably from Mir Zakah hoard, Afghanistan, 1st century B.C.–A.D. 1st century. Gold with carnelian and turquoise inlays, 14.6 × 12.7 cm.

sword (fig. 10; see also Hickman essay fig. 2).[14] Their helmets look more like bonnets with ribbons, but such helmets were often stylized in this manner in the Greek world. The man's profile with its bulging brow looks familiar—just like Alexander himself, whose image was well known in the east, often rendered on coins and sculpture. These clasps were worn by an oriental princess buried at the site, located in an area recently occupied by Greeks.

One of the most iconic Graeco-Oriental images from Tillya Tepe (fig. 11; see also Francfort, fig. 13)[15] depicts a central figure who has acanthus leaves below his belt rather than legs. This is a fairly common concept in the Greek world, especially in the east, for various divine figures, more often female but also male, who denote a version of divinity perhaps associated with wealth as well as with power. Our figure is wearing a battlement crown, as did some Greek divinities representing cities, and it is this type of crown that will have a long history in the east; he has a cast mark on his forehead, which in Central Asia signified divine status; he has slanting, slit eyes and wears a Chinese kaftan jacket—altogether oriental. He is controlling two divine horses. Their identity as horses had been disputed, in favor of dragons or divine felines of the type shown controlled by a king or god in Mesopotamia (see Francfort essay, p. 97).[16] Certainly, from the west come the little twisted horns and wings, a sign of divinity. But the mane runs along the crest of the neck, the bodies and the legs are slim, while the feet are clearly equine, marking the hoof and fetlock, and not feline. The slim tail is nondescript, the muzzle long, also not feline. The identity is even clearer on another version of the subject, which is larger, reportedly found in Gandhara at Mir Zakah with a coin hoard, and so far the only indicator of this "Tillya Tepe style" to the south (fig. 12).[17] On it the equine hoof is unmistakable.

The identification prompts other thoughts. In the last centuries B.C. the Chinese were themselves visiting the area adjacent to Bactria, Ferghana to the northeast, where Indo-Greeks had once settled. They were seeking the large "divine" horses, which "sweated blood" and had been bred there for centuries, to use them in their fight at home against the nomads, whose horses were barely more than ponies. I cannot but think that the image somehow reflects this Chinese interest in the west, one devised by artists—to whom both the history and the environment were very familiar, as were the horses and their purchasers. The subject was expressed in an essentially Greek way, transforming the oriental Master of Animals into a Master of Divine Horses.

The echoes of east and west in northern Afghanistan are loud and strong. We see floral decoration that would not have disgraced a Greek court, often an odd conflation of Greek ovolo pattern and Indian lotus; and we find a degree of animal realism that in its way outdoes the Greek and represents yet another facet of Central Asian art that is only slowly being recognized. It stands comparison with the best of Greece or China and vividly contrasts with what we commonly associate with the steppes of Asia.

1. The prime source is Sarianidi 1985, which has appeared in various languages and titles. Boardman 2003a and 2003b deal with most of the finds discussed here.
2. Boardman 2003b, pp. 370–71.
3. Sarianidi 1985, p. 23: "a plaited basket containing an iron pickaxe and two Siberian-style daggers," in the coffin of a woman.
4. Afghanistan 2008, no. 106.
5. See Boardman 2010, pp. 9–10.
6. Sarianidi 1985, 6.38, p. 259 (ill. 147).
7. Afghanistan 2008, no. 136.
8. Ibid., no. 107.
9. E.g., Errington and Cribb 1992, no. 97. For the remainder of the find, see Baratte 2001.
10. Artamonov 1966, fig. 286.
11. Note that the Ariadne of our figure 4 also wears sleeves. For a man riding a lion and carrying a cup, on a Gandhara palette, see Marshall 1951, pl. 144.72; for a child, see Boardman 2003b, p. 366, fig. 22 (relief in Peshawar).
12. Afghanistan 2008, no. 36.
13. Boardman 2003b, p. 360, fig. 8, for comparable figures in the east and in India.
14. Afghanistan 2008, no. 79.
15. Ibid., no. 61.
16. Boardman 2003b, pp. 357–58, on their identity.
17. Described in Bopearachchi and Flandrin 2005, p. 156. This must be the piece on the London art market (Christie's, 25 April 2001, lot 28), illustrated in Boardman 2003b, p. 356, fig. 6 (drawing), where it was mistakenly considered to have escaped from Tillya Tepe.

Denise Patry Leidy

Links, Missing and Otherwise: Tillya Tepe and East Asia

The Chinese, or Chinese-inspired, goods, manufacturing techniques, and imagery found at Tillya Tepe in northern Afghanistan raise interesting questions about the nature of the relationship between the six individuals buried in the tombs there and the artistic traditions and peoples found farther east. As is often the case in steppe burials, the women in Tombs II, III, and VI were interred with Chinese mirrors placed above their chests.[1] This practice follows longstanding Chinese traditions, traceable to at least the sixth century B.C., in which mirrors were placed in burials, at times as part of cosmetic sets, but more commonly as protective devices symbolic of light, longevity, and immortality. The three mirrors, which are made from a high-tin bronze and are similar in size, have identical decoration, including a series of raised dots in the interior, and the same inscriptions, referring to the apotropaic properties of light, in the borders. Mirrors of this type, which were widely produced in northern China, were common from the second century B.C. to the first century A.D., and have been found throughout China, in Inner Mongolia, and in Korea. The fact that the three at Tillya Tepe are identical suggests that they share a common place and date of manufacture and raises the possibility that the individuals at Tillya Tepe had direct ties either to China or to people with such ties and had, thereby, acquired the mirrors as a group, rather than assembling them through random exchanges on the steppes.

Also found in Tomb III, a stamp seal (fig. 1) shows an intriguing combination of ancient western seal-carving traditions with the use of jade, a quintessentially Chinese material that was often imported from such areas as Khotan on the southern edge of the Taklimakan Desert. Jade, like the hard stones worked in Mesopotamia and Iran, must be laboriously abraded with sand or some similar substance. The rudimentary animal—possibly a zebu—on the Tillya Tepe stamp seal was most likely created by grinding sand with a stick in a fashion that could have ultimately derived from the ancient Near Eastern technique used for the making of drilled-style seals; it could also have been inspired by the sophisticated jade-working technologies long found in China.

The elegant boot buckles worn by the man interred in Tomb IV (fig. 2), on the other hand, were the product of a method

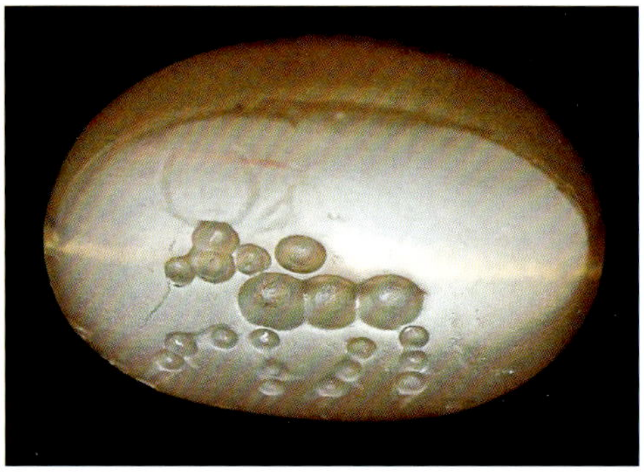

Fig. 1. Stamp seal with an animal, possibly a zebu. Tillya Tepe, Tomb III, second quarter of 1st century A.D. Nephrite jade, 2.1 × 1.6 × 1 cm. National Museum of Afghanistan, Kabul (04.40. 242)

of manufacture that can be traced to the east. The impressed or woven patterns on the backs (fig. 3) indicate that they were produced with the "lost wax–lost textile" technique found in China (see also the essays in this volume by Jane Hickman and John Boardman) and in the northeastern reaches of the steppes among the many pastoralists that inhabited those regions.[2] In this technique, which is a variant of the indirect lost-wax casting method, the wax model used in the casting is reinforced with a piece of coarse fabric, and the patterns on the back of the buckles are duplicates in relief of the textiles that fortify the model. The decoration on the buckles shows a Chinese-looking figure, wearing Chinese clothing and riding in a Chinese-style chariot drawn by leonine creatures; and it seems likely that the buckles, which are among the most beautifully made works from the Bactrian hoard, were cast either in China or in a border zone between China and the steppes, probably as a gift to, or for trade with, members of a pastoralist confederation based farther north.

The dagger and sheath worn by the man in Tomb IV also show familiarity with Chinese imagery, and it remains unclear—as is true of most of the material found at Tillya Tepe—where such an implement was produced. The bear on the pommel (fig. 4) is also found in nomadic and western Asiatic imagery; however, the posture—the animal stands on its hind legs, while the front ones are outstretched—is similar to representations in Chinese art of bears and wolves, particularly in scenes with astral overtones.[3] A prowling dragon, a classic Chinese motif, is depicted among the creatures in the combat scene on the surface of the sheath (fig. 5), further attesting to Chinese inspiration, if not workmanship.

The long, sinuous body, curling horn, and short wings of the dragon on the sheath parallel those found in the rendering of the mythical hoofed creatures controlled by the figure in the center of one of a pair of ornaments worn by the woman buried

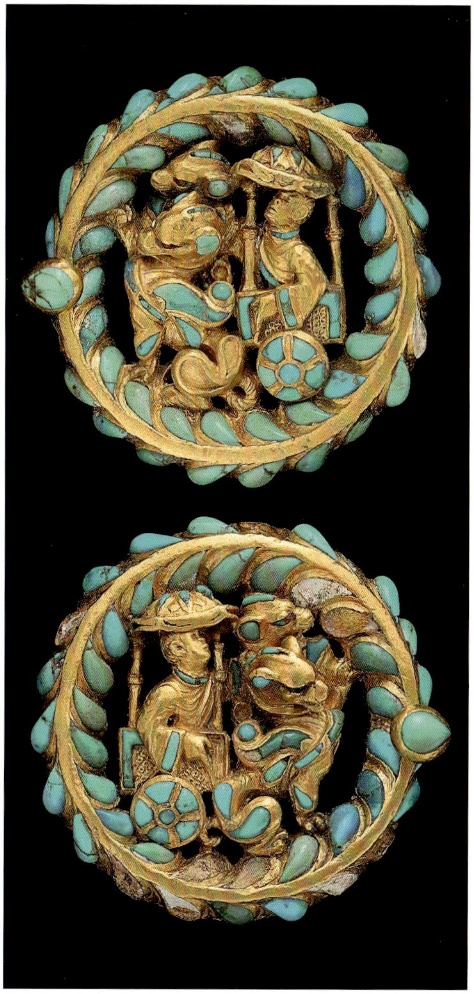

Fig. 2. Boot buckles with men in a carriage drawn by dragons. Tillya Tepe, Tomb IV, second quarter of 1st century A.D. Gold, turquoise, and carnelian, H. 1.1 cm, D. 5.5 cm. National Museum of Afghanistan, Kabul (04.40.383)

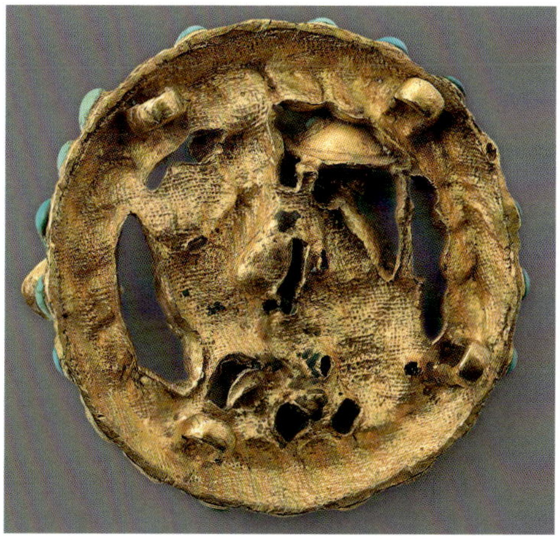

Fig. 3. Back view of boot buckle. Tillya Tepe, Tomb IV, second quarter of 1st century A.D. Gold, turquoise, and carnelian, H. 1.1 cm, D. 5.5 cm. National Museum of Afghanistan, Kabul (04.40.383)

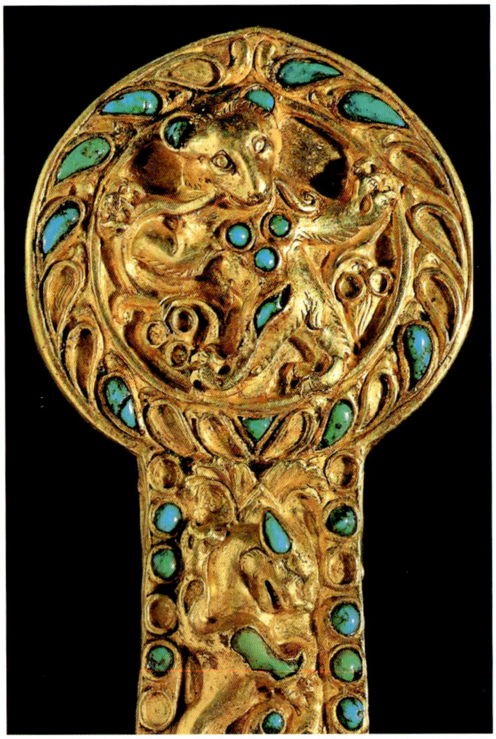

Fig. 4. Dagger (detail) with a bear on pommel. Tillya Tepe, Tomb IV, second quarter of 1st century A.D. Iron, gold, and turquoise, H. 37.5 cm. National Museum of Afghanistan, Kabul (04.40.387)

in Tomb II (see Francfort essay, fig. 13). Although this imagery can be traced to the ancient western Asiatic Master of Animals motif, the horse-dragons are reminiscent of similar creatures in the art of the Western Han dynasty (209 B.C.–A.D. 9) in China, such as that seen on the frontlet of a bridle excavated in 1999 in Shandong Province (fig. 6).[4] The twisted hindquarters of the horse-dragons in both works derive from longstanding steppe traditions; the elongated and narrow bodies follow traditional Chinese depictions of dragons (see also the discussions in Francfort, p. 97, and Boardman, pp. 110–11).

The spectacular crown (fig. 7) from Tomb VI at Tillya Tepe provides further fascinating parallels with eastern artistic traditions. Made of gold sheet, it consists of a thin band and five removable elements in the shapes of trees or antlers that are further embellished with openwork patterns, some in the shape of hearts, a motif commonly found

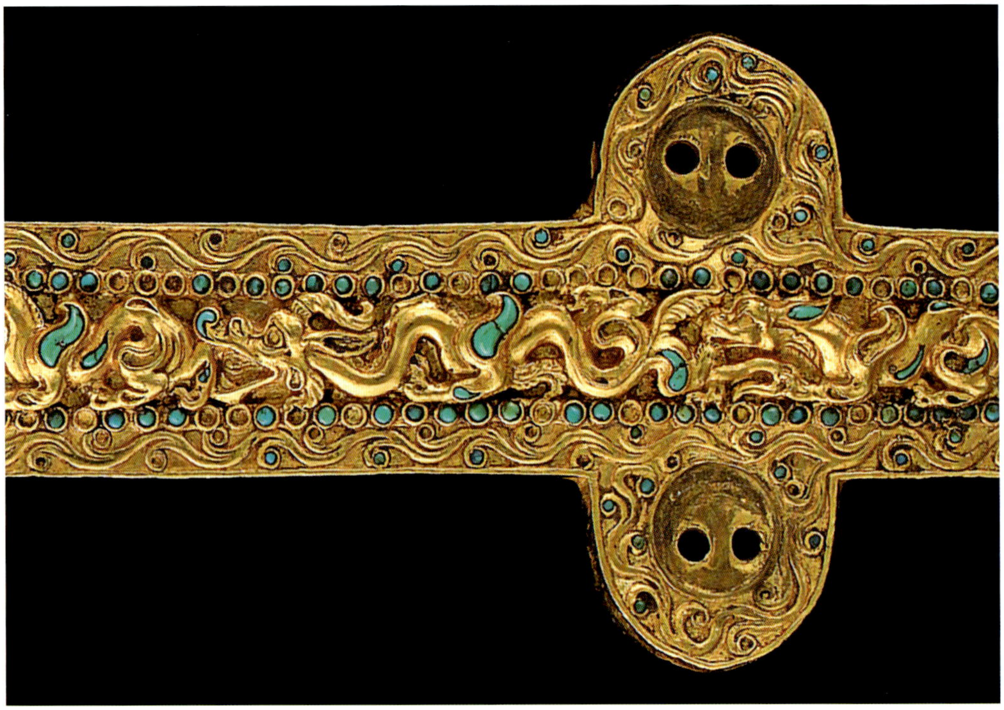

Fig. 5. Dagger sheath (detail) with prowling dragon. Tillya Tepe, Tomb IV, second quarter of 1st century A.D. Gold and turquoise, 23.5 × 9 cm. National Museum of Afghanistan, Kabul (04.40.382)

at Tillya Tepe. Both the tree antlers and the supporting band are decorated with twenty raised rosettes with granulated surfaces, each of which once held inlays intended to mimic turquoise. They are further encrusted with round leaves that have been attached with thin gold wires. This particular method of manufacture (described in Jane Hickman's essay, pp. 84–85), in which spangles are attached to a thin gold sheet with gold wires, is also found in China in the third and fourth centuries and in Korea in the fifth and sixth centuries A.D.

Examples of this type of metalwork have also been excavated at several sites in Inner Mongolia as well as in Jilin and Liaoning provinces in northeastern China and are associated with a nomadic confederation known, in Chinese historical records, as the Xianbei. Part of a larger and more amorphous group referred to generically as the "eastern barbarians," or *donghu*, the Xianbei first appear as an independent confederation in the mid-first century B.C., during a period of internecine strife among the Xiongnu, which was the dominant group on the vast eastern steppes from the third century B.C. to the first century A.D. By the mid-first century A.D., the Xianbei had become more powerful and were demanding payments of goods and monies from the court of the Eastern Han (A.D. 25–220). Some records suggest that payments to the Xianbei exceeded the tribute sent to the Xiongnu at the same time.[5] In the mid-second century, under the leadership of the chieftain Tanshihuai, numerous smaller clans were briefly united into a large confederacy. Despite the quick dissolution of this group, different branches of the Xianbei continued to play an important role on the steppes and within China in the third and fourth centuries. Some briefly controlled small polities in northern China. Others served in the cavalry and other forces deployed by the various warring factions that ruled in China during the tumultuous, and aptly named, Sixteen Kingdoms period (A.D. 304–439). Members of one branch,

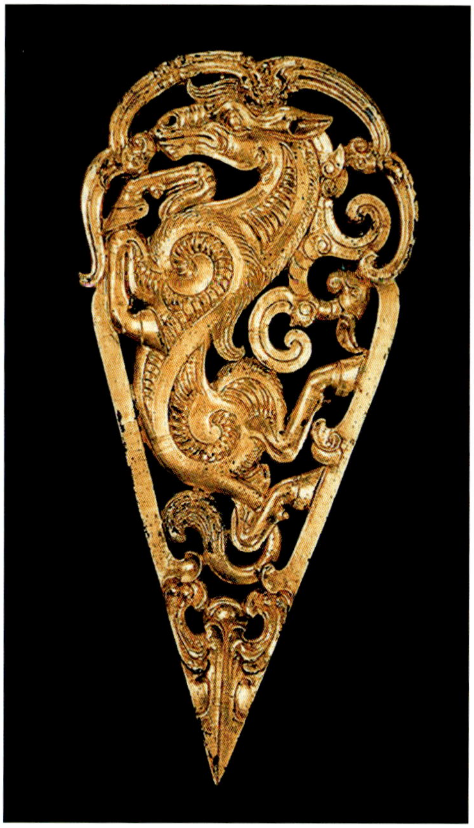

Fig. 6. Frontlet of a bridle with a horse-dragon. Shandong Province, 1st century B.C.–A.D. 1st century. Gilt bronze, L. 16.5 cm. Jinan Municipal Museum

known as the Murong Xianbei, rose to prominence in the fourth century, when they controlled various small states, such as the Former Yan (337–70), Later Yan (384–409), and Northern Yan (407–36), which were based in the northeast and centered in Jilin and Liaoning provinces.

Archaeological discoveries in China indicate that the Xianbei can be associated with the development of a distinctive first–second century A.D. variant of steppe art, which is characterized by an interest in geometric, almost abstract, rendering of animals such as horses and deer.[6] Moreover, unlike that of the Xiongnu, Xianbei imagery

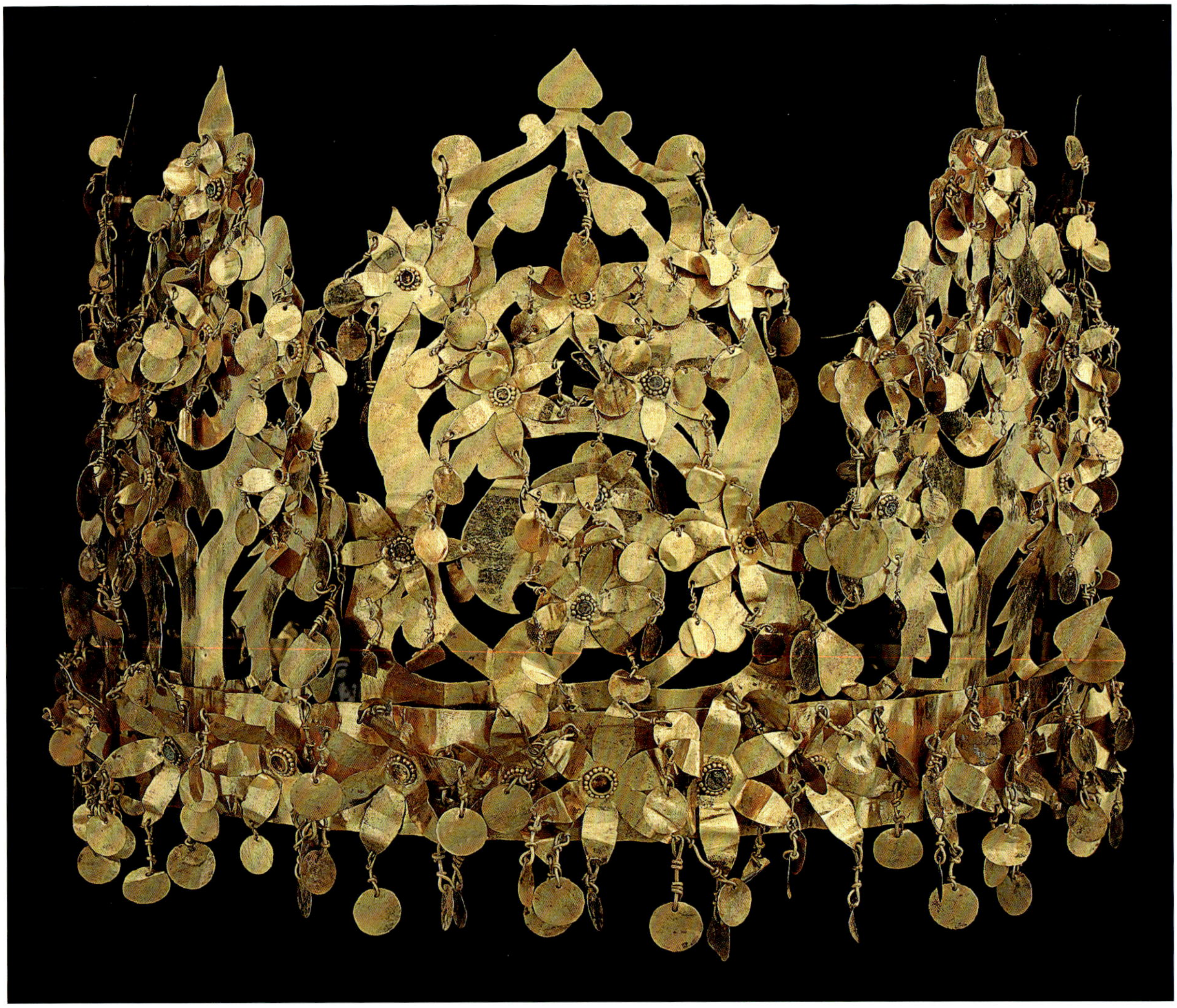

Fig. 7. Crown. Tillya Tepe, Tomb VI, second quarter of 1st century A.D. Gold and imitation turquoise, 45 × 13 cm. National Museum of Afghanistan, Kabul (04.40.50)

shows a preference for real as opposed to mythical creatures, such as the dragon. The one exception is a fantastic horse-like creature with wings and a horn-like snout, not dissimilar to the composite animal of the pendant in Tomb II at Tillya Tepe mentioned above (see Francfort essay, fig. 13, and Boardman essay, pp. 110–11 and fig. 11). In later Chinese records, such as the sixth-century *History of the Wei* (*Wei Shu*), a heavenly beast in the shape of a horse, which has an ox-like bellow, is identified as the creature that led the Xianbei from their ancestral lands near the Hinggan Mountains in Heilongjiang Province, south to the pastures of Inner Mongolia, and ultimately into China. Such winged and hoofed animals, possibly the descendants of the beast shown on the bridle front from Shandong (see fig. 6), are depicted on belt plaques and other objects produced for members of the Xianbei confederation.[7]

Other pieces found in Inner Mongolia and in Liaoning and Jilin provinces illustrate artistic traditions that can be linked specifically to the Murong Xianbei. These include a plaque, found in Liaoning Province in 1957, which is decorated with gold spangles attached to a gold sheet further embellished with openwork patterns and was most likely worn at the front of a headdress (fig. 8). Additional examples of this type of ornament have also been excavated.[8] Pieces found in archaeological sites also include adornments in the shape of antlers or trees that would have been worn on headdresses or diadems,[9] again similar to what was found in Tomb IV at Tillya Tepe and thought to have decorated the crown worn by the male figure in that tomb.[10] One of the most interesting excavated pieces associated with the Murong Xianbei is a small decorative plaque found in Inner Mongolia in 1990 that shows a standing figure with two dragon-like beasts to either side (fig. 9), a design that, again, is reminiscent of the Master of Animals pendant from Tomb II at Tillya Tepe (see Francfort essay, fig. 13). Like the Xianbei ornaments discussed earlier, the imagery of this plaque reflects continuing ties between the Xianbei in northeastern China and peoples based farther west.

The use of thin gold sheets embellished with spangles supported by gold wires appears to have disappeared in China after the mid-fifth century A.D., when the Murong Xianbei polities were incorporated into the Northern Wei empire (386–534), which was established by the Tuoba Xianbei and controlled all of northern China. It is interesting to note, however, that this distinctive method of working gold continued on the Korean peninsula, which is contiguous to the Murong lands in Jilin and Liaoning provinces and which, during the third and fourth centuries, experienced an influx of horse-riding peoples, some of whom may have been Xianbei or had ties to that group.[11] Examples of this type of metalworking have been found at sites throughout Korea, but the most dramatic are works found in tombs in the southeast of the peninsula that are associated with the rulers of the Silla kingdom (57 B.C.–A.D. 668), one of four polities that controlled the peninsula during the Three Kingdoms period. The others are Goguryeo (37 B.C.–A.D. 668) in the north, Baekje (18 B.C.–A.D. 668) in the southwest, and the smaller, and less well-studied, Gaya (42 B.C.–A.D. 562) nestled between Silla and Baekje. In the mid-seventh century, with the help of the Tang dynasty (618–907) in China, the peninsula was united under the rule of the Unified Silla dynasty (668–935).

The noticeably larger number of objects preserved from the Silla kingdom is due

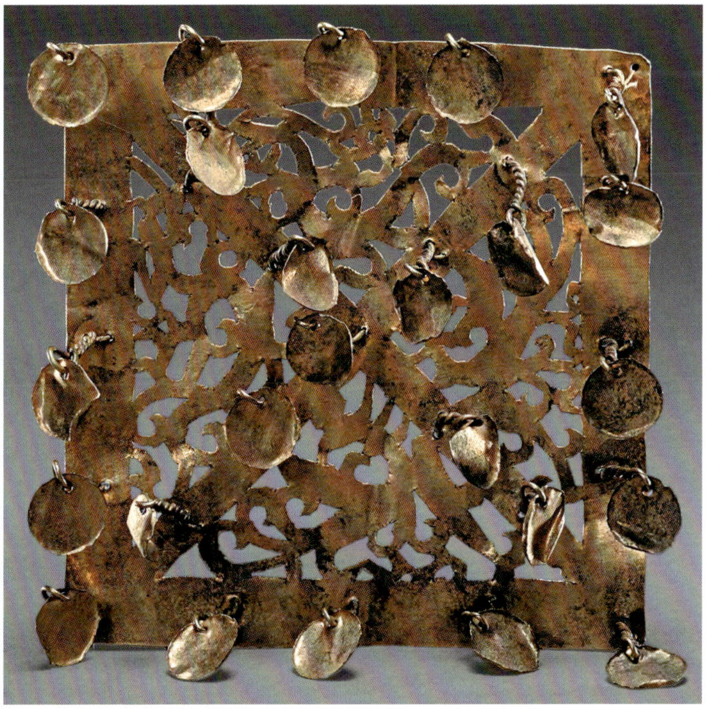

Fig. 8. Headdress ornament with pendants. Liaoning Province, Fangshen, Beipiao, 4th century A.D. Gold, 9 × 9 cm. Liaoning Provincial Museum

Fig. 9. Plaque with a figure and animals. Inner Mongolia Autonomous Region, Jerim League, Horqin Zuoyizhong Banner, 3rd–4th century A.D. Gold, 5.8 × 10 cm. Jerim League Museum, Tongliao

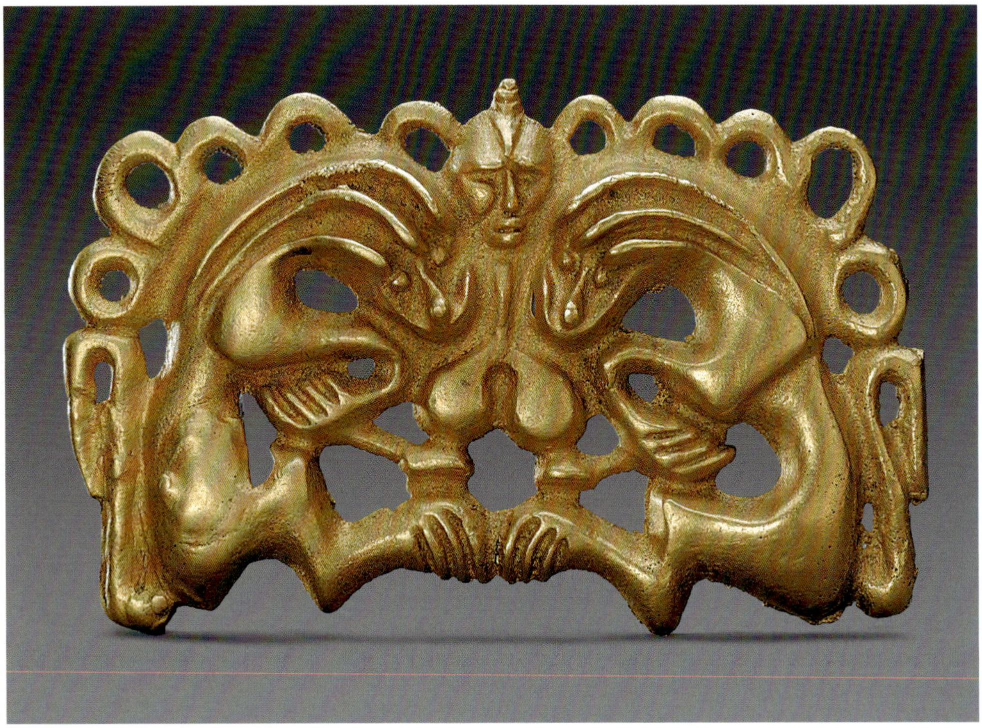

in large part to the inaccessible structure of the tombs from this period. Most likely introduced by the horse-riding people that moved into the peninsula in the early fourth century, the tombs are comparable to the kurgans found in the Altai region and elsewhere in Central Asia and southern Russia. They consist of a wood chamber, which houses one or two coffins, sometimes placed on a stone platform. Some also contained burial chests filled with goods. The chambers were first filled and covered with a large number of stones and, then, with mud, sod, and grass to create the large mounds that identify the tombs. Over one hundred have been identified in the region of present-day Gyeongju, the center of both the Silla kingdom and the United Silla dynasty. Not all have been excavated.

In addition to an astonishing array of gold implements and adornments, Silla kingdom–period tombs have yielded visual evidence for the continuation of horse-riding traditions from the fifth to the sixth century, as well as for the existence of ties to regions at the western edges of the steppes and with the Murong and Tuoba Xianbei in China. Members of the Silla elite, who were most likely buried in cemeteries based on clan affiliations, had gold caps, headdress ornaments, and crowns, as well as elaborate belts, horse gear, and a range of vessels (including gold and silver) in their tombs. In addition, several of the individuals in Korean tombs were buried with large gold shoes or soles,[12] comparable to the pair of gold soles found in Tomb IV at Tillya Tepe.[13]

Western Asian works excavated in these tombs include a unique silver bowl showing animals and recumbent hunters,[14] an extraordinary dagger that is very similar to one found in Kazakhstan,[15] and glass vessels and beads.[16] Moreover, several of the high-fired earthenware vessels found in these burials are in the shape of drinking horns or rhyta,[17] a type often associated with western Asia. It is interesting to note that most of the drinking horns found in Korean tombs are placed on stands, like a glass rhyton with a stand found in the Afghan site of Begram (see Whitehouse essay, fig. 4),[18] located to the south of Tillya Tepe. Moreover, the shape and style of both the belts and saddles found in Korean tombs show parallels to those excavated in Xianbei sites in China.[19] Both the belt plaques and the saddle also share a taste for hexagonal patterns in their decoration, as does the necklace found in Tomb II at Tillya Tepe.[20] Use of granulation is found also in Korean material, such as earrings and headdress ornaments,[21] in Xianbei artifacts,[22] as well as in the jewelry found at Tillya Tepe.[23]

Finally, the Old Silla tombs of the fifth to sixth century A.D. have yielded gilt bronze, silver, and gold crowns that are strikingly similar in manufacture and appearance to the one, dating centuries earlier, found in Tomb VI at Tillya Tepe. The gold crown from the Heavenly Horse Tomb (fig. 10) is further enhanced by the long pendants that would have framed the face, much like the adornments worn by the woman in Tomb VI (see Francfort essay, fig. 20).[24] Typical of Korean crowns, it consists of a thin diadem with three tree-like finials in the center and two additional antler-shaped pieces at the ends. Like the Tillya Tepe crown, the Korean examples are embellished with round spangles that have been tied to thin gold sheets with gold wires. Unlike those from Tomb VI, however, the finials on the Korean examples are not removable. Moreover, they are embellished with pieces of jade in the shape of commas, a shape that is also found in other materials at Tillya Tepe.[25] The complexity of exchanges in Central and East Asia at this time is reflected in studies by several scholars, who believe that the jade used in the production of Korean crowns was imported from Japan, which had also experienced an influx of horse-riding peoples and a change in burial practices and goods in about the fourth to fifth century.[26]

The similarities between the method of manufacture and the appearance of the gold crown found at Tillya Tepe and of those excavated in Korea are striking and raise a host of intriguing, if unanswerable, questions. It may be that ornaments with such decorative gold spangles were produced over a wide geographic range, as well as over the course of several centuries, and that the material from Afghanistan, Inner Mongolia, China, and Korea represents a

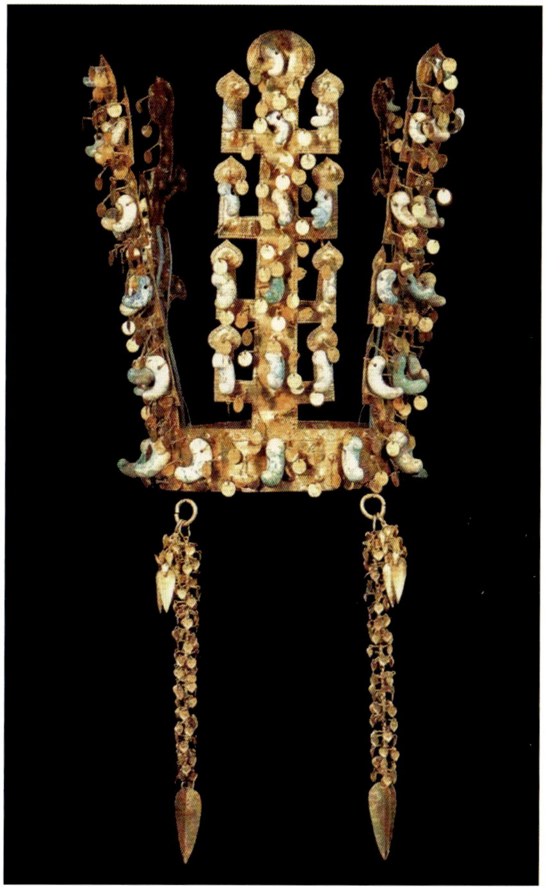

Fig. 10. Crown from the Heavenly Horse Tomb. Korea, Silla dynasty, 6th century A.D. Gold, H. 32.5 cm. Gyeongju National Museum

minute fraction of what was originally made. It is also possible that this particular style of ornamentation can be linked to one group of the many nomadic or pastoralist confederations found in the eastern reaches of Central Asia. In this light it might be noted that of the six crowns of this type found in Korea, five were found in women's burials, while the identity of the figure in the sixth tomb remains uncertain.[27] Both the Chinese *History of the Later Han Dynasty* (*Hou Han Shu*), compiled in the sixth century but addressing the period from the first to the third century, and *History of the Three Kingdoms* (*Sanguozhi*), which is contemporaneous and written in the third century, state that Xianbei women who were of marriageable age wore a headdress known as a *jujue*,[28] made of gold and decorated with precious stones—a reasonable description of the crowns in question. These citations help link the decoration of the crowns not only to the Xianbei but also to women, providing another parallel to the material from Tillya Tepe.

The identity of the woman buried in Tomb VI, and that of her companions at Tillya Tepe, remains unclear, as does that date of their interment, which is usually placed in the first century A.D. based on the evidence of a coin from the reign of the Roman emperor Tiberius (A.D. 14–37) in Tomb III.[29] The first-century date has led to the suggestion that the individuals buried at Tillya Tepe may have had ties to the Kushans, who ruled parts of Afghanistan as well as Pakistan and much of northern India from the first to the third century A.D. The name Kushan is a westernized rendering of the Chinese term *Guishuang*, and the Kushans are the descendants of one branch of an eastern confederation of nomad-pastoralists known in Chinese sources as the Yuezhi. Based in China's northwest, the Yuezhi first appear in records as traders in horses and jade. In the early second century B.C. they were pushed out of their territories by the powerful Xiongnu, and at least some portion of the confederacy moved first into Kazakhstan and ultimately into the Oxus River region and northern Afghanistan.

It is possible that the six people buried at Tillya Tepe were members of a Yuezhi confederation that chose to continue a nomadic-pastoralist lifestyle, while others, at the same time, adopted a settled existence and ruled as the Kushans. Alternatively, the people at Tillya Tepe may represent individuals who lived a sedentary life, but chose a more traditional means of burial. They may also represent a mixed nomadic group, partially Yuezhi, and partially others, some of whom may have come from the east. It is possible that the woman in Tomb VI was either a Xianbei or of Xianbei descent and had joined the chieftain in Tomb IV—and the other members of the clan—as part of an alliance that reflected the growing power of the Xianbei in the first and second centuries. (For Greek and steppe associations of this female, see Boardman, pp. 105–7, and Francfort, pp. 96–99) This suggestion is admittedly speculative, but it does help to explain the technical and visual similarities between the crown in her tomb, works of art produced in parts of China under the control of the Xianbei, and related traditions preserved in Korea from the fifth to the sixth century. Moreover, such a situation would also help to explain the strong presence of Chinese imagery in the complicated visual world of the Tillya Tepe nomads and of Chinese-made mirrors, boot buckles, and possibly other goods.

1. Sarianidi 1985, pp. 203, 235, and 258.
2. Bunker 1994, pp. 41–42.
3. Sturman 1988.
4. Jinan and Shandong 2004.
5. Jagchid and Symons 1989, p. 63.
6. Bunker et al. 1997, pp. 279–83.
7. Su 1977; Bunker et al. 1997, p. 304, figs. W16 and W17.
8. Watt et al. 2004, cat. no. 36.
9. Ibid., cat. no. 35.
10. Yatsenko 2001, pl. 10.
11. Ledyard 1975.
12. Gyeongju 2008, p. 37.
13. Afghanistan 2008, no. 89.
14. Gyeongju 2008, pp. 52–53.
15. Nara 2004, cat. no. 31.
16. Ibid., cat. no. 42-1; Gyeongju 2008, pp. 69–75 and 92–99.
17. Gyeongju 2008, pp. 58–68.
18. Afghanistan 2008, no. 170.
19. Watt et al. 2004, cat. no. 25; Yi 2004, pp. 192–226.
20. Pak 1988; Afghanistan 2008, p. 253, no. 78.
21. Gyeongju 2008, pp. 24–25, 32.
22. Watt et al. 2004, cat. nos. 26–28.
23. Afghanistan 2008, nos. 42, 44, 46, 51, 54, 78, 90, 104, 122, and 143.
24. Yatsenko 2001, pl. 11.
25. Afghanistan 2008, nos. 51, 72, and 74.
26. It may be worth noting that movements of horse riders are also attested in the western part of the steppes in about 400 A.D. In this case, the peoples in question are known by the names Hepthalites and Kidarites.
27. The status of the woman in question is beyond the scope of this essay, although it seems likely that, at least in the case of the women buried in Korea, they had both political and religious status.
28. Pulleyblank 2000, p. 72.
29. Afghanistan 2008, no. 95.

Bibliography

Abdullaev 2007. Kazim Abdullaev. "Nomad Migration in Central Asia." In Cribb and Herrmann 2007, pp. 73–98.

Afghanistan 2008. *Afghanistan: Hidden Treasures from the National Museum, Kabul*, edited by Fredrik Hiebert and Pierre Cambon. Washington, D.C.: National Geographic Society.

Afghanistan 2011. *Afghanistan: Crossroads of the Ancient World*, edited by Fredrik Hiebert and Pierre Cambon. London: British Museum Press.

Akishev 1978. Kemal Akishev. *Kurgan Issyk*. Moscow: Iskusstvo.

Amiet 2001. Pierre Amiet. "La sculpture susienne à l'époque de l'empire parthe." *Iranica Antiqua* 36, pp. 239–91.

Anthony 2007. David Anthony. *The Horse, the Wheel and Language: How Bronze-Age Riders from the Eurasian Steppes Shaped the Modern World*. Princeton: Princeton University Press.

Antiquities of Southern Uzbekistan 1991. Kh. Sh. Abdusamatov, K. Takamatsu, G. A. Pugachenkova, and others. *Antiquities of Southern Uzbekistan* [in Russian and Japanese]. Tokyo: Soka University Press.

Artamonov 1966. Mikhail I. Artamonov. *Sokrovitsa Skiphskich Kurganov* [Treasures from Scythian kurgans]. Praga: Artia; Leningrad: Sovetskij hudožnik.

Aruz et al. 2000. Joan Aruz, Ann Farkas, Andrei Alekseev, and Elena Korolkova. *The Golden Deer of Asia: Scythian and Sarmatian Treasures from the Russian Steppes*. New York: The Metropolitan Museum of Art.

Aruz, Benzel, and Evans 2008. Joan Aruz, Kim Benzel, and Jean M. Evans. *Beyond Babylon: Art, Trade, and Diplomacy in the Second Millennium B.C.* New York: The Metropolitan Museum of Art.

Aruz, Farkas, and Valtz Fino 2006. Joan Aruz, Ann Farkas, and Elisabetta Valtz Fino. *The Golden Deer of Eurasia: Perspectives on the Steppe Nomads of the Ancient World*. New York: The Metropolitan Museum of Art.

Arveiller-Dulong and Nenna 2000. Véronique Arveiller-Dulong and Marie-Dominique Nenna. *Les verres antiques du Musée du Louvre*. Vol. 1: *Contenants à parfum en verre moulé sur noyau et vaisselle moulée, VIIe siècle avant J.-C.–1er siècle après J.-C.* Paris: Réunion des Musées Nationaux.

Askarov 1977. A. A. Askarov. *Drevnezemledel'cheskaya Kul'tura Epokhi Bronzi Iuga Uzbekistana* [*The ancient agricultural culture of Bronze Age southern Uzbekistan*]. Tashkent: Fan.

Ball 1982. Warwick Ball. *Archaeological Gazetteer of Afghanistan: Catalogue des sites archéologiques d'Afghanistan*. Paris: Éditions Recherche sur les civilisations.

Baratte 2001. François Baratte. "Orient et Occident: le témoignage d'une trouvaille d'argenterie d'époque parthe en Asie centrale." *Journal des Savants* (no. 2), pp. 249–307.

Barfield 2010. Thomas Barfield. *Afghanistan: A Cultural and Political History*. Princeton: Princeton University Press.

Barkova and Pankova 2005. Ludmilla Barkova and S. V. Pankova. "Tattooed Mummies from the Large Pazyryk Mounds: New Findings."

Archaeology, Ethnology and Anthropology of Eurasia 22, pp. 48–59.

Bartol'd 1966 (1907). Vasily V. Bartol'd. Review of *Explorations in Turkestan: Expedition of 1903*. In *Sochineniia: Raboty po Arkheologii, Numizmatike, Epigrafike i Etnografii*, pp. 141–53. Moscow: Nauka.

Beningson and Liu 2005. Susan L. Beningson and Cary Y. Liu. *Providing for the Afterlife: "Brilliant Artifacts" from Shandong*. New York: China Institute.

Berger and Fünfschilling 1986. Ludwig Berger and Sylvia Fünfschilling. "Ein gläserner Askos aus Martigny/Schweiz." *Journal of Glass Studies* 28, pp. 19–23.

Bernard 1968. Paul Bernard. "Chapiteaux corinthiens hellénistiques d'Asie centrale découverts à Aï Khanoum." *Syria* 45, pp. 111–51.

Bernard 1969. Paul Bernard. "Quatrième campagne de fouilles à Aï Khanoum (Bactriane)." *CRAI* 113, pp. 313–55.

Bernard 1970. Paul Bernard. "Sièges et lits en ivoire d'époque hellénistique en Asie centrale." *Syria* 47, pp. 327–43.

Bernard 1971. Paul Bernard. "La campagne de fouilles de 1970 à Aï Khanoum (Afghanistan)." *CRAI* 115, pp. 385–452.

Bernard 1972. Paul Bernard. "Campagne de fouilles a Ai Khanoum (Afghanistan)." *CRAI* 116, pp. 605-32.

Bernard 1976. Paul Bernard. "Les traditions orientales dans l'architecture gréco-bactrienne." *Journal Asiatique* 264, pp. 245–75.

Bernard 1978. Paul Bernard. "Campagne de fouilles 1976-1977 à Aï Khanoum (Afghanistan)." *CRAI* 122, pp. 421–63.

Bernard 1981. Paul Bernard. "Problèmes d'histoire coloniale grecque à travers l'urbanisme d'une cité hellénistique d'Asie Centrale." In *150 Jahre Deutsches Archäologisches Institut 1829–1979*, pp. 108–20.

Bernard 1982. Paul Bernard. "An Ancient Greek City in Central Asia." *Scientific American* 246, no. 1, pp. 148–59.

Bernard 1985. Paul Bernard. *Fouilles d'Aï Khanoum 4. Les monnaies hors trésors. Questions d'histoire gréco-bactrienne* (MDAFA 28). Paris: Boccard.

Bernard 1987a. Paul Bernard. "Les nomades conquérants de l'empire gréco-bactrien. Réflexions sur leur identité ethnique et culturelle." *CRAI* 131, pp. 758–68.

Bernard 1987b. Paul Bernard. Review of Pugachenkova and Rempel' 1986. *Abstracta Iranica* 10, pp. 67–69.

Bernard 1990. Paul Bernard. "L'architecture religieuse de l'Asie Centrale à l'époque hellénistique." In *Akten des XIII. internationalen Kongresses für Klassische Archäologie, Berlin, 1988*, pp. 51–59. Mainz: Zabern.

Bernard 2001. Paul Bernard. "Aï Khanoum en Afghanistan hier (1964–1978) et aujourd'hui (2001): un site en péril. Perspectives d'avenir." *CRAI* 145, pp. 971–1029.

Bernard 2009. Paul Bernard. "La découverte et la fouille du site hellénistique d'Aï Khanoum en Afghanistan: comment elles se sont faites." *Parthica* 11, pp. 33–56.

Bernard et al. 1973. Paul Bernard et al. *Fouilles d'Aï Khanoum 1, 2 (Campagnes 1965, 1966, 1967, 1968)* (MDAFA 21). Paris: Boccard.

Bernard et al. 1976. Paul Bernard, Henri-Paul Francfort, Jean-Claude Liger, Bertille Lyonnet, and Serge Veuve. "Fouilles d'Aï Khanoum (Afghanistan): Campagne de 1974." *Bulletin de l'Ecole Française d'Extrême-Orient* 76, pp. 5–58.

Bernard et al. 1980. Paul Bernard et al. "Campagne de fouille 1978 à Aï Khanoum (Afghanistan)." *Bulletin de l'Ecole Française d'Extrême-Orient* 68, pp. 1–103.

Bernard and Abdullaev 1997. Paul Bernard and Kazim Abdullaev. "Nomady na granice Baktrii: k voprosu etnicheskoj i kul'turnoj identifikacii" [Nomads on the border of Bactria: on the question of ethnic and cultural identification]. *Rossijskaja Arkheologija* [1], pp. 68–86.

Bernard, Besenval, and Marquis 2006. Paul Bernard, Roland Besenval, and Philippe Marquis. "Du 'mirage bactrien' aux réalités archéologiques: nouvelles fouilles de la Délégation archéologique française en Afghanistan (DAFA) à Bactres (2004–2005)." *CRAI* 150, pp. 1175–1248.

Bernard, Jarrige, and Besenval 2002. Paul Bernard, Jean-François Jarrige, and Roland Besenval. "Carnet de route en images d'un voyage sur les sites archéologiques de la Bactriane afghane (mai 2002)." *CRAI* 146, pp. 1385–1428.

Bernard, Pinault, and Rougemont 2004. Paul Bernard, Georges-Jean Pinault, and Georges Rougemont. "Deux nouvelles inscriptions grecques de l'Asie centrale." *Journal des savants* (no. 2), pp. 227–356.

Besenval and Marquis 2008. Roland Besenval and Philippe Marquis. "Les travaux de la Délégation archéologique française en Afghanistan: résultats des campagnes de l'automne 2007–printemps 2008 en Bactriane et à Kaboul." *CRAI* 152, pp. 973–95.

Bivar 2007. A. D. H. Bivar. "Gondophares and the Indo-Parthians." In *The Age of the Parthians*, edited by Vesta Sarkhosh Curtis and Sarah Stewart, pp. 26–36. London: I. B. Tauris.

Boardman 2000. John Boardman. *Persia and the West: An Archaeological Investigation of the Genesis of Achaemenid Art*. New York: Thames and Hudson.

Boardman 2003a. John Boardman. "Three Monsters at Tillya Tepe." *Ancient Civilizations from Scythia to Siberia* 9, nos. 1–2, pp. 133–46.

Boardman 2003b. John Boardman. "The Tillya Tepe Gold: A Closer Look." *Ancient West & East* 2, no. 2, pp. 348–74.

Boardman 2007. John Boardman. "Central Asia: West and East." In Cribb and Herrmann 2007, pp. 9–28.

Boardman 2010. John Boardman. *The Relief Plaques of Eastern Eurasia and China: The "Ordos Bronzes," Peter the Great's Treasure, and Their Kin.* Oxford: Archaeopress.

Boardman forthcoming. John Boardman. "A Scythian Maenad on the Black Sea." *Il Mar Nero.*

Bonomi and Tagliaferro 2006. S. Bonomi and C. Tagliaferro. "Uno *pseudo-diatretum* da Padova." In *. . . Ut . . . rosae . . . ponerentur: Scritti di archeologia in ricordo di Giovanna Luisa Ravagnan*, edited by E. Bianchin Citton and M. Tirelli, pp. 105–11. Rome: Quasar-Canova.

Bopearachchi 1991. Osmund Bopearachchi. *Monnaies gréco-bactriennes et indo-grecques. Catalogue raisonné.* Paris: Bibliothèque nationale.

Bopearachchi 1993. Osmund Bopearachchi. *Indo-Greek, Indo-Scythian, and Indo-Parthian Coins in the Smithsonian Institution.* Washington, D.C.: Smithsonian Institution, National Numismatic Collection.

Bopearachchi 1995. Osmund Bopearachchi. "Découvertes récentes de trésors indo-grecs: nouvelles données historiques." *CRAI* 139, pp. 611–30.

Bopearachchi 1998. Osmund Bopearachchi. *Sylloge Nummorum Graecorum: The Collection of the American Numismatic Society*, pt. 9: Graeco-Bactrian and Indo-Greek Coins. New York: American Numismatic Society.

Bopearachchi 2007. Osmund Bopearachchi. "Acroliths from Bactria and Gandhara." In *On the Cusp of an Era: Art in the Pre-Kuṣāṇa World*, edited by Doris M. Srinivasan, pp. 119-32. Leiden: Brill.

Bopearachchi and Flandrin 2005. Osmund Bopearachchi and Philippe Flandrin. *Le Portrait d'Alexandre le Grand: Histoire d'une decouverte pour l'humanité.* Monaco: Edition du Rocher.

Bowersox and Chamberlin 1995. Gary W. Bowersox and Bonita E. Chamberlin. *Gemstones of Afghanistan.* Tucson, AZ: Geoscience Press.

Brosseder 2009. Ursula Brosseder. "Xiongnu Terrace Tombs and Their Interpretation as Elite Burials." In *Current Archaeological Research in Mongolia. Papers from the First International Conference on "Archaeological research in Mongolia," Held in Ulaanbaatar, August 19th–23rd, 2007*, edited by J. Bemmann, H. Parzinger, E. Pohl, and D. Tseveendorzh, pp. 247–80. Bonn: Vor- und Frühgeschichtliche Archäologie.

Bühler 1894. Georg Bühler. "Votive Inscriptions from Sanchi Stūpas." *Epigraphia Indica*, 2, pp. 87–115, 386–407.

Bunker 1988. Emma C. Bunker. "Lost Wax and Lost Textile: An Unusual Ancient Technique for Casting Gold Belt Plaques." In *The Beginning of the Use of Metals and Alloys*, edited by Robert Maddin, pp. 222–27. Cambridge, Mass.: MIT Press.

Bunker 1994. Emma C. Bunker. "The Metallurgy of Personal Adornment." In *Adornment for Eternity: Status and Rank in Chinese Ornament*, edited by Julia M. White and Emma C. Bunker, pp. 31–54. Denver: Denver Art Museum.

Bunker et al. 1997. Emma C. Bunker, with Trudy S. Kawami, Katheryn M. Linduff, and Wu En. *Ancient Bronzes of the Eastern Eurasian Steppes* *from the Arthur M. Sackler Collections*. New York: Arthur M. Sackler Foundation.

Bunker, Chatwin, and Farkas 1970. Emma C. Bunker, C. Bruce Chatwin, and Ann R. Farkas. *Animal Style Art from East to West*. New York: Asia Society.

Bunker and Ternbach 1970. Emma C. Bunker and Joseph Ternbach. "A Variation of the 'Lost-Wax' Process." *Expedition* 12, no. 3, pp. 41–43.

Callieri 2005. Pierfrancesco Callieri. "The Sakas in Afghanistan: Evidence from the Glyptics." In *Tsentralnaia Aziia. Istochniki, Istorija, Kultura* [Central Asia: sources, history, culture], edited by E. A. Davidovich et al., pp. 359–64. Moscow: Russian Academy of Sciences.

Calligaro 2006. Thomas F. Calligaro. "Analyse des matériaux, Tillia tepe, étude des incrustations et de l'or." In Cambon and Jarrige 2006, pp. 292–93.

Cambon 2006. Pierre Cambon. "Tillia tepe, la connexion de l'Est." In Cambon and Jarrige 2006, pp. 295–97.

Cambon 2008. Pierre Cambon. "Begram: Alexandria of the Caucasus, Capital of the Kushan Empire." In Afghanistan 2008, pp. 145–61.

Cambon and Jarrige 2006. Pierre Cambon and Jean-François Jarrige, eds. *Afghanistan, les trésors retrouvés. Collections du musée national de Kaboul*. Paris: Réunion des Musées Nationaux.

Canali De Rossi 2004. Filippo Canali De Rossi. *Iscrizioni dello Estremo Oriente Greco: un repertorio (Inschriften griechischer Städte aus Kleinasien*, vol. 65). Bonn: Habelt.

Casal 1961. Jean-Marie Casal. *Fouilles de Mundigak*. Paris: Klincksieck.

Casson 1989. Lionel Casson. *The Periplus Maris Erythraei: Text with Introduction, Translation, and Commentary*. Princeton: Princeton University Press.

Chabouillet 1867. Anatole Chabouillet. "L'Eucratidion: Dissertation sur une médaille d'or inédite d'Eucratide, roi de la Bactriane." *Revue Numismatique* 12 (n.s.), pp. 382–415.

Clarysse and Thompson 2007. Willy Clarysse and Dorothy J. Thompson. "Two Greek Texts on Skin from Hellenistic Bactria." *Zeitschrift für Papyrologie und Epigraphik* 159, pp. 273–79.

Conolly 1834. Arthur Conolly. *Journey to the North of India, Overland from England, through Russia, Persia, and Affghaunistaun*. 2 vols. London: Richard Bentley.

Cowell 1895–1913 [1973]. Edward B. Cowell. *The Jātaka; or, Stories of the Buddha's Former Births*. Cambridge: Cambridge University Press [London: Routledge & Kegan Paul].

Cribb 2007. Joe Cribb. "Money as Marker of Cultural Continuity and Change in Central Asia." In Cribb and Herrmann 2007, pp. 333–76.

Cribb and Herrmann 2007. Joe Cribb and Georgina Herrmann, eds. *After Alexander: Central Asia before Islam*. Oxford: British Academy for OUP.

Čugunov, Parzinger, and Nagler 2006. Konstantin V. Čugunov, Hermann Parzinger, and Anatoli Nagler. *Der Goldschatz von Aržan. Ein Fürstengrab der Skythenzeit in der südsibirischen Steppe*. Munich: Schirmir/Mosel.

Curiel and Fussman 1965. Raoul Curiel and Gérard Fussman. *Le Trésor monétaire de Qunduz*. Paris: Klincksieck.

Dales 1977. George F. Dales. "Hissar IIIC Stone Objects in Afghan Sistan." *Mountains and Lowlands: Essays in the Archaeology of Greater Mesopotamia*, edited by Louis D. Levine and T. Cuyler Young Jr., pp. 17–27. Malibu, CA: Undena Publications.

Dalton 1964. Ormonde Maddock Dalton. *The Treasure of the Oxus, with Other Examples of Early Oriental Metal-Work*. London: Trustees of The British Museum.

Davidson 1971. J. Le Roy Davidson. "Begram Ivories and Indian Stones." *Marg* 24, no. 3, pp. 31–45.

De Cardi 1951. Beatrice De Cardi. "A New Prehistoric Ware from Baluchistan." *Iraq* 13, no. 2, pp. 63–75.

Desroches 2003. Jean-Paul Desroches, ed. *Mongolie. Le premier empire des steppes*. Arles: Actes sud; Paris and Ulaanbaatar: Mission archéologique française en Mongolie.

Downey 1988. Susan Downey. *Mesopotamian Religious Architecture: Alexander through the Parthians*. Princeton: Princeton University Press.

Dupree et al. 1972. Louis Dupree et al. *Prehistoric Research in Afghanistan (1959–1966).* Philadelphia: American Philosophical Society.

Dupree and Kolb 1972. Louis Dupree and Charles Kolb. "Ceramics from Aq Kupruk, Darra-i Kur and Hazar Gusfand." In Dupree et al. 1972, pp. 33–42.

During Caspers 1981. Elisabeth C. L. During Caspers. "The Indian Ivory Figurine from Pompeii: A Reconsideration of Its Functional Use." In *South Asian Archaeology 1979: Papers from the Fifth International Conference of the Association of South Asian Archaeologists in Western Europe Held in the Museum für Indische Kunst der Staatliche Museen Preussischer Kulturbesitz, Berlin*, edited by Herbert Härtel, pp. 341–53. Berlin: D. Reimer.

Dwivedi 1976. V. P. Dwivedi. *Indian Ivories: A Survey of Indian Ivory and Bone Carvings from the Earliest to the Modern Times.* Delhi: Agam Prakashan.

Elisséeff 1954. V. Elisséeff. "Les laques chinois de Begram." In Hackin 1954, pp. 151–56.

Errington and Cribb 1992. Elizabeth Errington and Joe Cribb, eds. *The Crossroads of Asia: Transformation in Image and Symbol in the Art of Ancient Afghanistan and Pakistan.* Cambridge: Ancient India and Iran Trust.

Fairservis 1956. Walter Ashlin Fairservis. *Excavations in the Quetta Valley, West Pakistan.* New York: American Museum of Natural History.

Fenet 2010. Annick Fenet. *Documents d'archéologie militante. La mission Foucher en Afghanistan (1922–1925).* Paris: Boccard.

Frachetti 2009. Michael D. Frachetti. *Pastoralist Landscapes and Social Interaction in Bronze Age Eurasia.* Berkeley: University of California Press.

Francfort 1984. Henri-Paul Francfort. *Fouilles d'Aï Khanoum 3: Le sanctuaire du temple à niches indentées 2. Les trouvailles* (MDAFA 27). Paris: Boccard.

Francfort 1989. Henri-Paul Francfort. *Fouilles de Shortughaï: recherches sur l'Asie centrale protohistorique.* Paris: Boccard.

Francfort 2007. Henri-Paul Francfort. "Choix des nomades et choix des sédentaires en Asie Centrale dans l'adaptation de thèmes et de motifs des arts de la Perse achéménide." In *Mobilités, immobilismes. L'emprunt et son refus*, edited by Pierre Rouillard, Catherine Perlès, and Emmanuel Grimaud, pp. 267–82. Paris: Boccard.

Francfort, Ligabue, and Samashev 2000. Henri-Paul Francfort, Giancarlo Ligabue, and Zainullah Samashev. "La fouille d'un kourgane scythe gelé du IVe siècle av. notre ère à Berel' dans l'Altaï (Kazakhstan)." CRAI 144, pp. 775–806.

Francfort, Ligabue, and Samashev 2007. Henri-Paul Francfort, Giancarlo Ligabue, and Zainullah Samashev. "The Gold of the Griffins: Recent Excavation of a Frozen Tomb in Kazakhstan." In Aruz, Farkas, and Valtz Fino 2006, pp. 114–27.

Gardin and Scour 1998. Jean-Claude Gardin and Hélène Scour. *Prospections archéologiques en Bactriane orientale (1974–1978), vol. 3, Description des sites et notes de synthèse.* Paris: Éditions Recherche sur les civilisations.

Gardin and Lyonnet 1978–79. Jean-Claude Gardin and Bertille Lyonnet. "La prospection archéologique de la Bactriane Orientale (1974–1978): Premiers résultats." *Mesopotamia* 13–14, pp. 99–154.

Gentelle 1978. Pierre Gentelle. *Etude géographique d'Ai Khanoum et de son irrigation depuis les temps antiques.* Paris: Éditions du CNRS.

Gentelle 1989. Pierre Gentelle. *Prospections archéologiques en Bactriane orientale (1974–1978), vol. 1, Données paléogéographiques et fondements de l'irrigation.* Paris: Boccard.

Ghirshman 1962. Roman Ghirshman. *Iran. Parthes et Sassanides.* Paris: Gallimard.

Ghirshman 1979. Roman Ghirshman. "La ceinture en Iran." *Iranica Antiqua* 14, pp. 167–96.

Ghose 2005. Madhuvanti Ghose. "A Rare Image of the Goddess Nanā from Afghanistan." In *Afghanistan, ancien carrefour entre l'Est et l'Ouest*, edited by Osmund Bopearachchi and Marie-Françoise Boussac, pp. 259–70. Turnhout (Belgium): Brepols.

Grenet 1991. Frantz Grenet. "Mithra au temple principal d'Ai Khanoum?" In *Historie et cultes de l'Asie centrale préislamique. Sources écrites et documents archéologiques*, edited by Frantz Grenet and Pierre Bernard, pp. 147-51. Paris: Éditions du CNRS.

Grenet 2001. Frantz Grenet. "Mithra, dieu iranien: nouvelles données." *Topoi* 11, pp. 35-58.

Grose 1989. David F. Grose. *Early Ancient Glass: Core-formed, Rod-formed, and Cast Vessels and Objects from the Late Bronze Age to the Early Roman Empire, 1600 B.C. to A.D. 50.* New York: Hudson Hills Press.

Guillaume 1983. Olivier Guillaume. *Fouilles d'Aï Khanoum 2: Les propylées de la rue principale* (MDAFA 26). Paris: Klincksieck.

Gyeongju 2008. *Silla So Asia rul mannada* [Silla meets West Asia]. Gyeongju: Gyeongju and Cheju National Museums.

Hackin and Hackin 1939. Joseph Hackin and J. R. Hackin. *Recherches archéologiques à Begram, chantier no. 2 (1937)* (MDAFA 9). Paris: Les Éditions d'art et d'histoire.

Hackin 1954. Joseph Hackin. *Nouvelles recherches archéologiques à Begram, ancien Kâpicî, 1939–1940, rencontre de trois civilisations, Inde, Grèce, Chine* (MDAFA 11). Paris: Imp. Nationale.

Harden and Price 1971. Donald B. Harden and Jennifer Price. "The Glass." In *Excavations at Fishbourne 1961–1969*, vol. 2, *The Finds*, edited by Barry W. Cunliffe, pp. 317–68. London: Society of Antiquaries.

Herrmann 1968. Georgina Herrmann. "Lapis Lazuli: The Early Phases of Its Trade." *Iraq* 30, pp. 21–57.

Hiebert 1994. Fredrik T. Hiebert. *Origins of the Bronze Age Oasis Civilization in Central Asia.* Cambridge, MA: Peabody Museum of Archaeology and Ethnology.

Hiebert 2003. Fredrik T. Hiebert, with Kakamurad Kurbansakhatov. *A Central Asian Village at the Dawn of Civilization: Excavations at Anau, Turkmenistan.* Philadelphia: University of Pennsylvania Museum of Archaeology and Anthropology.

Hilgers 1969. Werner Hilgers. *Lateinische Gefässnamen: Bezeichnungen, Funktion und Form römischer Gefässe nach den antiken Schriftquellen.* Düsseldorf: Rheinland-Verlag.

Holt 1981. Frank Holt. "The Euthydemid Coinage of Bactria: Further Hoard Evidence from Aï Khanoum." *Revue Numismatique* 23, pp. 7–44.

Holt 1984a. Frank Holt. "The So-Called 'Pedigree Coins' of the Bactrian Greeks." In *Ancient Coins of the Graeco-Roman World: The Nickle Numismatic Papers*, edited by Waldemar Heckel and Richard Sullivan, pp. 69–92. Waterloo, Ont.: Wilfrid Laurier University Press.

Holt 1984b. Frank Holt, ed. *The Greeks in Bactria and India* by W. W. Tarn, 3rd ed. Chicago: Ares Press. (See also Tarn 1938.)

Holt 1999a. Frank Holt. "Mimesis in Metal: The Fate of Greek Culture on Bactrian Coins." In *The Eye Expanded: Life and the Arts in Greco-Roman Antiquity*, edited by Francis B. Titchener and Richard F. Moorton, pp. 93–104. Berkeley: University of California Press.

Holt 1999b. Frank Holt. *Thundering Zeus: The Making of Hellenistic Bactria.* Berkeley: University of California Press.

Holt 2000. Frank Holt. "Did King Euthydemus II Really Exist?" *Numismatic Chronicle* 160, pp. 81–91.

Holt 2005. Frank Holt. "The Problem of Poseidon in Bactria." In *Tsentralnaia Aziia. Istochniki, Istorija, Kultura* [Central Asia: sources, history, culture], edited by E. A. Davidovich et al., pp. 721–26. Moscow: Russian Academy of Sciences.

Invernizzi 2007. Antonio Invernizzi, ed. *Sulla via di Alessandro: da Seleucia al Gandhara.* Turin: Edizioni Silvana Editoriale.

Jagchid and Symons 1989. Sechin Jagchid and Van Jay Symons. *Peace, War, and Trade along the Great Wall: Nomadic-Chinese Interaction through Two Millennia.* Bloomington: Indiana University Press.

Jain 1984. J. C. Jain. *Life in Ancient India as Depicted in the Jain Canon and Commentaries, 6th Century* B.C. *to 17th Century* A.D. 2nd rev. ed. New Delhi: Munshiram Manoharlal.

Jettmar 1967. Karl Jettmar. *Art of the Steppes: The Eurasian Animal Style.* London: Methuen.

Jinan and Shandong 2004. Jinan shi kaogu yanjiu suo, Shandong daxue kaogu xi, Shandong sheng wenwu kaogu yanjiusuo, and Zhangqiu shi bowuguan. "Shandong Zhangqiu Luozhuang Hanmu peizang keng de qingli" [Summary report of the Han tomb and accompanying burial pits at Luozhang, Zhangqui, Shandong]. *Kaogu* 8, pp. 3–16.

Kabul Museum 1995. "Looting and Destruction in the Kabul Museum." *Far Eastern Economic Review*, September 23. (Online at www.hartford-hwp.com/archives/53/005.html.)

Keller and Schorta 2001. Dominik Keller and Regula Schorta, eds. *Fabulous Creatures from the Desert Sands: Central Asian Woolen Textiles from the Second Century B.C. to the Second Century A.D.* Riggisberg: Abegg-Stiftung.

Kim and Pearson 1977. Kim Won-Yong and Richard Pearson. "Three Royal Tombs: New Discoveries in Korean Archaeology." *Archaeology* 30, pp. 302–13.

Koryakova 2006. Liudmila Koryakova. "On the Northern Periphery of the Nomadic World: Research in the Trans-Ural Region." In Aruz, Farkas, and Valtz Fino 2006, pp. 102–13.

Koryakova and Epimakhov 2007. Liudmila Koryakova and Andrej Epimakhov. *The Urals and Western Siberia in the Bronze and Iron Ages.* Cambridge: Cambridge University Press.

Koster and Whitehouse 1989. Annelies Koster and David Whitehouse. "Early Roman Cage Cups." *Journal of Glass Studies* 31, pp. 25–33.

Kruglikova 1984. Irina T. Kruglikova. "Bully iz Dzhiga-Tepe." In *Drevnjaja Baktrija 3: Materialy Sovetsko–Afganskoj Arkheologicheskoj Ekspedicii* [Ancient Bactria 3: materials from the Soviet-Afghan expedition], edited by Irina T. Kruglikova, pp. 141–51. Moscow: Nauka.

Kruglikova and Mustamandi 1970. Irina T. Kruglikova and Shahibye Mustamandi. "Résultats préliminaires des travaux de l'expédition archéologique afghano-soviétique en 1969." *Afghanistan* 23, pp. 84–97.

Kuz'mina and Sarianidi 1982. Elena Kuz'mina and Viktor Sarianidi. "Dva golovnykh ubora iz pogrebenij Tilljatepe i ikh semantika" [Two headdresses from the Tillya Tepe burials and their semantics]. *Kratkie Soobshchenie* 170, pp. 19–27.

Lawler 2009. Andrew Lawler. "Going the Distance to Uncover the Roots of Trade in the Near East." *Science* 324 (5928), p. 717.

Lecuyot 1993. Guy Lecuyot. "Résidences hellénistiques en Bactriane, résidences parthes en Iran et en Mésopotamie. Diffusion ou communauté d'origine?" *Mesopotamian History and Environment, series 1, Northern Akkad Project Reports* 8 (Ghent), pp. 31–45.

Lecuyot 2007. Guy Lecuyot. "Ai Khanum Reconstructed." In Cribb and Herrmann 2007, pp. 155–62.

Lecuyot and Ishizawa 2005. Guy Lecuyot and O. Ishizawa. "NHK, TAISEI, CNRS: une collaboration franco-japonaise à la restitution 3D de la ville d'Aï Khanoum en Afghanistan." In *Virtual Retrospect 2005*, edited by Robert Vergnieux and Carolina Delevoie, pp. 121–24. Pessac Cedex: Ausonius. (Online at http://archeovision.cnrs.fr/pdf/vr05_pdf/05_lecuyot.pdf.)

Ledyard 1975. Gari Ledyard. "Galloping Along with the Horseriders: Looking for the Founders of Japan." *Journal of Japanese Studies* 1, pp. 217–54.

Leriche 1986. Pierre Leriche. *Fouilles d'Aï Khanoum 5: Les remparts et les monuments associés* (MDAFA 29). Paris: Boccard.

Lerner 2003–4. Jeffrey D. Lerner. "Correcting the Early History of Ay Kanom." *Archäologische Mitteilungen aus Iran und Turan* 35–36, pp. 373–410.

Levi d'Ancona 1950. M. Levi d'Ancona. "An Indian Statuette from Pompeii." *Artibus Asiae* 13, pp. 166–80.

Linduff 2009. Katheryn M. Linduff. "Production of Signature Artifacts for the Nomad Market in the State of Qin during the Late Warring States Period in China (4th–3rd century BCE)." In *Metallurgy and Civilisation: Eurasia and Beyond*, edited by Jianjun Mei and Thilo Rehren, pp. 90–96. London: Archetype.

Liu 1994. Liu Xueyao. *Xianbei Shi lun* [Xianbei history]. Taipei: Nantian Press.

Livshits 2003. Vladimir Livshits. "Three Silver Bowls from the Isakovka Burial-Ground No. 1 with Khwarezmian and Parthian Inscriptions." *Ancient Civilizations from Scythia to Siberia* 9 (nos. 1–2), pp. 147–72.

Longpérier 1839. Adrian de Longpérier. "Collection numismatique du Général Court." *Revue Numismatique* 4 (ser. 1), pp. 81–88.

Lyonnet and Gardin 1997. Bertille Lyonnet and Jean-Claude Gardin. *Prospections archéologiques en Bactriane orientale (1974–1978)*, vol. 2, *Céramique et peuplement du chalcolithique à la conquête arabe*. Paris: Recherche sur les civilisations.

Majidzadeh 2003. Youssef Majidzadeh. *Jiroft: The Earliest Oriental Civilization*. Tehran: Ministry of Culture and Islamic Guidance.

Majidzadeh 2008. Youssef Majidzadeh. "Excavations at Konar Sandal in the Region of Jiroft in the Halil Basin: First Preliminary Report (2002–2008)." *Iran* 46, pp. 69–103.

Marshall 1951. John Hubert Marshall. *Taxila, an Illustrated Account of Archaeological Excavations Carried Out at Taxila Under the Orders of the Government of India between 1931 and 1934*. Cambridge: Cambridge University Press.

Martinez-Sève 2010. Laurianne Martinez-Sève. "À propos du temple aux niches indentées d'Aï Khanoum: quelques observations." In *Paysage et réligion en Grèce antique. Mélanges offerts à Madeleine Jost*, edited by Pierre Carlier and Charlotte Lerouge-Cohen, pp. 197–207. Paris: Boccard.

Massabò 1999. Bruno Massabò. *Magiche trasparenze: I vetri dell'antica Albingaunum*. Milan: Mazzotta.

Masson 1956. V. M. Masson. "Raspisnaya keramika iuzhnoi Turkmenii po raskopkam B. A. Kuftina" [Painted pottery of southern Turkmenistan on the basis of V. A. Kuftin's excavations]. *Trudi IuTAKE* 7, pp. 291–373.

Masson and Pugachenkova 1982. Mikhail E. Masson and Galina A. Pugachenkova. *The Parthian Rhytons of Nisa*. Florence: Le Lettere Licosa.

Mehendale 1997. Sanjyot Mehendale. "Begram: New Perspectives on the Ivory and Bone Carvings." Ph.D. diss., University of California, Berkeley. (Online at www.ecai.org/begramweb.)

Menninger 1996. Michael Menninger. *Untersuchungen zu den Gläsern und Gipsabgüssen aus dem Fund von Begram (Afghanistan)*. Würzburg: Ergon.

Merkelbach and Stauber 2005. Reinhold Merkelbach and Josef Stauber. *Jenseits des Euphrat. Griechische Inschriften. Ein epigraphisches Lesebuch*. Munich, Leipzig: K. G. Saur.

Miller 1956. Mikhail Miller. *The Archaeology of the U.S.S.R.* New York: Praeger.

Miniaev and Sakharovskaya 2007a. Sergei Miniaev and L.M. Sakharovskaya. "Elitnyj kompleks zakhoronenij Sjunnu v Padi Caram" [An elite complex of Xiongnu burials in the Tsaraam valley]. *Rossijskaja Arkheologija* 1, pp. 159–66.

Miniaev and Sakharovskaya 2007b. Sergei Miniaev and L.M Sakharovskaya. "Khanskaja kolesnica iz mogil'nika Caram" [A Han chariot from the Tsaram cemetery]. *Arkheologicheskie Vesti* 14, pp. 130–40.

Moshkova 1992. Marina Moshkova. *Stepnaja polosa Aziatskoj chasti SSSR v skifo-sarmatskoe vremja* [The steppe zone of USSR Asia in the Scythian era]. Moscow: Nauka.

Nara 2004. *Ōgon no Kuni Shiragi: ōryō no shihō* [The golden kingdom of Silla: Treasures from Korean royal tombs]. Nara: Nara National Museum.

Narain 1957. A. K. Narain. *The Indo-Greeks*. Oxford: Clarendon Press.

Ogden 1982. Jack Ogden. *Jewellery of the Ancient World*. London: Trefoil; New York: Rizzoli.

Olbrycht 1998. Marek J. Olbrycht. "Die Kultur der Steppengebiete und die Beziehungen zwischen Nomaden und der sesshaften Bevölkerung (der Arsakidische Iran und die Nomadenvölker)." In *Das Partherreich und seine Zeugnisse (Historia Einzelschriften*, 122), edited by Josef Wiesehöfer, pp. 11–43. Stuttgart: F. Steiner.

Oliver 1967. Andrew Oliver, Jr. "Late Hellenistic Glass in the Metropolitan Museum." *Journal of Glass Studies* 9, pp. 13–33.

Pak 1988. Pak Young-sook. "The Origins of Silla Metal Work." *Orientations* (September), pp. 44–53.

Pearson et al. 1989. Richard Pearson, Jong-wook Lee, Wonyoung Koh, and Anne Underhill. "Social Ranking in the Kingdom of Old Silla, Korea: Analysis of Burials." *Journal of Anthropological Archaeology* 8, pp. 1–50.

Perrot 2010. Jean Perrot. *Le palais de Darius à Suse. Une résidence royale sur la route de Persépolis à Babylone*. Paris: PUPS.

Pfrommer 1996. Michael Pfrommer. "Die Gräber von Tillya-Tepe: Eine späthellenistischfrühkaiserzeitliche Nekropole zwischen achämenidischem Erbe, griechischer Tradition und nomadisch-zentralasiatischer Gegenwart." In *Hellenismus: Beiträge zur Erforschung von Akkulturation und politischer Ordnung in den Staaten des hellenistischen Zeitalters*, edited by Bernd Funck, pp. 91–120. Tübingen: J. C. B. Mohr (Paul Siebeck).

Piggott 1950. Stuart Piggott. *Prehistoric India to 1000 B.C.*. Harmondsworth (Middlesex): Penguin Books.

Pirazzoli-t'Serstevens 2008. Michèle Pirazzoli-t'Serstevens. "Inner Asia and Han China: Borrowings and Representations." In *New Frontiers in Global Archaeology: Defining China's Ancient Traditions*, edited by Thomas Lawton, pp. 1–20. New York: Arthur M. Sackler Foundation for the Arts, Sciences, and Humanities.

Pitschikjan 1992. Igor Pitschikjan. *Oxos-Schatz und Oxos-Tempel. Achämenidische Kunst in Mittelasien*. Berlin: Akademie Verlag.

Polos'mak 2001. Natalia Polos'mak. *Vsadniki Ukoka* [Ukok horsemen]. Novosibirsk: Infolio Press.

Pottier 1984. Marie-Hélène Pottier. *Material Funéraire de la Bactriane méridionale de l'âge de bronze*. Paris: Recherche sur les civilisations.

Prinsep 1835. James Prinsep. "Further Notes and Drawings of Bactrian and Indo-Scythic Coins." *Journal of the Asiatic Society of Bengal* 4, pp. 327–48.

Prinsep 1838. James Prinsep. "Additions to Bactrian Numismatics and Discovery of the Bactrian Alphabet." *Journal of the Asiatic Society of Bengal* 7, pp. 636–58.

Pugachenkova 1966. Galina A. Pugachenkova. *Khalchaian: k probleme khudozhestvennoi kup'tury Severnoi Baktrii* [Khalchaian: the problem of the artistic culture of northern Bactria]. Tashkent: Fan.

Pugachenkova 1971. Galina A. Pugachenkova. *Skul'ptura Khalchaiana* [The sculpture of Khalchaian]. Moscow: Izdatel'stvo "Iskusstvo."

Pugachenkova 1978. Galina A. Pugachenkova. *Les trésors de Dalverzine-Tépé*. Leningrad: Aurore.

Pugachenkova and Rempel' 1986. Galina A. Pugachenkova and L. I. Rempel'. "O 'zolote bezymjannykh carej' iz Tillja-Tepe (k probleme stilja i svjazej)" [On the "gold of the unknown czars" of Tillya Tepe: problem of style and connections]. In *Iz istorii kul'turnykh svjazej narodov Srednej Azii i Indii* [History of cultural connections of Central Asian and Indian peoples], edited by P. G. Bulgakov, P. G. Aripov, and I. M. Khashimov, pp. 5–24. Tashkent: Fan.

Pulleyblank 2000. Edwin G. Pulleyblank. "Tribal Confederations of Uncertain Identity." In *History of the Turkic Peoples in the Pre-Islamic Period*, edited by Hans Robert Roemer and Wolfgang-Ekkehard Scharlipp, pp. 52–96. Berlin: Klaus Schwarz Verlag.

Pumpelly 1903. Raphael Pumpelly. "Archaeological and Physico-Geographical Reconnaissance in Turkestan." In *Explorations in Turkestan, with an Account of the Basin of Eastern Persia and Sistan. Expedition of 1903, under the Direction of Raphael Pumpelly*. Washington, D.C.: Carnegie Institution of Washington, pp. 3–22.

Pumpelly 1908. Raphael Pumpelly. *Explorations in Turkestan. Expedition of 1904*. Washington D.C.: Carnegie Institution of Washington.

Pumpelly 1918. Raphael Pumpelly. *My Reminiscences*. New York: Henry Holt.

Rapin 1992. Claude Rapin. *Fouilles d'Aï Khanoum 8: La trésorerie du palais hellénistique d'Aï Khanoum. L'apogée et la chute du royaume grec de Bactriane* (MDAFA 33). Paris: Klincksieck.

Rapin 2007. Claude Rapin. "Nomads and the Shaping of Central Asia. From the Early Iron Age to the Kushan Period." In Cribb and Herrmann 2007, pp. 29–72.

Rapin, Isamiddinov, and Khasanov 2001. Claude Rapin, M. Isamiddinov, and M. Khasanov. "La tombe d'une princesse nomade à Koktepe près de Samarkand." *CRAI* 145, pp. 33–92.

Rapoport, Nerazik, and Levina 2000. Yuriy A. Rapoport, Elena E. Nerazik, and Larissa M. Levina. *V nizov'jakh Oksa i Jaksarta. Obrazy drevnego Priaral'ja* [The lower reaches of the Oxus and Jaxartes: ancient images from the pre-Aral region]. Moscow: Indrik.

Rea, Senior, and Hollis 1994. John R. Rea, R. C. Senior, and A. S. Hollis. "A Tax Receipt from Hellenistic Bactria." *Zeitschrift für Papyrologie und Epigraphik* 104, pp. 261–80.

Rosén 2009. Staffan Rosén. "Korea and the Silk Roads." *The Silk Road* 6, no. 2, pp. 3–14.

Rosen [Stone] 1974–75. E. Rosen [Stone]. "The Begram Ivories." *Marsyas* 17, pp. 39–49.

Rosenfield 1967. John Rosenfield. *The Dynastic Arts of the Kushans.* Berkeley: University of California Press.

Rougemont 2012. Georges Rougemont. *Inscriptions grecques d'Iran et d'Asie centrale* (*Corpus Inscriptionum Iranicarum* II, 1, 1). London: School of Oriental and African Studies.

Rtveladze 1993–94. Edvard Rtveladze. "Coins of the Yuezhi Rulers of Northern Bactria." *Silk Road Art and Archaeology* 3, pp. 81–96.

Rtveladze 1995. Edvard Rtveladze. "Parthia and Bactria." In *In the Land of the Gryphons: Papers on Central Asian Archaeology in Antiquity*, edited by Antonio Invernizzi, pp. 181–90. Florence: La Lettere.

Rtveladze 2007. Edvard Rtveladze. "Monetary Circulation in Ancient Tokharistan." In Cribb and Herrmann 2007, pp. 389–98.

Rubinson 2008. Karen S. Rubinson. "Tillya Tepe: Aspects of Gender and Cultural Identity." In *Are All Warriors Male? Gender Roles on the Ancient Eurasian Steppe*, edited by Katheryn M. Linduff and Karen S. Rubinson, pp. 51–63. Lanham, MD: Alta Mira Press.

Rudenko 1960. S. I. Rudenko. *Kul'tura naselenija Tsentral'nogo Altaja v skifskoe vremja* [The culture of the population of the Altai in the Scythian era]. Moscow–Leningrad: USSR Academy of Science.

Rudenko 1969. S. I. Rudenko. *Die Kultur der Hsiung-Nu und die Hügelgräber von Noin Ula.* Bonn: Habelt.

Rudenko 1970. S. I. Rudenko. *Frozen Tombs of Siberia: The Pazyryk Burials of Iron Age Horsemen.* London: Dent.

Samashev et al. 2000. Zainullah Samashev, Gallja Bazarbaeva, Gyulja Zhumabekova, and Henri-Paul Francfort. "Le kourgane de Berel' dans l'Altaï kazakhstanais." *Arts Asiatiques* 55, pp. 5–20.

Sampaolo 1986. Valeria Sampaolo. "Le pitture." In *Le collezioni del Museo Nazionale di Napoli: I mosaici, le pitture . . .*, edited by Maria Rosaria Borriello et al., pp. 39–75 and 124–73. Rome: De Luca.

Sarianidi 1976. Viktor I. Sarianidi. "Issledovanie pamyatnikov dashlinkskogo oazisa" [The study of sites of the Dashli oasis]. *Drevnjaja Baktrija 1 (Materialy Sovetsko–Afganskoj Ekspedicii, 1969–73)*, pp. 21-86. Moscow: Archaeological Institute.

Sarianidi 1977. Viktor I. Sarianidi. *Drevnie Zemledel'tsi Afganistana (Ancient agriculturalists of Afghanistan).* Moscow: Nauka.

Sarianidi 1984. Viktor I. Sarianidi. "Raskopki monumentalnikh zdanii na Dashli-3." In *Drevnjaja Baktrija 3: Materialy Sovetsko–Afganskoj Arkheologicheskoj Ekspedicii*) [Ancient Bactria 3: materials from the Soviet-Afghan expedition], edited by Irina T. Kruglikova, pp. 5–32. Moscow: Nauka.

Sarianidi 1985. Viktor I. Sarianidi. *The Golden Hoard of Bactria: From the Tillya-tepe Excavations in Northern Afghanistan.* New York: Abrams, and Leningrad: Aurora. (Also published in Leningrad [1985] as *Bactrian Gold: From the Excavations of the Tillya-tepe Necropolis in Northern Afghanistan* and as *L'or de la Bactriane. Fouilles de la nécropole de Tillia-Tépé en Afghanistan septentrional*).

Sarianidi 1986. Viktor I. Sarianidi. *Die Kunst des Alten Afghanistan: Architektur, Keramik, Siegel, Kunstwerke aus Stein und Metall.* Leipzig: E. A. Seeman Verlag.

Sarianidi 1989. Viktor I. Sarianidi. *Khram i nekropol' Tilliatepe* [The temple and cemetery of Tillya Tepe]. Moscow: Nauka.

Sarianidi 1990. Viktor I. Sarianidi. "The Golden Hoard of Bactria." In *National Geographic* 177, no. 3, pp. 50–75.

Sarianidi 1998. Viktor I. Sarianidi. *Myths of Ancient Bactria and Margiana on Its Seals and Amulets.* Moscow: Pentagraphic Ltd.

Sarianidi 2002. Viktor I. Sarianidi. *Margush: Ancient Oriental Kingdom in the Old Delta of Murghab River.* Ashgabat: Turkmen Dowlet Habarlar.

Sarianidi 2008. Viktor I. Sarianidi. "Ancient Bactria's Golden Hoard." In Afghanistan 2008, pp. 211–17.

Sarianidi and Koshelenko 1982. Viktor I. Sarianidi and Gennadi Koshelenko. "Monety Tilljatepa" [Coins from Tillya Tepe]. In *Drevnjaja*

Indija. Istoriko-kul'turnye svjazy [Ancient India: historical-cultural links], edited by G. M. Bongard-Levin, pp. 307–18. Moscow: Nauka.

Savoie 2007. Denis Savoie. "Le cadran solaire grec d'Aï Khanoum: la question de l'exactitude des cadrans antiques." *CRAI* 151, pp. 1161–90.

Schiltz 1994. Véronique Schiltz. *Les Scythes et les nomades des steppes. VIIIe siècle avant J.-C.–Ier siècle après J.-C.* Paris: Gallimard.

Schiltz 2006. Véronique Schiltz. "Tillia tepe, la 'Colline de l'or,' une nécropole nomade." In Cambon and Jarrige 2006, pp. 69–79 and pp. 270–83.

Schneider 2007. Rolf Schneider. "Friend *and* Foe: The Orient in Rome." In *The Age of the Parthians*, edited by Vesta Sarkhosh Curtis and Sarah Stewart, pp. 50–86. London: I. B. Tauris.

Seyrig 1938. Henri Seyrig. "Armes et costumes iraniens de Palmyre." *Antiquités Syriennes* 2, pp. 45–73.

Shaffer 1971. Jim G. Shaffer. "Preliminary Field Report on Excavations at Said-Kala-tepe." *Afghanistan* 24 (no. 2/3), pp. 89–127.

Sherwin-White and Kuhrt 1993. Susan Sherwin-White and Amelie Kuhrt. *From Samarkand to Sardis: A New Approach to the Seleucid Empire.* London: Duckworth.

Stern 1954. Philippe Stern. "Les ivoires et os découverts à Begram. Leur place dans l'évolution de l'art de l'Inde." In Hackin 1954, pp. 17–54.

Sturman 1988. Peter C. Sturman. "Celestial Journeys: Meditations on (and in) Han Dynasty Painted Pots in the Metropolitan Museum of Art." *Orientations* 19 (May), pp. 54–67.

Su 1977. Su Bai. "Dongbei Neimenggu diqu de Xianbei yiji" [Vestiges of the Xianbei people in Manchuria and Inner Mongolia]. *Wenwu* 5, pp. 42–54.

Tarn 1938. W.W.Tarn. *The Greeks in Bactria and India.* Cambridge: Cambridge University Press. (See also Holt 1984b.)

Tarzi 1996. Zemaryallaï Tarzi. "Jules Barthoux: le découvreur oublié d'Aï Khanoum." *CRAI* 140, pp. 595–611.

Thierry 2005. "Yuezhi et Kouchans. Pièges et dangers des sources chinoises." In *Afghanistan, ancien carrefour entre l'Est et l'Ouest*, edited by Osmund Bopearachchi and Marie-Françoise Boussac, pp. 421–539. Turnhout (Belgium): Brepols.

Tokyo 2005. *Shin Shiruku Rōdo ten: maboroshi no miyako Rōran kara eien no miyako Seian e* [Treasures of the Silk Road: recent discovery from Xinjiang and Shaanxi], edited by Nobuyuki Matsumoto. Exh. cat. Tokyo: NHK.

Tosi and Wardak 1972. Maurizio Tosi and Rauf Wardak. "The Fullol Hoard: A New Find from Bronze Age Afghanistan." *East and West* 22, pp. 9–17.

Treister 2009. Mikhail Treister. "Silver Phialai from the Prokhorovka Burial-mound No. 1." *Ancient Civilizations from Scythia to Siberia* 15, pp. 95–135.

Troickaja 1997. Tatiana N. Troickaja. "Kollektivnye pogrebenija v kurganakh konca skifskogo i nachala gunno-sarmatskogo vremeni" [Collective kurgan burials at the end of the Scythian and the beginning of the Hunno-Sarmatian era]. In *Chetvertye istoricheskie chtenija pamjati Mikhaila Petrovicha Grjaznova* [The fourth of historical readings in memory of Mikhail Petrovich Griaznov], edited by V. I. Matjushchenko et al., pp. 167–70. Omsk: Izd. OmGU.

Van Lith 1991. Sophia M. E. Van Lith. "First-Century Cantharoi with a Stemmed Foot: Their Distribution and Social Context." In *Roman Glass: Two Centuries of Art and Invention*, edited by Martine Newby and Kenneth Painter, pp. 99–110. London: Society of Antiquaries.

Vavilov 1951. Nikolai I. Vavilov. *The Origin, Variation, Immunity, and Breeding of Cultivated Plants: Selected Writings of N. I. Vavilov.* Waltham, MA: Chronica Botanica Co.

Veuve 1987. Serge Veuve. *Fouilles d'Aï Khanoum 6: Le gymnase: architecture, céramique, sculpture* (MDAFA 30). Paris: Boccard.

Wang 1987. Wang Binhua. "Recherches historiques préliminaires sur les Saka du Xinjiang ancien." *Arts Asiatiques* 42, pp. 31–44.

Wang 2001. Wang Binhua, ed. *The Ancient Corpses of Xinjiang: The Ancient Peoples of Xinjiang and Their Culture* [in Chinese]. Ürümqi: CIP.

Watt et al. 2004. James C. Y. Watt, An Jiayao, Angela F. Howard, Boris I. Marshak, Su Bai, and Zhao Feng. *China: Dawn of a Golden Age, 200–750 A.D.* New York: The Metropolitan Museum of Art.

Whitehouse 1989. David Whitehouse. "Begram, the Periplus and Gandharan Art." *Journal of Roman Archaeology* 2, pp. 93–100.

Whitehouse 1997. David Whitehouse. *Roman Glass in The Corning Museum of Glass.* Vol. 1. Corning, NY: The Corning Museum of Glass.

Whitehouse 2001a. David Whitehouse. "[Begram:] The Glass." *Topoi* 11, pp. 437–49.

Whitehouse 2001b. David Whitehouse. *Roman Glass in The Corning Museum of Glass.* Vol. 2. Corning, NY: The Corning Museum of Glass.

Widemann 2009. François Widemann. *Les successeurs d'Alexandre en Asie centrale et leur héritage culturel. Essai.* Paris: Riveneuve.

Winkelmann 2006. Sylvia Winkelmann. "Waffen und Waffenträger auf parthischen Münzen." *Parthica* 8, pp. 131–52.

Wolff 1845. Joseph Wolff. *Narrative of a Mission to Bokhara, in the Years 1843–1845, to Ascertain the Fate of Colonel Stoddart and Captain Conolly.* London: J. W. Parker.

Wonacott 2009. Peter Wonacott. "The Keeper of the Keys and the Mystery of the Bactrian Gold: Afghan Banker Who Risked His Life to Save Treasure from the Taliban Finally Gets His Due." *The Wall Street Journal* (Aug. 12), p. A1.

Wood 1841. John Wood. *A Personal Narrative of a Journey to the Sources of the River Oxus by the Route of the Indus, Kabul, and Badakhshan, performed under the Sanction of the Supreme Government of India, in the Years 1836, 1837, and 1838.* London: John Murray.

Xinjiang 2001. Xinjiang Uygur Autonomous Region Museum and Xinjiang Institute of Archaeology. *Sampula in Xinjiang of China. Revelation and Study of Ancient Khotan Civilization* [in Chinese]. Ürümqi: Xinjiang People's Publishing House.

Yatsenko 2001. Sergey A. Yatsenko. "The Costume of the Yueh-Chihs/Kushans and Its Analogies to the East and to the West." *Silk Road Art and Archaeology* 7, pp. 73–120.

Yi 2004. Yi Han-sang. *Hwanggeum ui nara Silla* [The golden kingdom of Silla: treasures from Korean royal tombs]. Gyeongju: Kimyosa.

Young 1955. Rodney Stuart Young. "The South Wall of Balkh-Bactra." *American Journal of Archaeology* 59, pp. 267–76.

Zeymal and Davidovich 1983. Evgeny V. Zejmal and E. A. Davidovich. *Drevnie monety Tadzhikistana* [Ancient coins of Tajikstan]. Dushanbe: Izd.-vo "Donish."

Zeymal 1999. Evgeny V. Zeymal. "Tillya-Tepe within the Context of the Kushan Chronology." In *Coins, Art, and Chronology: Essays on the Pre-Islamic History of the Indo-Iranian Borderlands*, edited by Michael Alram and Deborah E. Klimburg-Salter, pp. 239–44. Vienna: Verlag der Österreichischen Akademie der Wissenschaften.

Photograph and Illustration Credits

Massoudi: figs. 1–4: Jolyon Leslie; figs. 5–8, 12: Courtesy of the National Museum of Afghanistan; figs. 9, 10: © Kenneth Garrett/National Geographic Society; fig. 11: The Metropolitan Museum of Art, New York

Hiebert: fig. 1, Anandaroop Roy; fig. 2: Casal 1961, pl. XVa; fig. 3: adapted from Casal 1961, figs. 49, 50, 51, 54, 58, 62, 64, 66, 108; fig. 4: © Thierry Ollivier, Courtesy of the National Museum of Afghanistan; fig. 5: courtesy of Walter Fairservis; figs. 6, 7: Sarianidi 1977, figs. 11, 15; fig. 8: Sarianidi 1976, fig. 46; fig. 9: adapted from Sarianidi 1984, fig. 16; fig. 10: adapted from Francfort 1989, pls. 54, 56, 60; fig. 11: V. I. Sarianidi; figs. 12, 13: Fredrik T. Hiebert

Holt: figs. 1, 3-13: Osmund Bopearachchi; fig. 2: Frank L. Holt

Bernard: figs. 1, 2, 5, 9, 14, 15, 17 (right); Paul Bernard; figs. 3, 12: J.-C. Liger, G. Lecuyot; figs. 4, 8: 3-D reconstruction by G. Lecuyot; figs. 6, 11, 13: J.-C. Liger; fig. 7: J.-C. Liger and R. de Valence; figs. 10, 16, 17 (left), 18: © Thierry Ollivier, Courtesy of the National Museum of Afghanistan

Whitehouse: figs. 1, 2, 4, 6, 8, 9, 11–13: © Thierry Ollivier, Courtesy of the National Museum of Afghanistan; fig. 3: Courtesy of the National Museum of Afghanistan; figs. 5, 10: Whitehouse 1997, figs. 184, 395; figs. 7, 14: Whitehouse 2001b, figs. 866A, 867

Mehendale: figs. 1, 2, 7, 8, 9, 11–14, 18: © Thierry Ollivier, Courtesy of the National Museum of Afghanistan; figs. 3, 4, 15: Pierre Hamelin, in Hackin 1954, figs. 636, 652, 638; figs. 5, 10: Hackin 1954, figs. 141, 39; fig. 6: courtesy of Elisabeth During Caspers; fig. 16: Antiquities of Southern Uzbekistan 1991, cat. no. 92 ; fig. 17: Hackin and Hackin 1939, fig. 190; fig. 19: Dwivedi 1976, pl. 47

Hickman: figs. 1–16: Michael Furlong and Leslie Furlong for Jane Hickman

Francfort: figs. 1a, 9: Cribb 2007, figs. 43, 67; fig. 1b: Ghose 2005, fig. 3; fig. 1c: Sarianidi 1984, fig. 3; figs. 2, 8, 13, 20: © Thierry Ollivier, Courtesy of the National Museum of Afghanistan; figs. 3, 15: Sarianidi 1985, pp. 6, 224; figs. 4, 6: Miniaev and Sakharovskaya 2007a, figs. 1, 3; fig. 5: Sarianidi 1989, fig. 30; figs. 7, 19: Rosenfield 1967, pl. 1, nos. 4, 8; fig. 10: Tokyo 2005, no. 51; fig. 11: Rudenko 1969, pl. LXIV; fig. 12: Mission archéologique française en Asie central; fig. 14: Sarianidi 1989, fig. 37; fig. 16: Aruz et al. 2000, cat. no. 185; fig. 17: Bunker et al. 1997, fig. A55; fig. 18: Christoph von Viràg, in Keller and Schorta 2001, fig. 1

Boardman: figs. 1–4, 6–11: John Boardman; fig. 5: © Thierry Ollivier, Courtesy of the National Museum of Afghanistan; fig. 12: © Christie, Manson & Woods, Ltd. (2001), Fine Antiquities Catalogue, 4/25/2001, pp. 22-23, no. 28

Leidy: figs. 1, 2, 4, 5, 7: © Thierry Ollivier, Courtesy of the National Museum of Afghanistan; fig. 3: Michael Furlong and Leslie Furlong for Jane Hickman; fig. 6: Beningson and Liu 2005, cat. no. 1; figs. 8, 9: courtesy of Hu Chui, in Watt et al. 2004, nos. 36, 35; fig. 10: reproduced with permission of the Gyeongju National Museum